SPEAKING FOR OURSELVES

EDITED BY
MAXINE ALEXANDER

 PANTHEON BOOKS, NEW YORK

SPEAKING FOR OURSELVES

❧ WOMEN OF THE SOUTH

Library of Congress Cataloging in Publication Data
Main entry under title:

Speaking for ourselves.
    1. Women—Southern States—Social conditions—
Addresses, essays, lectures.   I. Alexander, Maxine,
1944–
HQ1438.A13S63   1984   305.4′0975   84-7088
ISBN 0-394-72275-2 (pbk.)

Since this copyright page cannot accommodate all
acknowledgments, they can be found on the following page.

BOOK DESIGN BY GINA DAVIS

Manufactured in the United States of America

First Edition

❧ CONTENTS

In the poetry and works of fiction that appear in this volume, no reference to any person, living or dead, is intended or should be inferred.

The time has come, Lillian Smith wrote in 1962, for women to risk the "great and daring creative act" of discovering and articulating their own identities. Three years later, Southern women of a younger generation, fortified by the skills and self-respect earned in the black-freedom struggle, issued the first manifesto of a new feminism. Their words landed with explosive force, setting off cultural reverberations that have shaken the lives of men and women alike. A little more than a decade after that, an issue of *Southern Exposure* called "Generations: Women in the South" began to take form.

As an advocate of racial justice, Lillian Smith belonged to a clear, if beleaguered, tradition of Southern liberalism. When she began to write abut sexual oppression in the 1940s and 1950s, however, her words seemed to come out of nowhere. Similarly when the young women of the civil rights movement groped for words to express their own situation, they could draw guidance from no readily available feminist heritage. Appearing in the spring of 1977, "Generations" sought to place Southern women in the context of a tradition that has managed to evolve despite repeated interruption and suppression.

The women who emerged in those pages exhibited many forms of integrity, courage, and spiritual grace. Their labor in the household, the fields, the factories, and the schoolrooms was crucial to the economic life of the region. They built a network of voluntary organizations that provided the cement of Southern communities. They formed a secret sisterhood of storytellers and comic artists whose humor functioned as sex education, social criticism, and shared delight. "Cooking, quilting, and making do," they were the anonymous artists of everyday life.

The women who spoke there did more than survive from day-to-day. They took risks, fought back, assumed a place in the forefront of insurgency. They played key roles in the labor movement and in the struggle for racial justice in the region. In the process, they forged a bond of common womanhood across class and racial lines that remains a model for our own time. Creativity, subversion, survival skills—a soft heart and a thick skin—those were all parts of the legacy we claimed.

The experience of women in the South has much in common with that of American women generally. Victorian ideals, the impact of industrialization, the rise of feminism—most of the main themes of women's history find some variation or counterpart in the region. Yet these commonalities do not offset the fact of distinctiveness. If Southern women share aspects of both strength and oppression with their sisters elsewhere, they have nevertheless been set apart, their lives shaped by a peculiar regional heritage.

Since "Generations" appeared, the process of reclaiming the heritage of Southern women has intensified. In 1977, the only contemporary study focused exclusively on women in the South was Anne Firor Scott's *The Southern Lady.* Our efforts were influenced by her example, by the insights of the new feminism, and by the development of women's studies throughout the country. Our work, in turn, has served as an inspiration for others. Books prefigured by *Southern Exposure* articles have now been published, among them Sara Evans's *Personal Politics,* my own *Revolt Against Chivalry,* Roseann Bell, Bettye J. Parker, and Beverly Guy-Sheftall's *Sturdy Black Bridges: Visions of Black Women in Literature,* and others. Conferences sponsored by a wide range of civic, religious, educational, and political organizations continue to generate a rich pool of unpublished writing. Even Hollywood—in *Norma Rae* and *Coal Miner's Daughter*—has chosen Southern women for two of the strongest female roles in recent years. This book combines the best of those early statements with work by and about women from the five years since we began. We believe it can lead us to the next stage of collective struggle to re-envision the past and create the future.

—JACQUELYN DOWD HALL

❧ ACKNOWLEDGMENTS

Thanks to my mother, Docey Harrell Alexander,
for inspiring the love of home that gave me the
desire to work on this anthology. And thanks to
my daughter, Taifa Bartz, for accepting me as a
person, which gave me the courage.

I am especially grateful to an endless list of
people but must mention these:
Heather Mee for giving so freely of her time
    and talent;
Barbara Neely for having the foresight to found
    the Third World Women Writers Workshop
    and for staying on my case;
the editors of "Generations: Women in The
    South." The *Southern Exposure* special issue
    that was the foremother of this book:
    Jacquelyn Hall, Candace Waid, and
    Susan Angell;
Wendy Wolf, editor at Pantheon, for almost
    endless patience;
the staff, volunteers, and interns at the Institute
    for Southern Studies for a continuous learning
    experience—and good food;
the writers and contributors to this book, who
    offered much encouragement and support,
    even when they didn't know I needed it.

LEGACY: MOTHER RICH

~ PART ONE

One of the most exciting results of the insurgent women's movement of the seventies has been the conscious and serious attempt by women to define and reevaluate the meaning of our heritage *as* women. Not so surprisingly, many are finding, when they look back, that our grandmothers and their generation were sensitive to many elements of the feminist perspective emerging today—if not explicitly, then in the way they lived their lives. In a sense, we have found that the women's movement is perhaps not so new after all —women we once dismissed as economically dependent and socially oppressed often demonstrated a very real sense of independence that transcended their legal and economic status.

Many of the media images of women's struggles for equal rights suggest that we have rejected all traditionally defined women's roles as nurturers, purveyors of culture to the young, healers, and social stabilizers. But what has actually happened is that we now look at our old definitions of and about inferiority and powerlessness with new eyes. We have begun to see that the work women perform—ordinary, tedious, and thankless, dismissed or despised —can have its own intrinsic and undeniable value. It is at the very heart of the experience of a community. Devotion to family, to the land, and to survival itself are traits that endure and bind us together. And, along with those more "earthy" attributes, we have discovered intellectual and social achievements on both a grand and a small scale.

Many of the poorer Southern women who are now writing, particularly African Americans, Chicanas, and Indians, are the first, and sometimes the only, members of their families to have access to formal education. As these women gain the mobility to move between classes, their reflections give us first-hand reports on the ways the social orders are changing around us. We have also been fortunate that, in this generation, newly literate groups often seek to explore rather than obscure their origins. Their links to the generations now gone are indispensable if we are to think clearly about the future we are forging for ourselves.

Taking with them the new tools of oral history, women are returning to their old communities, their own pasts and families to record the everyday conversations, activities, and personal awakenings at a place called home. Many of us were schooled in the "great men of history" approach that assumes that all our past can be understood simply by recording the deeds of the ruling classes. In these pages we read an utterly different set of facts, presented in highly individualized autobiographical explorations. None are definitive statements of the "truth," but each has its own import or drama. Whether a glimpse from a journal or letter, a conversation on a front porch, or a passing scribble, they reveal our own potential and, we hope, inspire others to review and value their own lives. We celebrate the skills, the insights, the humor, and the endurance of our foremothers, and by so doing, we ourselves find the strength to endure.

CELEBRATE EMMA

❧ MAUDY BENZ

For Emma Catharina Zahn Benz
August 12, 1883–June 30, 1969

Grandmother
I pray to your bones now dust
like the dried rose petals
I keep in boxes
that I may stand as woman
and fall
when I am dark and ripe
from the branches of my own tree.

Grandmother
I pray to the veins in your hands
that I may swim
in the rivers of your blood
and feel your waters rising
for the farmer who lay beside you
Grandmother
I pray to walk in the fields
of your fathers
blessing my peasant feet
deep into the earth.

Grandmother
I pray to the umber in your eyes
and the flecks of sun that float there
that I may rest and rise   rest and rise
to remember

how our faces meet one another
in the mirror
that I may rest and rise   rest and rise
like the yeast you kneaded firmly into bread.

Grandmother
I pray to you
for all those floured fingers touching air
for Regina   Mary   Louise   Lucille
I cease my silence
for the womb in each woman before me
breaking with pride   I speak
for the woman child emerging
in sheaths of yellow water
and skin like membranes opening
in the rain   I pray to you

Grandmother
I pray to you
for you are my only Grandmother
whose hands ride on the loins of the lioness
whose tongue talks in the wind.

LEGACY: MEMORIES OF OUR FOREMOTHERS

✣ DEE GILBERT

We called them Granny, *Mémère,* and all variety of nicknames, and many of us were given our heritage on our grandmother's lap. Their stories give us a look back to a time long past, a world dramatically different from our own. They also give us a look inward, revealing a personal history inherited from them that influences our way of looking at and living in this changed world. Each of us fortunate enough to have known her grandmother might trace a particular way of speaking, a certain style of cooking, an individual concept of life to our foremothers. Whether they nurtured us or scared us, they are powerful presences in our lives. We still hurt from harsh words, still laugh at old family anecdotes; still mourn the death of a grandmother or great-grandmother, gone perhaps five, perhaps fifty years and more.

So for Mommee, Mary Una Jones Fory, and Nanow, Bertha Lee Roberts Gilbert Heard, here is our legacy.

Mable Wiggins; her great-grandmother, Sally McDaniels; her grandmother, Eliza Finger; and her father lived in a farmhouse in Harding County, Tennessee. Mable talks of the season farm chores in the country; hog killing, molasses making, digging out the water wells, logrolling, and quilting bees. "Just families a-helping families, that's the way they did it back then, to get big jobs done. That's the only way it could be done." Grandmother Eliza was the caretaker of the family, working all day long, all year 'round. As Mable says, "That's just what it took to please her—she was 'making family go.' "

Her hair was dark brown; she never cut it. People was always talking to her about her hair. "Tell us your recipe," they'd say. When she washed it, she'd sit out on the back porch and have a little tub sitting up there and have wash water in it and rinse water in another one, just like she was washing clothes. I'd just get fascinated sitting around watching just what she'd do to it. On that same porch the sun would come in good and she'd sit there and sun-dry it. It would take a long time.

Mostly we used the soap that she made. We had a fireplace and we'd burn hickory and oak—hardwood, you know. Everyday we'd clean out the ashes and put them in a wooden barrel out in the backyard. When she'd get the barrel up about two thirds full, she'd start putting water in there and put a drip pan under this elevated base it was on and it would drip out through the barrel and it would be lye. It's strong and dark, almost like iodine. And the hog-killing time would be once a year, when it was cold weather because we had no refrigeration. She'd take the lard from the hog meat and then boil this lye in there and the lard and the lye come out to be soap. There was such of a trick to it.

She'd wash clothes with a tub and washboard and a little jar of the soap. You'd reach your hand down and rub that soap on the dirty clothes like a coat of jelly. And boy, would it suds! It would take the skin off your fingers, it was so strong with lye. You needn't go to wash with no delicate fingers 'cause you'd have them skinned to the bleed.

We'd grow and can the vegetables, and then we had fruit that growed in the orchards and we'd take it out in the sun and let it dry. We'd dry beans. We made our own meal out of corn; we'd take it to the grist mill and have it ground into meal.

But the sewing, that's what I was most interested in. They didn't weave by the time I come up, but great-grandmother used to. I heard somebody talking to her about the Civil War. How when the soldiers come through, they'd break into the house, pour out the molasses and sugar, drag the meat in the dirt—all kind of crazy things. She told about weaving. She was making some cloth to make her menfolks clothes. She's sitting out in the yard, so she could see. If the soldiers was to come, she was going to hide it. They came and she jumped up and hid it under a big flowerbush.

They had quilting parties going pretty well all the year. We raised the cotton, picked it, took it to the gin to get the seeds out of it, and then we'd card it on combs and make it into batts to go in the inner linings of quilts they had pieced. They had quilting frames hanging from the ceilings or on chairs. In between the other chores, they had quilts rolled up, waiting for them to have time to do a few more stitches. All the neighbors would get together and go in and quilt out somebody's quilt. And they'd go to somebody else and do theirs, and just go all the way around the community. In the winters you'd pile five and six quilts on top of you at a time in the nighttime—and then you'd still get cold!

My grandmother, she had her way about sewing. When I'd go to school, I'd see others, how they had their clothes made. She didn't make mine like that. Well, I wanted her to let me sew. One day she had the patterns all spread out, material cut out, and she had to go start some cooking in the kitchen. When she got away from that pattern, where the neck would be left up high, I got the scissors and I cut it way down this a way! She come back to it and found it all cut and she says, "Now if you can do this, you can just finish it now!" I learned to sew from that.

Great-grandmaw died when she was ninety-six. They called it dropsy. It was fluid, like she was drowning. She died in early morning. My cousin come and waked me up and said, "Grandmaw's passing away, don't you want to get up?" I didn't understand, but I got up and was holding her hand when her head dropped and her last breath came.

The women of different families of our neighbors come together and made her some new clothes that they buried her in. Each one was doing some different part of the dress. It just fascinated me how fast they put it together.

But in a way I was scared of what they was doing to her. I was thinking now, what if she was just asleep and not dead? What if she's not dead and they're putting her down in the deep hole? I couldn't get rid of that.

Well, now, I've told off a great big rigamarole I didn't know I knew.

Hilda Murdock, from Terrebonne Parish, takes pride in the fact that her family is well educated. "We had doctors and lawyers and ministers, even in the old times. They were very strict about us respecting other people's rights. And they always taught us to let each tub —I'm telling you like they told me—let each tub stand on its own bottom."

My great-grandmother, Priscilla Smith, said her people always worked in the boss's house. So I think that is one of the reasons why they were educated. The children would teach them to read and write. In a way, they thought they were more than the rest of the slaves because they had to be kept clean to work in the house. She said she'd wear this big white rag on her head with these white aprons, and all these petticoats that had to be starched. So the other slaves sort of envied them, you know.

She said they had to sneak in the woods somewhere and have church service. They didn't allow them to have church. The boss man, see, was supposed to be the god. So all in all my family was very religious from the slaves on down to us.

My great-grandparents jumped over the broom. She said they had a big ceremony and somebody played the guitar and somebody played the harp and the preacher says, "Now!" and they jumped over and hugged and kissed and were pronounced man and wife. But my great-grandparents, being as civilized as they were, he being educated, they repeated the marriage vows. Everybody thought they were smart.

They went on to do pretty good after Freedom because we still have some property in Terrebonne Parish that they bought. He bought enough to give some to build a church. My great-grandfather could read a Bible. My great-grandmother couldn't, but late in her life the government had this project and she went to school. She wrote us all a letter before she died.

My grandmother was Mary Smith Hall. We called her Mama. We all attributed it to our family as having a guardian angel because of her and her religious beliefs.

One of my aunts was blinded when she was two years old, and my step-grandfather would bring her every other week to the hospital in New Orleans. So my grandmother says she was just sitting in the rocking chair one day and the door opened and a big light came in and this light was a lady, all in white, who told her, "Mary, if you want your child's sight back, christen her over and call her Eve." Her name was Eva. Well, they christened her over, and on the way home from the hospital, she got her sight. So we began to believe in this guardian angel. I have never seen her, none of us has ever seen her, but Mama made it so clear to us, you could just see her.

She used to sit on the stoop in the afternoons and she'd throw this big, beautiful towel around her and she smoked a pipe. All the children in the neighborhood would be around her and she'd be telling them tales.

She'd tell how during slavery they would keep my grandfather's grandfather in a cage for hours without food or water because he was always doing something to antagonize the boss. His grandmother would drink water and go to the cage and kiss her husband and put water in his mouth.

We would make it a point to go to church every New Year's Eve night, from babies on up. And she would have the prayer meeting at her house. We'd hide our little bottles under the step, so she wouldn't see us. She would make eggnog and spike it. She would pray for us, each and every one of us. I still tell everybody that I'm still living on my grandmother's prayers.

Annabel Gros Feigel was one of sixteen children, born in Donaldsonville, Louisiana, and raised in New Orleans. Her grandmother, Virginia Guidry, was born in 1843 of wealthy parents and educated in France. In later years she lived on a widow's pension from the Civil War. Annabel, her grandmother, parents, and brothers and sisters all lived together.

I can't lie about it, my grandmother Mémère—that's French—didn't have a nice disposition, she really didn't.

She had owned a home in Clottsville, Louisiana, on Bayou Lafourche and a pretty home at that. My uncle got a little money hungry and went and sold the house from under my grandmother's feet. Then he didn't want her after that. He kept her for a couple of months, you know, the usual thing, and then she came to live with us.

She didn't like New Orleans and I think she would have wished to be back in the country, where she was born and raised. They'd had acreage, a garden, a cow, everything for their living. She had so much. But, of course, then, when she moved with my parents, everything was gone, more or less. I think my grandmother had really gotten hurt when she had to move. She had no friends. She did nothing but sit on that rocking chair on the porch from morning to night. Watched, that's all she did.

She was selfish. My grandmother wore these big old skirts, that go down to the floor, all gathered, and she would sit on the front porch in her big old skirt and the fruit man would pass. So she'd buy herself oranges. She loved oranges. But instead of giving the kids one, she'd stick them under her skirt and then she'd eat one after another until she had every one of them gone. And my brothers'd say, "Gee whiz, we hope she chokes on them oranges!"

My grandmother hated my sister Virgie with a purple passion. I kind of stayed away from her, but Virgie was a son-of-a-gun, she could care less. Virgie loved to play "alaria." It's a ball game—you throw the ball up and your leg goes over the ball and you'd say, "One, two, three, alaria, four, five, six, alaria" and so on. She would play that around my grandmother and Mémère would sit there and wait for the opportunity for Virgie to throw that ball down. She couldn't stand for Virgie to play ball around her! When Mémère died, my mother found fifty balls in her trunk that she had taken away from Virgie. Fifty balls!

Mémère got very, very sick, and she lay on the bed many months, maybe a year. My mother had to take care of her. We slept right there in the room with her. Then when she died, I remember it as if it was yesterday. The embalmers came in with their buckets and all—it was horrible! We lived in a two-story house, and they carried her stiff body down the steps and then they laid her on that cold slab. They waked her in the house.

The next day my folks took her to Clottsville to bury her and us kids had to stay home. All that stuff stayed there; the slab stayed till maybe the day after. Oh, it was absolutely horrible!

We had to go upstairs to that bedroom where she had died. We cried and said we weren't going to sleep in that room but my father said, "Just forget about it." I tell you, we just cried and cried all night because we were afraid. I'm glad they changed that because something stayed with you all your life.

It's a shame to be talking about a person like that when they're in their grave. But you just don't lie. It might have been her unhappiness that made her act that way. You just can't uproot old people.

Olga Roos Brooks visited her grandmother, Elizabeth Roach, in New Orleans every summer to be near her childhood sweetheart. She eloped at age fifteen, and she and her husband joined a traveling vaudeville troupe, later getting parts in silent movies. She almost didn't get married at all because when the first minister they tried asked her if she had relatives to vouch for her age, she naively replied, "Oh, yes, I have my grandmother, Mrs. Eugene Roach." "My God, that's my best friend, she sings in our church. I couldn't think of marrying her granddaughter without her presence!" She and her sweetheart swiftly retreated, hopped the ferry across the Mississippi River, and were secretly married.

My grandmother had a wonderful voice. She was a renowned singer and sang in five different languages. The critics said her voice was greater than Adelina Patti. She sang in a concert at Christ Church Cathedral when she was only fifteen years old.

She had *so* many offers to go to the Metropolitan Opera Company, but she bore fifteen children, nine of whom survived. I remember when I was a little girl, grandmother sang at the Presbyterian Church up on Prytania Street. She was holding my hand and we were going to the church this Sunday morning and she had on a black taffeta dress with great big leg-o'-mutton sleeves and she rustled along as we walked. I was sitting in the front pew, and when she sang the tears just started rolling down my eyes.

She was so refined and ladylike. One time I met her in Holmes Department Store and I was walking down the aisle trying to catch up with her and I hollered, "Grandma, how are you?" She turned around and said, "Olga, is that ladylike? When you are in public be sure to speak in a whisper."

Many years passed and her nine children came to visit her New Year's Eve 1919 and asked her to sing an aria from *Carmen.* She hadn't sung in five years, but she lifted up her voice and it never cracked and never broke. As she sang she took this pain in her heart and later that night passed away.

Mallie Weathersby talks of her grandmothers, Fannie Steele Walker and Amanda McLauren, as she busily mixes up a skillet of cornbread for her daughter and newborn grandson. Mallie and both of her grandmothers are from a little town called Pineola in Mississippi.

Life was hard, but then, it didn't seem hard because that was what you had to do just to live, and everybody seemed to enjoy it. It was just like neighbors in the community—there'd be a white family here, maybe the next house would be a black family. But yet and still, when it come work time all of those families took an interest in each other. They called it "working through and through."

Now, my grandmother Fannie, I hadn't ever met anybody as clean as she was. Her main trouble was trying to keep clean.

You see, back then, people didn't clean house but twice a year. If it was too cold for Christmas, they'd wait till springtime. But most of the time, it was revival time in August. They didn't call it revival in them days; they called it "protract-a-meeting."

The way she would clean her house was to boil big pots of water and take a big gourd dipper full of lye soap and put it in the pot and then clean from top to bottom. Them walls would almost sparkle, you thought they could talk to you. Her floors, they just had the board floors. When she got ready to rinse that floor, she'd rinse it until the water that run off looked like you could drink it, it'd be so clean. Absolutely, she'd work you to death.

And she'd make some powerful lye soap. We'd have to go in the woods where cattle had died, take the bones, and put them in the soap pot. That lye in that pot would eat those bones up; they would disappear. And then she would test it. She would get a feather from a chicken and stick it in there and take it out and if it eat those fringes off, it was too strong. My granddaddy's overalls, she would rub them white. Absolutely the truth, they looked like they had been coated with Clorox—and it would be nothing but her fist on that washboard.

And would she fuss if there'd be some dirt on my dress. Oh, my goodness, she'd want to strap me up! She'd say she was going to put the whippings on the shelf—she'd save them for you. I don't ever remember her doing it, but she wanted to.

The ladies would gather in the evening, and, my goodness alive, they could really do some neat quilting. They mostly did it at my grandmother's house because Mandy didn't have no children and all the other ladies had children around and they'd be under the quilt, bumping heads, you know. They'd say, "You going to get your head cracked with a thimble!" I got mine cracked many a day.

My grandmother could piece some stars, I'm going to tell you right now. It wasn't shabby, not a bit. It was up-to-date. She had the Double Wedding ring. I don't know how long it took her to piece it, but when she quilted it it was some beautiful.

And I did *hate* it, I did hate cutting up material in those little bitty pieces and then sewing it back together. It didn't make sense to me—while they were together, let them stay together. If I could take big squares of material, put them on the machine, and sew them up, I had plenty of quilts. They wasn't beautiful, but I told them mine kept me just as warm as theirs.

My grandmother liked to fish, and sometimes she would go and she would have her work in her apron. She would be sitting down on the riverbank, and she would take and stick them poles right in the bank. She would put her leg across that pole, and when the fish bit it, she'd know. All the time, be sitting up there piecing them scraps.

Back then, it didn't mean so much to me, but now it does.

PIPSISSEWA, CALAMUS, AND PENNYROYAL

✣ CONSTANCE GARCIA-BARRIO

As fast as stores can shelve them, books on herbal remedies have poured off the press in recent years. Yet herbal cures, for many blacks, are an oral heirloom to be had for the listening.

My great-grandmother, Rose Ware, or just Maw, was born in slavery in Spotsylvania County, Virginia. Maw spent her 113 years in Spotsylvania County, but part of the family—including my mother, once she was grown—moved to Pennsylvania. She brought Maw's herbal remedies with her and passed them on to me. Many of her methods have been proven valuable by modern science.

Maw's remedies followed the rhythm of the seasons. In early spring she picked pipsissewa and used the whole plant to brew a bittersweet tea. Everyone drank a quarter of a cup each night to cleanse the body and tone it for the months of farming ahead.

Later in the spring a tea made with the flowers and seeds of the tansy plant would rid children of worms. The pleasant-tasting leaves, eaten raw, were good for an upset stomach.

In the warm months stomach remedies grew potent and plentiful. Maw used the mint that leapt up in July to calm queasiness. Calamus, too, thrived in nearby ditches; chewing its roots quickly settled the stomach.

Roses flourished on the farm in the mid-summer heat, and Maw would use the flowers to make rose water. Rose water and lard were the chief ingredients in her homemade cold cream. Later in the season Maw used the rose hips to make a healthful tea, which we now know is rich in vitamin C.

Summer might bring trouble like athlete's foot, but it also

brought the cure. The white liquid from the milkweed pod, when rubbed on the peeling foot, hastened healing. Other hot-weather plants fought other ills. Dandelions were death to warts. For fast results Maw would bruise the stem and rub the liquid inside right on the wart.

Pennyroyal leaves, rubbed on the skin, kept mosquitoes away. Pennyroyal kept away other things, too. Maw and Aunt Ilsie Ellis, the plantation midwife, believed that a woman who drank plenty of pennyroyal tea never had more babies than she wanted.

When the fall colors ran riot over the countryside Maw would pick the deep-purple berries of pokeweed. She used to pour whiskey over the berries and let them stand for months. The whiskeyberry essence stood ready to deal with bouts of winter rheumatism. Maw soaked wild cherry bark in whiskey to make another popular rheumatism remedy. A few spoonfuls gave much relief.

When warm weather gave way, resistance might, too. A remedy made from red oak bark loosened the grip of many a cold. Maw would steep the bark in hot water, then the cold-sufferer gargled with the liquid. It drew phlegm from the throat, leaving it clear.

Earache, another winter worry, had two home treatments. The old folks would stuff corn silk into a pipe, light it, then blow smoke directly into the aching ear. If that failed, Maw would press hot salt wrapped in a burlap bag against the ear.

Yellow onions cured chest colds. Maw chopped up the onions, stirred in lots of sugar or molasses, and let the mixture simmer for hours near the fire. The sick person ate a cupful for two or three nights. Maw might also make a poultice by mashing more onions, then adding goose grease or mutton tallow. Rubbed on the chest, this mixture speeded recovery. Scientists have shown that all members of the onion family contain a natural antibiotic.

Throughout the winter pine tags (needles) served to make cough medicine. Maw put them in scalding water and let them stand. She removed the needles, added molasses to the essence, and made a soothing syrup. A tea made with dried mullein leaves and sweetened with honey also helped stop a hacking cough.

Roots, leaves, bark, and homemade wisdom: Maw left me a legacy for all seasons.

GENEALOGY

🌿 RUTHANN ROBSON

Almost better to be an orphan

than to be a woman holding sea-rotted
twigs and looking for her ancestors;
clutching a driftwood divining rod that
will never discover a grand matriarch or
patron of the arts. My mothers had to work.

I come from a family of white trash;
of women with double first names and dubious
surnames; of half-sisters with half-told
stories; of women who erase their pasts
and use their family trees for firewood.

We have no leather bibles glorifying
the mother-daughter lines. In fact,
the custom among us has been to burn
birth certificates, to change names
like clothes stolen from someone else,

to hide from husbands and bad debts.
We moved across oceans and mountains and
never learned how to write a letter home.
You could say I have no history.
Of course, I could send to England
for my genealogy, my family crest.

The rich spent years writing history
and now they need the cash.

I say what I have is heritage:
a different child and one that does not
come so cheaply. She has been birthed
by women without regard for the borders

of blood relation patrolled by men.
She does not require bright red
markers to buoy her up.
She is clear and blue.

She is a woman caring for her daughter dying of childbed
     fever,
and a woman quilting while coughing of black lung, and
a woman on trial for miscegenation, and a chinese woman
ironing white boys' shorts, and a woman rolling other
women's hair on saturdays and cigars during the week, and

a woman sewing in a cold garment factory, waitressing in
Birmingham and whoring in New Orleans. She is a blind
woman selling newspapers and a woman with one leg who
     wanted
to love other women but was afraid and a woman whose
     family
changed their names in disgrace and moved away, looking

for work. She is a woman whose only goal in life is
to survive. She blooms like the sea, feeding
on the salt of women who could not write
their true names, even if they knew them.
She is born of the sweat of poor women, but

she is mother rich. I am her daughter.

MAGNOLIAS GROW IN DIRT:
THE BAWDY LORE OF
SOUTHERN WOMEN

❧ RAYNA GREEN

I heard my first bawdy stories from Southern women; they told them in the appreciative company of other women and children, male and female. Usually, this storytelling occurred when we city folk went "down home" for holidays to visit relatives in East Texas (a Southern enclave in the Southwest). All the women would assemble after dinner to talk about family matters and tell tales. The men were engaged in the same enterprise out in the yard, except that they didn't talk family; they talked politics. And they didn't "set" to talk; they stood or hunkered.

We girls and all the boys who were too young to go out with the men had been put to rest near the women, but we were always very much awake. No one really expected us to go to sleep, and we were allowed to listen as long as we didn't intrude. It was called being "seen and not heard." Ordinarily, we had been called upon to perform earlier, but when our songs and recitations and the men's mealtime politics talk were done, the women had their turn. When things got a bit too racy, someone would put a finger to her lips and say "little pitchers have big ears." The content would be adjusted for cleanliness for a while, but not for long.

Of course, some of what they said was meant for children, and it was calculated to send us into shrieks of shocked delight. The very advice traditionally given to children was comic, bawdy, and just the reverse of proper.

"Now that you're going off to college," an aunt advised my best friend, "don't drink out of any strange toilets." And my granny warned the girls many times, "Before you marry any ol' hairy-legged boy, be sure to look carefully into his genes [jeans]."

For such wonderful advice, we did indeed have big ears, and we carried away material for our future repertoires as grown women. Such performances gave my sisters and cousins something to share, expand, and treasure as much as we treasured the more conventional and publicly acceptable Southern woman's store of knowledge about cooking, quilting, and making do.

One of the first bawdy stories I remember was about a newly married couple who spent their first week with the girl's parents. Late one morning her mother went upstairs to see why the couple hadn't come down for breakfast, and she returned to the kitchen with orders for Paw to call the doctor. When he inquired why they needed one, she replied, "Oh, they come down in the middle of the night for the lard and got your hide glue instead."

The woman who told that story and many others was my grandmother. She continued to fill my big ears with a large and delightfully ribald store of tales, songs, jokes, and sayings for the next thirty years. Grandmother was an unusually good storyteller, but her bawdiness was not remarkable in our family. Her sisters, my mother, my sisters, cousins, and aunts all engaged in the perpetuation of the bawdy tradition. I have noted this family pattern elsewhere and have heard similar material from Southern friends and colleagues in folklore and from those marvelous teachers professional folklorists call "informants." I continue to hear such material from family members; since I don't travel home very often, Ma Bell has to serve as the communicative vehicle. I'm certain her corporate Yankee ears would turn pink if she knew what my sisters told me long distance.

Many folks in the South would vigorously deny that any women would engage in such naughtiness. Certainly there are some, perhaps many, who would no more traffic in bawdry than in flesh. And there are others who would not even participate by listening. As my best friend's aunt would say, "She wouldn't say 'shit' if she had a mouth full!" The South believes in and reinforces its own mythology, and the bawdy material simply would not aid women in maintaining the Mammy/Miss Melly image. Between the accepted image and the rigid sanctions of Protestant church life, I doubt many women would revel in a public reputation that included being a good trashy storyteller.

One way my family acknowledged the hypocrisy was to tell bawdy stories about it. A favorite from my mother concerns a group of ladies discussing sex. One said she'd heard that you could tell how much a woman liked sex just by examining the size of her mouth. "Waal [and here the teller opens her mouth wide and bellows], ah just don't believe that," said Mrs. Priss, the minister's wife. And "Ooooh [here the teller purses her lips], is that sooo!" said Mrs. Belle, the red-headed beauty operator.

The reason few know about Southern women's bawdy lore is that most scholars of pornography, obscenity, and bawdry are male. Unlike folklorist Vance Randolph—who had the good fortune, good sense, and credibility to collect such materials from women—most collectors received bawdy lore from men. Women sang them child ballads and lullabies and men told them bawdy tales and songs that could not, until recently, be printed at all. Men not only collected bawdry from men, but they often sought it only from certain kinds of men—usually urban black males on the street or in prison. They knew Southern white males tell racy racist material, and being rightfully offended by the existence of an endless Rastus and Liza joke cycle, they never thought to ask what else there was. Had they gone collecting the stuff from women they'd have either got it, been shot trying, or ruined their reputation with the men out by the pick-up.

I recall the stunned surprise of two male colleagues in folklore when, during a visit to my home, my female relatives treated them to a display of sisterly trust and verbal indiscretion the like of which they'd never been otherwise privileged to hear. Few husbands, brothers, or fathers would have sent male collectors to a female relative if the agenda was dirt. So, the dirt stays in the kitchen where men and women prefer to keep it.

You might expect most bawdry lore to come from lower- and lower-middle-class women, but I have mingled with wealthy and upper-class women enough to know that we are all sisters under the skin. Hearing the stories they have to tell and sharing trashy talk certainly moved us to a common denominator. Genteel rich ladies fulfill one's wildest expectations, and the stories of the Southern female horse set (the Manassas manure crowd, as one Washington journalist tabbed them) would give any Derby hooker a run for the money on this particular track. One of the loveliest of their stories comes from my aunt, an elegant horsey lady who loves train stories—the bawdier the better. She tells of the flashily dressed belle who boards a train in Memphis heading west. Two dark ladies seated across from her draw her attention, and she inquires after their exotic origins.

"Well," says the first one, "I'm a Navajo and my friend here, she's an Arapaho."

"Oh, that's just wonderful," says the berouged lady. "I'm a Dallas 'ho. We have so much in common."

Not to be outdone by elegant women, other women who operate outside the boundaries of social systems also take license in their storytelling. The various Southern "whore ladies," barmaids, snuff queens (Country-Western groupies), and other wicked ladies I have known and loved deliver the goods when it concerns bawdy tales. The trash-mouth "good old girl" has even surfaced in recent literary and cinematic treatments, such as the Cracker truck-stop waitress in *Alice Doesn't Live Here Anymore.* And two Southern madams and their repertoires have been immortalized in print. Pauline of Louisville's notorious bawdy house wrote her own delightful memoirs, and "Miss Hilda," the last of the Texas madams, appears with her tales in a 1973 *Journal of American Folklore* article. Miss Hilda illustrates part of the Southern paradox by telling outrageous stories at the same time she forbids her female employees and male clients to swear in her house. She might be a "Dallas 'ho," but some standards had to be maintained in order to keep up the proper image.

One final group that participates in bawdry, however, is less bound on keeping up the image. I have to confess that many of the women who tell vile tales are gloriously and affirmatively old! They transcend the boundaries—not by their station and employment, but by aging beyond the strictures that censure would lay on the young. The South, like many traditional cultures, offers an increase in license to those who advance in age, and those I have known take full advantage of it, delighting in presenting themselves as wicked old ladies. Once, when my grandmother stepped out of the bathtub and my sister commented that the hair on her "privates" was getting rather sparse, Granny retorted that "grass don't grow on a race track."

A number of stories I've heard concern old women's fancy for young men, and Randolph reports several of these in *Pissing in the Snow and Other Ozark Folktales.* As the Southern black comedienne, Moms Mabley, used to say: "Ain't nothin' no old man can do for me 'cept bring me a message from a young man." I confess I look forward to old age if I can be as bad as Granny and Moms.

Southern or not, women everywhere talk about sex—sex with young boys, old men, and handsome strangers—and sexual errors, both good and bad. Newly married couples are some of their favorite characters along with prostitutes, preachers, rabbis, nuns, Easterners, country boys and girls, foreigners, and traveling salesmen. In general, men are more often the victims of women's jokes than not. Tit for tat, we say. Usually the subject for laughter is men's boasts, failures, or inadequacies ("comeuppance for lack of uppcomance," as one of my aunts would say). One story my granny tells is about the two women who were arguing as to whether old men could satisfy women. They argued back and forth until one quieted the other by asking if she'd "ever tried to stuff spaghetti up a pig's butt?"

Preachers take the brunt of many jokes, and one can understand, given the Southern church's rigorous control over women's lives, why parson stories are true favorites. Preachers either get away with what they can never brag about or, worse, get caught with their clerical piety down. In a joke my aunt tells a young nun sits across from a prostitute on a train. When the sweet little nun inquires solicitously of the painted lady what she does to get such beautiful clothes, the lady replies that she is a prostitute.

"Oh, my," said the nun. "I've never met a prostitute. What do you do?"

"Well," the lady said, "I sleep with men for money."

"Oh, my goodness," gasped the nun, "how much do you charge?"

"Twenty-five dollars," said the lady.

"Twenty-five dollars," the nun said in surprise, "why, pooh on Father O'Brien and his cookies!"

Country boys and strangers are popular targets. The former are noted for their affections for sheep and their mothers and sisters. Strangers play tricks on local folk, most particularly for their efforts to get the farmers' daughters. In a story repeated in *Pissing in the Snow*, one of my Southern Indian-Kentucky migrant friends told of the onshore sailor who had the joke played on him. He visited a small-town prostitute, but was too drunk to know what he was doing. As he huffed and puffed in his efforts to get his money's worth, he asked how he was doing.

"Oh, about three knots," replied the lady.

"Three knots?" he asked.

"Yeah," she said. "It's not hard. It's not in. And you're not gonna get your money back."

My granny would tell us about the country boy who came to work with two black eyes. When his friend asked how he got them, he said, "Well, when we stood up in church yesterday morning, a fat lady in front of me had her dress tucked up between her buttocks. I thought to help her out so I pulled the dress straight and she turned around and hit me in the eye."

"But you have two black eyes."

And the country boy said, "Well, when she turned back around, I figured she must have wanted her dress like it was, so I put it back."

I have rarely heard from women material that I would consider to be deeply derogatory to women or men; I have as rarely heard racist sex tales from women, black or white. Thus, the women's repertoires, like those of other groups, are as distinctive for their omissions as for their inclusions. Southern men tell stories about many of the same characters as women, but their emphases and inferences are, I believe, quite different.

I cannot recall hearing many bawdy songs from women, but a kind of bawdy wordplay or word invention appears to be quite common among Southern women; here the content is often scatological rather than sexual. My mother's favorite curse is "shit fire and save matches." The comic naming of genital areas ("Possible" for: wash up as far as possible, down as far as possible, and then wash possible) offered women an enormous opportunity for bawdy language play. Here the many names were not in themselves bawdy though their immediate referent was. In my family a woman's pubic area was known as a "Chore Girl" or a "woolly booger." Here, I leave the reader to ponder the cultural significance of the terrifying "booger" in Southern life as well as the visual, metaphoric impact of the well-known (well-used and worn-out) scrub pad on women's imaginations. I never heard a woman use but one (twat) of the numerous derogatory terms for women's genitalia that Southern men use (gash, slash, pussy, cunt, etc.).

Our Chore Girls and woolly boogers were affectionately referred to, as were the male "tallywhackers." Again, I marvel at the richness of cultural interpretation possible as well as at the cynicism with which Chore Girls and tallywhackers were invented. So much for moonlight and magnolias. What is interesting in all the naming is that Southern ladies' reputed public preference for euphemisms (e.g., "he Critter" for "bull") travels to the private sector as well.

Southern women love to discuss death, disease, dying, and pain. But they also love to invent comic diseases accompanied by a comic definition of the disease. Just the shorthand name of the ailment said by one of my female relatives while we were in public or polite company could be guaranteed to send all the children into fits of laughter. Whenever one of us would complain of some unspecified ailment, Granny would say that we had the "hiergarchy"—that's when you usually fly high but have to light low to shit. Or when someone really behaved badly she would inform us that he had the "spanque" (pronounced span-Q). "That's when there's not enough skin on the ass to cover the hole," Granny would say. There were, of course, non-bawdy diseases like the "epizooty," applied to unspecified craziness or illness, but Granny seemed to know more people who had the spanque and the hiergarchy than the epizooty.

Bawdy material has many uses for many reasons. Obviously it's entertaining to those who use it and presumably to their audiences who continue to demand it. But why it entertains is something else again. I can scarcely develop a theory of humor here, but I can speculate on the uses of the material beyond the simple evocation of laughter. That function of evoking laughter, however, is an important one in the analysis of women's material since women, stereotypically, do not have reputations as humorists. Women themselves often say they cannot and do not tell jokes. The media comediennes stand alone in their presentation of women as inventors and perpetuators of humor, but even there few beyond Moms Mabley and Lily Tomlin, both from Southern cultures, have gone outside the boundaries of portraying women as humorous objects rather than as humorists. With bawdy lore, women can see themselves as comic storytellers and comic artists. In the women's world, as in the men's, the premier storyteller and singer—the inventive user of language—commands respect and admiration. And the ability to bring laughter to people is as much admired as the preacher's power to bring tears. Clearly, the material is educational, but in an unexpected way. Unlike the enormous repertoire of horror stories used to convince children (particularly young women) of the importance of maintaining the culture's public agenda ("Why, I know one girl who sat on a park toilet and got a disease and she could never marry"), the bawdy tales debunk and defy those rules. The very telling defies the rules ("Nice women shouldn't even know what a prostitute is much less what she does"). Women are not supposed to know or repeat such stuff. But they do and when they do, they speak ill of all that is sacred—men, the church, marriage, home, family, parents.

It is almost a cliché to say that humor is a form of social criticism, but the shoe certainly fits here. Southern women *ought* to get married and have children and like it, according to overt cultural prescriptions, but marriage and sex in bawdy lore are not always attractive states. In a story one woman told Vance Randolph, a young Cracker wife complains about her beekeeper husband's stinginess. He makes her lick old sour molasses off his pecker every night though he keeps three hundred pounds of strained honey in the house. Not a lovely portrait.

A standard comment on sex usually offered by married women is "I give it to him once a week whether he needs it or not." But some of the stories make sex, with whomever happens to be attractive, sound downright appealing, and that version differs from the duty-bound version ladies often purvey to prospective brides. So, in bawdy lore, women speak with disgust, relish, or cynicism about what they ought not to admit to in their socialized state. The bawdy lore gives a Bronx cheer to sacred cows and bulls.

But the bawdy lore itself is a form of socialization to the hidden agenda in Southern women's lives and thoughts. The tales and sayings tell young women what they can expect in private out of the men and the institutions they are taught to praise in public, and they inform them as they could never be informed in "serious" conversation. Poking fun at a man's sexual ego, for example, might never be possible in real social situations with the men who have power over their lives, but it is possible in a joke. The hilarity over the many tiny or nonperforming tallywhackers, or the foolish sexual escapades of drunken, impotent men form a body of material over which women vent their anger at males and offer alternative modes of feeling to the female hearers.

There is also a need for sex education, pure and simple, and bawdy lore serves that purpose as well as others. My granny's sayings about looking into a boy's genes/jeans made me ask about genes, which led to a discussion of why I couldn't marry my age-mate cousin and beget pop-eyed, slack-jawed kids. And those first bawdy stories about young married couples, lard, and hide glue led to inquiries about the *sex act* in general. Why, please, would anyone want to use lard or Vaseline in sex anyway? One may still ask that question, but posing it to my cousin got me a lot of information in return. The kind of sex education I got from the bawdy stories and from inquiries about them was no more erroneous or harmful than the "where babies come from" lecture, and it was a good deal more artistic and fun.

So participation in fun, rebellion, and knowledge-giving were all a part of what those naughty ladies gave me and what Southern women can continue to give new generations of women. For those who engage in bawdry, the reward comes from having been bad and good at it. The respect that her audiences give the bawdy female narrator backs up the delight she gets from the forbidden nature of it all. What she purveys is a closet humor, taken out and enjoyed whenever and wherever ladies meet—while they work together and while they relax together. Their humor requires no pick-up, no men's club, no coffee can for spitting, no coon hunt, no Mason jars full of whiskey, and no chaw of Red Dog Tobacco —just a kitchen, a porch, a parlor, and a private, willing audience of ladies. Next time you see a group of women in that particular set, don't assume they're sharing the latest recipe for peach cobbler. The subject may be other delights.

TRIBUTE TO MY HUSBAND

✢ MATTIE MAE NELSON

This is the autobiography of my life up until June 6, 1961.

I was born in Patrick County on February 22, 1909, near a little place called Stella. My father was Meggs Nelson and mother was Etta Tilley Nelson. We lived on Jeff Tilley's land and was a sharecropper for many years. There were ten of us children two of which died while we lived there. They were buried in a cemetery near where we lived. It has since been cleared out and a nice house built there. I attended a two-room school, called the Woods' School, until I was the age of eleven years old, and then we moved to Henry County. Near Mt. Pleasant School, which I attended until I was sixteen. My father died on July 22, 1922. There were eight of us children living then ranging in age from nine months to sixteen years old. So my brother that was sixteen got married the following October. So I was the oldest left at home there. My Grandfather Pink Nelson stayed with us the rest of that summer and helped us save our tobacco. So from then on until I was sixteen years old I had a hard time. Worked very hard in wheat and tobacco crops for people for anything they would give me. We lived near my grandparents on the Tilley side. They were very good to us. Helped us all they could and in return we helped them. So when I was fifteen years old I met a wonderful boy by the name of William Eliras Whitlock. We went together for about a year. And decided to get married. I did not have a decent dress for the wedding; he offered to get me one and I refused to let him get it. I was sixteen on February 22 and got married on March 27 in the year of 1925.

We were very happy although we lived with his parents for around three years and finely decided to move out to ourselves.

We still were poor but very happy and contented with what we had; we lived from place to place for several years and finely bought us a little place and built us a very cheap house. We lived in it until 1949 and then we remodeled it and made it comfortable. We still are poor in the sight of people, but underneath I feel like we are one of the richest couples in the world. We live a peaceful life and have a happy home. There's nothing in the world I wouldn't do for my husband (Bill) and I feel like he feels the same way about all of this as I do.

Couldn't anybody be any better to anyone than he is to me. So when I am gone which I feel like wont be much longer and he is left here. He wont have a thing to regret. I don't want him to forget me in a since of speaking. But I don't want him to worry anymore than he can help. So I would like this read at my funeral from where we remodeled the house. I would like for everybody to know what a wonderful person he is. If I could only be half as good as (he is. To everybody) I guess this would sound awful to other people. But to me it is just like music.

This document was contributed by Darnell Arnoult Stone, niece of Mattie Mae Nelson.

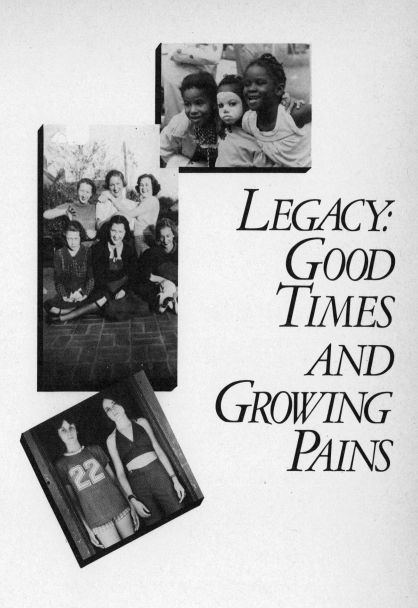

LEGACY: GOOD TIMES AND GROWING PAINS

 ❧ PART TWO

Coming of age in any culture is bound to have its ups and downs, and the experiences of the women in this section prove no exception. The scenes we watch move us through worlds which are very removed from each other, geographically and culturally, yet the themes enacted circle in and around us all. Again, we are witnessing events in the lives of "ordinary" people, but they demonstrate what it means to grow up with a drama as vivid as the saga of a more celebrated life. Contrast Mary Mebane, caught in the devastating web of class, sex, and color bias designed to keep her in her place—struggling to extricate herself through education—and Titter, immersed in the proscriptive deceptions and expectations of her class—unaware that there is anyplace else to go. Their stories tell us more about discrimination than any statistical analysis or polemic.

The period of national self-examination precipitated by the Southern black civil rights movement, expanded by the growing consciousness of the role racism played in the war against the Vietnamese in the sixties, has moved the pens of writers of the seventies and eighties. Our politics have been sharpened, radicalized, but so has the way we look at ourselves. Today we not only talk freely about topics once thought either trivial or taboo—sexuality, harassment, violence at home, segregation—in the context of adult lives; we also probe the process of indoctrination we underwent in childhood. The point is not to accuse but to understand, with the underlying hope that by sharing the pain and the memories of good times we can replace resentful silence with dialogue. In taking these bold steps into once forbidden territory, we may begin to tear down the walls of isolation.

Amelia Diaz-Ettinger shares a child's discovery of the human side of her formidable aunt, and Lily May Ledford brings back memories of the larger-than-life adults who inhabited and terrorized our childhood.

CORN SHUCKINGS, FIDDLE CONTESTS, SQUARE DANCES: ORAL HISTORY WITH LILY MAY LEDFORD

✒ ELLESA CLAY HIGH

Lily May Ledford was born in the Red River Gorge of eastern Kentucky. Part of the Daniel Boone National Forest today, the Gorge is a wilderness of cliffs and stone arches, dense woods and secluded hollers. From the late 1800s until the 1920s the seemingly endless resources of the Gorge itself, including one of the largest hardwood forests on earth, were able to support a thriving network of loggers and railroaders, fishers and trappers, farmers and an accompanying stream of sharecroppers.

However, when the logging companies had harvested their timber they left, taking their jobs with them and often closing down their railroads as well. Many families then had little choice but to leave also. Later, the Great Depression and the general migration of Appalachians to the urban North during the 1940s drew more people away. Aside from the sprinkling of established farmers who owned the narrow bottomlands by Red River, few could permanently support themselves in the area. Today, little remains of the mountain culture that flourished there.

As part of a tenant family with fourteen children, Lily May experienced growing up in the Gorge as a round of household chores and labor in the cornfields. But life there was also filled with strong family relationships, sustaining ties with the land—and, more importantly, a love of music. For her, the ballads, hymns, and mountain-shout songs of her youth meant more than casual entertainment. Music lent a sense of accomplishment and delight to a sharecropping life that otherwise may have seemed unremitting.

In 1936, at the age of nineteen, Lily May left the Gorge to begin a career as a professional musician, joining the "National Barn

Dance" at radio station WLS in Chicago. Then, as lead musician of the Coon Creek Girls, the first all-girl string band on radio, she continued performing in a field where few women previously had been successful. Soon after the band was formed they played for the Roosevelts and the king and queen of England at the White House. Later, she and the Coon Creek Girls spent eighteen years entertaining both live and radio audiences at Renfro Valley, Kentucky. Though she plays a variety of instruments, including the fiddle, bass fiddle, guitar, and mandolin, she is best known for her hard-driving, old-time mountain style of banjo playing.

When we lived at Chimney Top, in the Gorge, everybody around us lived much the same way as we did. Now some who owned their little pieces of land and didn't have to share half their crop with a landlord prospered more than we did. They was able to keep enough corn to go to the mill all summer and buy flour, too, and always have biscuits for breakfast. We didn't always have them, though we tried to as much as we could. We'd fry salt pork or side meat and make gravy to sop our biscuits in. Our hams we never did eat. We cured and sold them. We ate the shoulders and side meat, the jowls, but the hams we felt we just could not afford. So some would always carry biscuits with jam and butter, and ever once in a while cake or things we never could have had in our lunch pails, unless it was molasses cookies—what we called sweet cakes. Corn, of course, was the big crop, and I've hoed in ever little patch of ground up and down that river—if not at home, then for other people. We'd usually get paid about fifty cents a day for that. A lot of times we had corn bread for breakfast, made from our own corn that we'd take to the grist mill in Nada ever Saturday. We'd shell corn the night before and that was a party in itself.

The corn shellings, of course, would start in the fall at corn-gathering time. You couldn't gather it to store while it still had any milk. Saturday was always mill day because it was the only time the miller worked all day and the mill would be open from daylight till dark. So we'd have the parties on Friday nights. It'd usually just be our family, but once in a while somebody from way across Pinch-Em Tight Ridge would come three or four miles, carrying a lantern, to get in on it with us and have a chance to visit. They had to go to the mill the next day, too. They'd tell what little gossip they'd picked up from the outside world and talk about their illnesses and rheumatism. They'd bring their guns and hunt on the way home. Their dogs would always fight with ours so there'd be two or three dogfights, and the boys'd get out in the yard and have a cob fight in the night and cold, dodging and hiding behind the house and barn! And it was all fun.

Sometimes someone would bring a musical instrument if they had one. An old man and his boy that lived way across several mountains on Tarr Ridge were on a long walking trip and stopped to break the night. They brought their fiddle and banjo, and I heard three instruments playing together for the first time. And I can't tell you! Before that, Daddy just played the fiddle, and I felt a rhythm in me of some kind, but it was never carried out in my hearing. But when the banjo played along with the fiddles I began to feel something I'd never really felt before—a rhythm in music. And oh, my goodness! Now I don't know if we shelled corn that night or not!

Let me tell you about the first real instrument I owned. I had made me a bow. Things drifted back into the mountains from other places, and somewhere I'd gotten hold of a thick rubber string from an inner tube. I tied it to each end of a green willow stick, and I was going to shoot at targets with it, using sticks for arrows. I sat down to rest way up on a hillside and began to pluck on that string, and it made a nice "boing" sound, you know. Then I held it in my mouth so I could pick and hold it and kind of anchor it. But I found when I moved my mouth it would make a different tone and sound. So I commenced trying to play it, and before long I could do a whole tune on that thing. I knew my brothers, who teased us girls a lot anyhow, would laugh if I took it home, so I hid it under a ledge and would go back to it the next day and get away from Momma. It lasted quite a long time, until we moved on down the river from Chimney Top. I was about twelve, and we were still sharecropping about the same way.

One day I was down by the creek picking polk and a little boy came walking down the road. This was around 1929 and a car couldn't get through then—just horses and wagons. This boy had an old fiddle in his hands, and he was swinging it by the neck and batting weeds and branches with it! Now to me that fiddle was a sacred thing, like something alive. I was afraid he was going to damage it, and it'd already had all the damage it could take, I think. Anyway, I stopped him and asked him where was he going with that fiddle.

He said, "My uncle give it to me and I don't want it—I was just going to trade it off."

I said, "Would you sell it to me if I find you some things at home to trade with?" He said yes.

There was an old pair of gum boots, I remember, and a sling shot, and an old sweater belonging to one of my brothers, and a flashlight that had no batteries and maybe nothing else on it—just all the little old attractions I could find to get that fiddle away from him somehow. Finally he picked out the things he wanted. And there went my precious box of crayons—I drew and colored, too, and crayons was so hard to come by. They only cost a nickel, but how hard it was to come by a nickel in the first place! I could tell he felt he'd got the best end of the deal—I knew by the way he went strutting down the road, smiling to hisself. And I thought I'd got the best end of the deal, in fact I knew I had. That was one of the happiest days of my life, and I believe it was fate, because I never heard of or saw that boy again.

Well, that old fiddle didn't have nothing on it—no strings or keys or apron. I whittled that out myself. I made the apron rough cut and I don't remember how I fastened it onto the end of the fiddle, but I believe I wired it on a little knob. Then I burnt holes in it to hold on to the strings—I used a red hot wire like I'd seen my daddy do to get that done. And then I whittled my keys.

And Momma began to quarreling. She saw what was going to take place and she said, "Now the garden's got to be hoed, and there's water to carry, and I'm going to wash today, and I've got to have help, and you've got to take care of this baby, and you've got to help get dinner. . . ." She began to think of everything in the world. Well, I was determined that day to get my fiddle fixed up first. That had to be done—I couldn't wait. So I slipped off from poor old Momma again because I knew somebody else would do the work.

Finally I got everything I needed. I found some blue sticky mud and filled in the cracks in it. We had some old scraps of banjo strings around the house and I strung it with those. Then I made a bow out of a green willow stick and tied some of our old white work horse's tail on it. His name was Charlie, and he was just as dirty as he could be. The boys were always teasing him and had him kind of mean. They'd blow in his ear and pull his tail, and he'd bite and squeal at them. I was still small and hadn't ridden him much, and I was afraid of him. Well, I found him in the barn, with his backside pointed right at me. I climbed in a cow stall first, reached over with a pair of scissors, and chopped me out a big hunk of his tail. He kicked a little and swung his head around at me, but he didn't bite. So I tied each end of the hair to the stick and drew it tight. Of course, old Charlie's tail was greasy and I had to have some rosin, so I found some oozing out of a pine stump and I rosined my bow with that. Last I put a rattlesnake rattle inside the fiddle to improve the sound. All mountain fiddlers did that to pick up the tone quality.

Then I took my fiddle and went way up a mountain and behind a big boulder, hoping Momma couldn't hear me. I didn't want to hear her either. And I stayed up there the rest of the day. I learned how to play about three songs that first day—all that was in my head. We got a few primitive ballads from Momma, but her people were hard-shell Baptists and string music wasn't allowed in her house. I heard my daddy play every night. We'd shell corn or pop it or parch it, and he'd play his fiddle tunes. He also played the Autoharp till he traded it off to a kinsman. But he couldn't sing. He had no more than a half-octave range, and his voice would pop into a yodel. Then we'd go to laughing and he'd get mad.

Once this fiddle fell apart, somehow my daddy got enough money to order one. It was seven dollars from Sears and Roebuck. My little brother Coyen had been trying to play my old fiddle, and with the new one he began catching up and passing me in no time at all. He was a highly accomplished fiddle player at the age of twelve.

Both of us played the fiddling contests. Sometimes my brother'd win it and sometimes I would. But a trick thing I did would usually take away from him because it was judged on applause. I'd play my regular tunes, maybe "Mocking Bird" and "Cacklin' Hen," *then* I'd go out. I kept a pair of new overalls for the occasion, and I'd put them on over my dress. Then I'd come back and play "Pop Goes the Weasel." Where you pluck the strings twice and don't have to use the bow, and you can change the fiddle into different positions. Well, I'd play it through the regular way, then I'd play it in back of my head, then in back of my neck, and behind my back and behind my knees. I'd put the fiddle bow between my legs and rub the fiddle up and down on it, and then on the "pluck-pluck" I'd take it back up into position. Then I'd sit on the floor, fall back, and play under one knee, and then the other, and then under both of them, keeping my knees raised. Then I'd bow up a little and play under my back. When I'd hit the floor and finish my tune, of course, they'd tear the house down. That way I'd win the contest, which was unfair as it could be because it was Coyen that won it on purely good fiddling. I was about fifteen or sixteen years old. I didn't let Momma know I was doing that because she wouldn't have approved at all! I guess word got back to her, but she done found out she couldn't beat me and she had to let me go—course by that time she'd decided I wouldn't amount to nothing!

My sister Rosie was also getting hot on the guitar. Morgan Skidmore was real good on it, too, and Coyen was already sharp on the fiddle. So the four of us got up a little band and called ourselves the Red River Ramblers! And we began to be in demand all up and down the river for square dances.

Almost every weekend there'd be a square dance at different people's homes. But the biggest deal would be when we had a working to go with the dance. The men would mostly set the tobacco or clear the ground, but if there was single boys, some of us grown girls would help, too, and just let the mothers cook the big dinner. They'd fix thirty or forty dishes, and whoever was having the working would furnish the party. The women would have a quilting frame somewhere and talk in the afternoon. Everybody'd knock off about four o'clock to go home and do the chores, get cleaned up, and then get back for the square dance. Word would be passed up and down the river, and musicians and others would come clear from Cane Creek and off the ridges. Some walked for miles to get there—wade the river and everything else. The dances would start about dusky dark and go on until the parents told us to quit, since mostly only young folk came.

It was these square dances with the stringed music that scared Momma to death. She got that from her father, of course, that it was an idleness and therefore of the Devil and the Devil's workshop. She gradually let us go, but only if our brothers or Daddy would go with us. Sometimes us girls have waded the river to our waists to get to somebody's house on the other side, and it might be winter time. We'd carry our shoes and take along a dry rag to wipe our feet off right before we got there and put them back on.

Momma also didn't want us going because there was always so much work to do. Her mind was running a mile ahead of everybody else's. She had it laid out in her head ever night before she went to sleep, how the next day would go and what everybody's job would be. She announced it at the breakfast table or sometimes before she went to bed, and my daddy'd agree with her. But she was the main leader. We could have prospered with her, I believe, if my daddy hadn't done so many foolish things. Oh, lord, he traded us out of so much that we needed! Buddy, if he saw a gun he'd love to hunt with, he'd trade off the last milk cow we had. And poor old Momma, she just worried and fretted herself to death with his foolishness. Boy, she loved him, though, better than anything in this world, and she kind of had him for a pet, you know.

We didn't get any church until we moved on down the river, except for experiences with our momma and daddy. They had a big Bible and read aloud from it a great deal, especially my daddy. And it seemed like they preached the fear of God more than the love of God. My daddy's people were all Methodists, and as I've said, on my mother's side they were hard-shell or primitive Baptists, and they didn't allow stringed music. That's why we had such a hard time when we all started playing. But I'll swear, I still believe the fiddle was one thing that attracted Momma to my daddy. She loved to hear him play and thought it perfectly all right, him and his fiddle. And she had a few old songs. She was so workminded, one of them was typical of her: [sings] "We'll work till Jesus comes, we'll work till Jesus comes . . ." I believe in her mind she thought manual labor and the work she was doing was what was being referred to in the song—that was the kind of work we was supposed to do, as God had laid it out for us.

I'll never forget this. One night we tried to have a square dance and one of my uncles came in. Ever time he got drunk he thought he was a preacher, and he could climb up a tree, preach, and go on so! And, of course, string music and dancing was the Devil—you couldn't have it in your house. He was a man in his forties, and we hadn't seen him in a long time. He come in and said, "What's going on here, White?"

My daddy and momma was watching the little ones and sitting by the fireplace in the next room from where we were dancing. And Papa said, "We had a working today so we're having a square dance tonight."

He said, "Now I want that music stopped and these people out of here!"

And my daddy said, "Listen, it's none of your business what we do."

He said, "By God, that's my sister, though, and I know how she was raised. And I'm not going to have it!"

My daddy got down his gun and said, "Oh, yes, we will have it. And if you don't like it, you can leave here."

And boy, he got scared. He took off, and you could see that lantern running, absolutely flying through the cornfield the way he came!

There'd be a square dance nearly every Saturday night somewhere on the river, though seldom through the week. We'd sometimes have a little play-party games on Wednesday nights. When
they could finally find a preacher we'd hold a prayer meeting on
Wednesday night, too, and that was used as a social thing as well as
religious. So if we had anything extry at all, it would always be
then, to break the week.

A play-party was "Skip to My Lou," where you change partners
and sing as you go through the figures. But you didn't use music
and you didn't dance—it was more of a run-through: [sings to the
tune of "Skip to my Lou"]

> Hurry up, hurry up, this will never do,
> Hurry up, hurry up, this will never do. . . .

And you go back and forward, make a circle and hold hands. And
Momma permitted the kissing games—she was young. So we'd
have those and play-party for a while: "Skip to My Lou," "Paw-
Paw Patch," "Swing a Lady Up and Down," and everybody'd sing
while you did the figures.

We'd have these at one another's houses, whoever had a floor
big enough to circle in and dance. Ever body had to do the evening
chores, the milking and feeding, and then we'd go to gathering in
about dark. Sometimes we'd quit around eleven o'clock, and at
some places they danced all night. We'd just invite the closest families around, and we always made candy. There were some good
cooks down at the river, and the boys brought the brown and
white sugar we needed to go in it. Sometimes we'd have them buy
Karo Syrup to make peanut-butter roll, and they would have to go
to Bowen or Nada to get it.

So ever body'd be in the kitchen, watching us daub it out. Some
nights we poured pull-candy into shallow, buttered plates. Boys
and girls would pull together on that taffy, then swap ends till it
got real hard and pretty. They'd kind of court a bit, team up and
pull together, and I found myself pulling by myself most of the
time! Then we'd stretch the candy out and let it lay for just a minute, then take scissors and cut it into little pillows. We'd eat it all
up that night.

We'd usually play a while first because ever body wanted in on
the candy and we didn't start making it till later. So one of the
more forward ones would say, "Now let's 'Skip to My Lou,' " and
we'd go through that till we got tired of it. We'd waltz around, and

sometimes the boys would line up on one side and the girls on the other. A girl would come out of the corner for "Swing a Lady Up and Down"—it was like "The Virginia Reel," and we'd sing to accompany it. Then we'd make candy and eat it.

In a kissing game, like "Snap," only four was up on the floor till they'd all kissed. They went through some formations first, then they'd put their arms across one another's shoulders, all lean in and kiss their partner, then the opposite partner, and then their own again. Then they'd break up and leave one to choose the next three. When we'd get tired somebody'd say, "Now let's play 'Spin the Bottle' or 'Spin the Plate,'" and whichever one was spinning would kiss whoever it landed in front of or pointed to. A thimble brought on post-office kissing. I've forgotten how "Who's Got the Thimble" went. Maybe they'd pass another little object around— gravel or something. But two would have to go to a dark room and kiss, then they'd come out blushing, and we'd go through it again.

The older people would always be there and join in, the kissing games and all! Of course, to us they were old, but I imagine that most were in their late thirties. The young ones had to be brought along, but they'd set in the corner and be good. They didn't take part in the games—really, they were too busy fighting one another.

A square dance to us was a lot bigger deal. A big play-party had twelve people, but a crowd at a square dance was twenty-five. You had to have fiddles, guitars, and banjos. You may not be able to tell it now, but I was a good dancer and won some contests square dancing, but all I really ever wanted was to play. My great thrill was me and Coyen on the fiddle and four or five guitars around us.

Then every Sunday, since nobody else would go with me, I went by myself to Natural Bridge. That was about an eight-mile walk from Red River. I'd start out around daylight with my fiddle in a flour sack to protect it, go across the mountain, and walk up the railroad through the tunnel clear to Natural Bridge where an excursion train ran from Cincinnati every Sunday. They had a big pavilion built right by the track where the train stopped, and it had benches all around, a big dance floor, and a good roof.

I'd sit there and start playing by myself, and there'd be a few workers wandering around. But soon crowds would start pouring out of the hollers. Poor old plow boys would come with their little pints of moonshine stuck down in their shirt, the shirt a-bagging where it'd run down next to their belt. They'd always wear a long-billed cap or felt hat, and they'd stick a rose under each side of it.

And they'd wear a white shirt and a pair of overalls or some kind of khaki work pants as their Sunday best. They'd come first.

Then the excursion train would come and unload, well-dressed people would get off, and they'd all start square dancing. By then several other musicians would appear and start helping me. So I'd play all day, and most of the other musicians would, too. Some of the old people that later made it in radio, like Asa Martin, he'd come sometimes, and so would Shorty Hobbs, who made a fine mandolin player and comedian and lived up in Wolfe County. I think Asa was already in radio a little bit and recording at that time, but not Shorty. Then Ruby Mays's uncles, Carl and Tom, would come with their fiddle and banjo, and we'd play and they'd dance all day.

Somebody'd pass the hat, and we'd get ever thing in the world in it—a little money, all pennies and nickels and dimes; and bobbie pins; and sticks of chewing gum. And pretty soon all the old boys from around there would get drunk and go passing their caps and hats, and run off with the money! But I usually wound up with at least a couple of dollars every time I'd go.

So I would sit in that one spot the whole blessed day and play the fiddle. I never really thought about money or wanting to get up and dance, or getting me a drink of water or anything to eat—I had no money, of course, to eat on. Just playing music—that's all in the world I wanted to do.

GROWING UP SOUTHERN & SEXY

❧ MARIE STOKES JEMISON

I was a virgin when I got married. All my friends were, too, or at least they never told me if they weren't. Nice Southern girls did not go "all the way." We just drove boys crazy, blowing in their ears, letting them feel our bosoms, then shutting the door in their panting faces. The war changed everything and saved a lot of prostate glands.

The Depression laid on strong in Montgomery, Alabama, in the late 1930s, and there was no money to buy anything or go anywhere, making for a slow and boring life for privileged white teenagers in a sleepy South. All the big migrations were yet to come and in 1938 there was no reason to believe that the people with whom we grew up would not be friends for the rest of our lives. We would be in each others' weddings and be godmothers to each others' babies, just like our mothers before us. Girls grew into women aping their mothers, and boys shouldered fishing rods and guns under the tutelage of their fathers, just like always.

We were thirteen and full of beans; nothing much happened for us after school hours. Competitive sports were for boys and we were content to cheer for the home team from the sidelines. Each pert or pitiful girl-child dreamed the only dream we knew about the male sex: that the broadest available hunk of shoulders would swagger over and choose her to take to the drive-in and neck.

With no money and nowhere to go, but too restless to sit before the radio, we spent a lot of our free time between the ages of twelve and fourteen in Doc's drugstore, flirting and peeping at the dirty books the drugstore cowboys flashed around behind the shelves of Castoria and Sloan's liniment. The repulsive, cheap pictures of comic strip characters like Dick Tracy and Little Orphan Annie screwing each other gave us a charge.

Miss Rose Herndon was my best friend Winkie's mother. She stayed in bed all day, a female sight not unusual in our circle. Rose suffered from punishing "migraines" whenever she exerted herself to go to the grocery or drive the car. After Winkie was born she went to bed for good. When her husband, Sam, came home from the country club around nine or ten at night she departed her bed, put on a wrapper, and cooked him a hot dinner, all the while cursing "bastard" under her breath.

Sprawled on her bed, summer and winter, with us stretched out on the floor, Rose wove wonderful tales of her girlhood in a house full of sisters and the comings and goings of "beau lovers." Storytelling excited Rose. Her pale face took on a fevered pink as she called out frequently in a bright, strong voice, "Loula, bring me a beer." She enjoyed visualizing us as grown-up ladies and often pulled me up from the floor toward the long, goldleaf, pier mirror standing at the foot of the bed. Snatching my hair back or piling it up on top and bending her head to look critically, she would say, "My, but you are gonna be a knockout, sweetheart. Some man is gonna lose his mind over you." I believed her blandishments.

Rose never had any cash, but she could charge at the drugstore. Several times a week she would call out to Uncle T, the old black man who swept around and waited on Loula, "T, go get these children some ice cream and tell Doc to send me $25." A curious child, I questioned this arrangement. "What does it say on the bill, Miss Rose? Does it say, '$100 worth of ice cream,' or what?" "No, darlin'," she added, "he is the banker for the neighborhood wives. If Sam complains about the amount of medicine charged, I just tell him my migraines were worse. How would he know the difference? He is never home." And he rarely was.

Rose had an Aunt Carrie, who rustled in to sit on the bed and visit. She was a tall, skinny, elegant old lady of around fifty when we were twelve. We loved her visits when she swept in bearing the fresh apple muffins that were her cook's specialty. Dressed in romantic gray or purple chiffon that billowed out behind as she passed in front of the electric fan and always just back from a cruise on the Nile or full of talk about her next archeological dig in Greece, she dazzled us with her exotic glamour.

"Was Aunt Carrie ever married?" I asked Rose after that lady's flowing departure one afternoon.

"Yes, my precious, but long ago and not for long."

"How long?" we chorused.

"Less than a week," whispered Rose, averting her eyes.

"A week! What happened?"

Clearing her throat, Rose answered hesitantly, "It was one of those things you just don't ask. It was so long ago. I was your age and I remember. . . ."

"Go on, Mother," wailed Winkie.

"Well, something happened on the honeymoon."

"What was it?" insisted Winkie.

Rose could not bring herself to divulge Carrie's secret. "A beer, Loula." Panting a little and bravely whispering, she lay back murmuring, "Darlings, I have a beast of a headache." Drawing a wet cloth over her eyes from a bowl of water on the bedside table, she signaled the end of that conversation, whispering weakly, "It was so long ago."

My friend Tina's was a fascinating house to visit because of her mother, Florida—a small, blonde china doll with a brain like a steel trap. This was during the depression, and Florida's land was in South Alabama with taxes to pay. The red-brick-columned "Beauvior"—romantically placed among giant water oaks and hung with imported gray moss—was heavily mortgaged. There seemed to be no earthly way Florida could get the money she needed. But even with her worries, she found time to speculate on our futures. She would often grab one of us as we ran through the house and gently pat our emerging bosoms. "My, but it looks as if these will grow into small cantaloupes, angel. You are going to drive the men crazy."

Florida's husband, Oliver, was a patrician loser who drank too much, and had "given up." On hot summer afternoons Florida paced the upstairs hall in her girdle trying to think of a way to save the plantation. In the late summer of 1938 she found it. We sat on her bed while she packed lovely, thin, flowing pastel dresses and two big hats decorated with roses. "I am going to Long Island for the weekend," she told us.

When she returned she looked different, more relaxed. There was an air of mystery about her. When we asked if she had a good time she looked obliquely at us as if she held a secret. That mystery was quickly solved. Within two weeks a short, portly, and stern-looking older man, Mr. Hay, appeared in a long, chauffeur-driven, black car. Florida and her mother Gin had put on their long, filmy, low-cut frocks to entertain him on the veranda. It must have worked, for within three months Florida had divorced the loser and married a winner.

Mr. Hay had a town house on East 64th Street in New York City and a large estate in Locust Valley, Long Island. Florida's clothes got grander, her furs silkier, her body hung with jewels. The last time I saw her (she died of a heart attack soon after) was in the house on 64th Street. She was at one end of the long dining table and Mr. Hay was at the far end. I was sitting on her right, and she was telling me that she simply could not stand Mr. Hay. He was tightfisted, she said. There was a house in Nassau she wanted, but he said no. About that time Mr. Hay asked, down the length of the table, "Florida, what are you saying?" Butter wouldn't melt in Florida's mouth. "Darling, I was just telling Titter how much I loved you."

Lucy Belle Pearman was my second-best friend. Pudgy, fat, with a soft, white body that reminded me of a featherless pigeon, Lucy Belle (another only child) was the apple of her parents' eyes. Mr. Pearman, or Big Roy as we called him, did not appear to work and their source of income was a mystery. Somewhere along the way I was given to understand that Big Velma, Lucy Belle's mother, had the money. Her people had bought land cheap down on the Gulf Coast where Panama City grew and down Mobile way where the highway was coming through.

Big Roy might have worked at something, but he was always home when we got home from school about three, sitting in his undershirt by the radio drinking a beer. Our routine in their house comprised a dash to the kitchen to wolf down a piece of Big V's sunshine cake and a cola. Then back for a tease from Roy. "Come here, sugar," he winked at me. "Close your eyes and hold out your hand." Knowing well the next move I still giggled and squeezed my eyelids together. "Here's a present from Uncle Roy," and he dumped warm ashes from his smelly cigar into my outstretched hand. This had been no surprise since the first time, but I went along with the "trick" because it seemed a friendly gesture. It also gave Lucy Belle and me reason to release all that prepubescent pent-up energy. Screaming with laughter the next move was to jump on him and swap tickles.

My father never had any time to take us anywhere, but Roy Pearman did. Around age thirteen, we hit on a pastime that he enjoyed as much as we. The Red Light District was well defined in Montgomery, on the edge of "nigger town," and the trick was to drive slowly along the street with no car lights. The women stood in the doorways of the seedy houses barely covered by flimsy kimonos, their limbs in silhouette from the dim light behind. Occasionally men would stagger out, but nobody we knew.

In our still-small town the names of these "ladies of the evening," as my mother delicately called them, were known to all. On Wednesday night when Velma and Roy played bridge, Lucy Belle spent the night at my house and we entertained ourselves by calling the "ladies." Holding a handkerchief over the receiver to muffle the voice the caller attempted a low, male sound and whispered something devilish like, "How much does it cost under water?" Or, "Do you charge half price for midgets?" The poor victim was not destined to suffer long as we invariably got the giggles and hung up, so convulsed with laughter that we often wet our pants. We had no idea, of course, what these women really did or even how the sex act occurred. All our information was acquired by hearsay or from those dirty books passed around by the drugstore cowboys.

If I learned anything about sex at all in those protected years it was from my father and certainly not on purpose. Papa was a self-made man, an early rendition of a good old boy. From a plain South Alabama country family, orphaned as a baby, he was raised by older brothers and sisters, learning only to survive. After one year in college the money ran out and he had to go to work. Good-looking, bawdy-talking, and oozing charm, he snowed the patrician lady who became my mother. She was soft, gentle, and submissive and never quite got over marrying a man with whom she had so little in common.

Papa was an earthy man and loved horseplay. Grabbing me in his huge farmerlike hands, pinning me hard against his chest in a steel grip, he blew in my ears as I struggled helplessly, yelping with joy at the undocumented sensation. I never got too old to sit on his lap. Long after other fathers had self-consciously ceased this familial intimacy, Papa still pulled me down for snuggles. After age twelve and blossoming bosoms, it was embarrassing for me, but not for him. He never seemed shy that his breath came more quickly with me so close and for that I have come to be grateful. I learned what a man smelled like and what close proximity did in a hurry to his glands. My father taught me in a crude but valid way that sexual response is as natural as breathing.

When we got to be thirteen or fourteen, the picture show took up much of our time. We'd sit in the back row of the balcony, learning to soul kiss in the blackness. When a boy's hand started to steal up the thigh it was time to slap him, be insulted (of course) but not leave. At roadside joints with names like Moonwinks and The Green Lantern, dancing close to Tommy Dorsey's "Marie," when a male hand got hot on my back and I was pressed so close I could feel something hard against my leg, I was satisfied. I had driven him crazy. That was what girls were supposed to do to boys.

"Do you know what boys do when they get all heated up?" Winkie asked one sweltering summer day as we lay on our stomachs on the cool marble hall floor at my house. "What?" I asked, not really expecting her to know. "They take a room at the Jeff Davis Hotel. The cops don't bother the hotel, so the bellboy can bring in a couple of floozies." She wrinkled her nose in distaste. "It's cheaper than those old whorehouses, you know, the ones Big Roy used to drive us by. This way, with one floozie, they can prorate expenses."

Then there were always those stories about the fellow who, after heavy necking with his date on the back seat, could stand it no more. Turning up his collar he rushes painfully off to the whorehouse only to return with a "social disease," which meant no nice girl would ever go out with him again.

Ethel was the most worldly girl in our crowd. She had been known to order a highball on a date; she read books like *Moby Dick* and had been to Chicago to the World's Fair. As we finished our sophomore year in high school, she announced she'd had it with Hickville and was heading toward those bright lights up north. (When my father heard the news, he said scornfully, "Well, she can afford it. Her old man is the biggest mortgage banker in town.")

At the train station, when Ethel left on the old Crescent Limited, we cried and took on as if she was going off to slave labor in Siberia. At the long-anticipated spend-the-night party on her return at Christmas, she told us the big news. "I'm not a virgin anymore," she proudly proclaimed, brushing her auburn pageboy into place. After our communal gasp, she continued smoothly, "Daddy reserved a drawing room for me on the Crescent because I had some studying to do. I took my math book to the diner for dinner and there was this cute young steward. He offered to help me with that horrible 'trig,' and I could have used some, but," she laughed, "I didn't get *that* kind of help. After he finished up in the diner he came back to my room and brought a bottle of Early Times. We had a ball. He was really good at it," she said, rolling her eyes. Aghast, we stared speechless at our friend. Now she was different, nothing would ever be the same. All night long the shock flattened Winkie, Tina, Lucy Belle, and me, causing us to wail and weep intermittently for our friend's loss, while she lay sleeping with a smile on her face. Was it for her we mourned, or because of all those pent-up emotions of our own? So much emotion, so few outlets.

Mother finally brought herself to tell me the facts of life, after a fashion, when I was fifteen, but she didn't have to tell me. "If you let him go too far, you will have a baby." Or, "Sister, you know boys don't marry girls with whom they have had their way." This knowledge had been part of my bones; unspoken, but rooted as firmly in the female consciousness as if in cement, was the dictum, "Nice girls don't go all the way."

Sometimes circumstances might *explain* the guilt of the individual, but our code of ethics still did not *excuse* it entirely. I saw with my own eyes eighteen-year-old Bess Kirksey bulge down the aisle of St. Martin's Episcopal Church behind her bouquet of Talisman roses at high noon, and my shock had not subsided when the eight-pound baby arrived less than six months later. When Lucy Belle, Tina, and I came back from the wedding snickering at Bess's plight, my mother said, "The child never had a chance; her parents are divorced. Her poor mother takes in sewing to try to support those three children. That sorry father just walked off and left her." To my mother and her generation divorce was indulged in only by lesser mortals with no social position to protect. Exposed to such parents, how could Bess have known any better?

The only official word my friends and I received on sex from family, church, and school was inadequate or fraudulent. Protected, sheltered, and lied to, we had one objective: get a husband. It never occurred to us that marriage should be an equal partnership or that other career options were as desirable. Men were objects to tease, torment, tantalize, and use for a permanent meal ticket. If we dangled our charms just out of reach before their hungry eyes, they would go out of their minds with desire for the unattainable. And then they might seek the prize through the one and only legal means, sacred marriage.

Growing up in the 1930s has allowed us to witness and participate in a complete change in social attitudes. Sex can be more openly discussed, another possibility that didn't occur to us at the time, and we can see our own sons and daughters make more informed decisions about the nature of their relationships. In spite of the adjustments that the generations which followed us have had to make with their new knowledge, we can be almost certain that at least the opportunity to know is available and less clouded by the fables and fantasies that substituted for fact in our youth.

THREE MAXIMS IN THE LIFE OF MARY

⋊ MARY MEBANE

"Hard Work Never Killed Nobody"

It was summer 1949 and I needed a job. Everybody tried to "get on" at the tobacco factory during "green season," when lots of extra workers were hired to "work up" new tobacco—that is, process it for cigarettes. Some people made their chief money of the year during the ten-to-twelve-week green season. The factory paid more money than days work, so lots of women gladly left their housekeeping jobs and went to the factories. In Durham there were two major factories and several smaller ones. The major factories worked up tobacco, but they also made cigarettes and had a shipping department and research laboratories. The smaller factories mainly worked up tobacco for the larger ones in Durham and in other cities.

I wasn't eighteen, but I was tall and stocky and could pass for older, and besides, they never asked to see your birth certificate; so, a few months short of my sixteenth birthday I went to get work at the American Tobacco Company, makers of Lucky Strike cigarettes and other brands. From the start I knew that I wouldn't get a job on the "cigarette side." That was easy work, and I was told that mostly whites worked over there. I would get a chance on the belt on the "tobacco side." Several women in the neighborhood who had worked at the American during the green season instructed me about how to get on. I was told to get there early and stand on the sidewalk in front of the employment office and just as close as possible to it, so that when they came out to select workers I would be easily seen. Also I was told to say, if they asked me, that I had worked there before. Nobody ever checked the records. So on the morning that hiring began for green season, I went to Durham.

I accompanied neighbors who had received postcards informing them they could come to work. They left me outside while they went in. I was dismayed, for the whole street in front of the employment office was filled with black women. They crowded around the brick porch leading to the employment office; they were on the sidewalk; they overflowed the street and covered the sidewalk behind. They were directly in front of the office, spreading out fanwise in both directions from it. Nobody was allowed on the porch except those who already had cards.

A pudgy white man with a cigar in his mouth came and stood on the porch and said, "All those who have cards, come forward." Those who had cards held them up over their heads and started pushing through the crowd. Others quickly surged forward, trying to fill the space that was left, taking advantage of the confusion to try to push even nearer the office. The crowd continued to grow bigger by the minute as new arrivals came.

You could tell the veterans from the rookies by the way they were dressed. The knowledgeable ones had their heads covered by kerchiefs so that if they were hired tobacco dust wouldn't get in their hair; they had on clean dresses, that by now were faded and shapeless, so they wouldn't get tobacco dust and grime on their best clothes. Those who were trying for the first time had their hair freshly done and wore attractive dresses; they wanted to make a good impression, and they were soon crumpled in the crush.

Some women looked as if they had large families; they looked tired and anxious, but determined. Some looked single; they had on lipstick and eyebrow pencil, and some even wore black patent leather pumps with stockings.

The morning passed and the sun got hotter; there was no shade on the sidewalks or in the street. The street stayed full except when trucks edged their way in and the crowd gave way slowly.

After a while the pudgy white man with the big cigar came to the door and stood and looked. Instantly the whole mass surged forward. The shorter ones tried to stand on tiptoe to be seen over the heads of their taller sisters. Hands shot up in the air, trying to make him notice them. Those at the front who'd gotten shoved against the brick porch shouted, "Stop pushing, stop pushing, ya'll! You're hurting me!"

Finally the pudgy man spoke, standing on the porch with his cigar in his mouth. "Until ya'll stop pushing and shoving I'm not gonna hire none of ya'll." Then he stood for a moment to see what effect his words were having on the crowd. Sensing no discernible effect the man went back inside, and the surge forward stopped for the time being.

The women stood and stood; the sun grew hotter. Some grew tired of waiting. "I left my baby with a neighbor. I told her that if I didn't get on I'd be back before twelve. I gotta go." Others were just "tired of this mess." One woman said, "All ya'll might as well go home. He's got his number for today. Come back tomorrow when they'll know how many more they'll need." At that, even more women faded away. The mass shrunk, but it was still a mass.

Finally, shortly before noon, the pudgy man came quietly to the porch and pointed quickly to two women standing close by. Before the crowd knew it, the two women were on the porch and in the hall, following him. The crowd surged forward but the man was gone. "What time is it?" someone said. "Nigh noon" was the answer and everyone seemed to agree that there would be no more hiring until one or two o'clock, after lunch.

I went with some other women far down the street to sit on the grass and eat my tomato sandwich. They talked in front of me as if I were grown, so I knew that I would have no trouble if I got hired.

Word came over the grapevine that they needed some more helpers and would hire some more today. This gave everybody courage, so the crowd grew calm. Then the pudgy man made an announcement: "Any shoving, any pushing, and there'll be no more hiring today." The women grew quiet. Those who had been impatient hadn't come back from lunch, leaving those who were determined to get on.

The man selected two more women; the crowd gave a little surge forward, but nothing like the shoving and pushing of the morning. In another hour he came back for one more, and soon the word came that we might as well go home. The crowd started fading away, but the diehards didn't believe the grapevine and were determined to stay to see what was going to happen. I had no choice; I was staying until the people I rode with got off from work. It was now three o'clock and we all had been standing in the sun since eight o'clock in the morning.

I lay in bed that night, too tired to do anything else, and thought about the day. Hundreds of women had stood in the hot sun for seven or eight hours. There was no bathroom, no drinking fountain, no place to sit down. Those who had to leave lost their place in line and, thus, their chance for a job. Why was this? Because they needed work and the factory didn't need them. They could treat the surplus as they chose, and there was nothing that the women could do about it.

The next day I was there early and standing in place by the steps before the employment office opened. The crowd stretched out as far as it had the previous day, and the sun was already hot. I was close enough to see into the hall inside and the glass-faced wall of the employment office. It was shut off from the hall because it was air-conditioned. A slim man came to the door and watched as the pudgy man came back and stood over the crowd. He watched the crowd surge forward, and he stepped back a little as if all the energy would wash over him. It seemed to give him great satisfaction—he'd stand and watch for a while, then turn and go into the air-conditioned office.

More and more women were hired; the pudgy man would point here and there, then take them off. In an hour or so he'd come back and hire one or two more. Lunch came and the crowd scattered. I knew enough not to leave my good place near the porch, so I ate standing in the hot sun, along with the rest of the women who had good places. Around two o'clock the pudgy man came back and his eye fell on me and the woman standing beside me. He motioned us in. I was now a factory hand.

The air-conditioning in the office chilled me after the heat of the street as I gave up the necessary information. I made up a birthday and nobody questioned it. Then I was taken to a "line" on the first floor.

It was a cavernous room, long and tall. The boss came over to tell me what to do, but the machinery was so loud that I couldn't hear him and I was so startled by my new surroundings that I didn't really concentrate on what he said. I was afraid to take a deep breath because the room was so cloudy with tobacco dust that brown particles hung in the air. I held my breath as long as I could and then took a deep breath. I started to cough and my eyes watered.

My job had something to do with a conveyor belt. It was shaped like a child's sliding board, only it had a deep trough and it moved. Shredded tobacco was on this belt—I think it came from upstairs—and my job was to sit by the belt and pick out the pieces whose stems were too large. The belt was constantly moving, and obviously I couldn't pick out every single stem on the belt, so I looked at the others, but I couldn't see what method they were using. I was in misery, for this was my first "public" job and I didn't want to do badly on it. Soon the boss came and told me he was going to put me on the belt upstairs. I was glad, for my back hurt from bending over, trying to pick out the stems.

The air was full of tobacco dust there, too, but not as much as it had been downstairs; also, it was quieter. This belt moved horizontally, from right to left; women stood parallel to it, two women facing each other on the same side of the belt, with a barrel of tied tobacco leaves in front of them. They worked in pairs, taking the tobacco from the barrel, the hogshead, and putting it on the belt. The important thing, as my partner explained to me, was to make sure that the tied ends faced me, for the belt was on its way to the cutter and the machine would cut off the hard tied end, which would not go into the making of cigarettes, while the leaves went another way.

The job seemed easy enough as I picked up bundle after bundle of tobacco and put it on the belt, careful to turn the knot end toward me so that it would be placed right to go under the cutting machine. Gradually, as we worked up our tobacco, I had to bend more, for as we emptied the hogshead we had to stoop over further, then straighten up and put it on the belt just right. That's when I discovered the hard part of the job: the belt kept moving at the same speed all the time and if you didn't place the leaves on it at the same tempo, there would be a big gap where your bundle should have been. So that meant that when you got down lower, you had to bend down, get the tobacco, straighten up fast, make sure it was placed knot end toward you, place it on the belt, and bend down again. Soon you were bending down, up, down, up, down, up. All along the line, heads were bobbing—down, up, down, up—until you finished the barrel. Then you could rest until the men brought you another one.

To make sure that you kept the belt filled, there was a line boss, a little blond man who looked scared most of the time. You'd be working away, when suddenly behind you you'd hear this voice, "Put the tobacco on the belt, girls. Put the tobacco on the belt. No empty spaces, girl. No empty spaces." I noticed that no one paid him any mind. He could be standing right by the belt talking, and it was as if he were invisible.

The floor boss had charge of all the operations on the floor. He was the line boss's boss, and the line boss was clearly afraid of him. The big boss seldom came to the floor unless there was real trouble. Most of the women had never seen him, but some had and said that he was mean as the devil.

I bent and straightened and bent and straightened and thought that my back would break. Once in the afternoon I got a ten-minute break in the "house," or toilet. I went there and collapsed into a chair.

The most interesting thing about my job was the people on it. They were grown people that I was seeing for the first time as an equal, not as a child. Some of them commented that I sure looked young, but I smiled and didn't say much and they soon turned the talk to something else. I listened, fascinated.

One woman who worked on a different belt was a schoolteacher during the regular year, and now she had quietly slipped in to take a green-season job. Most of the women commented on her sardonically, not because she was a schoolteacher working in a tobacco factory but because she made sure they knew she was a teacher and was to be treated as such. She wore high-heeled shoes to work and smart cotton dresses and kept her hair in an upsweep, not tied in a kerchief like most of the women. At lunchtime she went out to eat. She earned the wrath of the whole floor when she attempted to discipline one of the "girls" for not doing her work properly, threatening to tell the boss and get her fired. At noon the girl involved told everybody what had happened and by the end of the day it had somehow been agreed that from now on we would just leave Schoolteacher alone. I used to look at her. She had been to college. I wanted to go to college, but I didn't want to be like her.

Sometimes in the late afternoon, near quitting time, the black men would come by the belt and tease some of the women. They'd say things about sex and soon the talk would get explicit. I was shocked the first day, but after that I listened. Here were men and women talking like the worse sinners in the world, and God didn't come out of the sky and cut them down; in fact, He didn't seem to be punishing them at all. I wondered about God and this question quite a bit, particularly when it came to Viola.

Viola was a "bad" woman. I had known some bad girls in school, but none of their activities even began to compare with Viola's. She was the first woman I'd met whose sense of her own worth was directly related to how many men wanted her in bed. There had been quite a number. She regarded herself as a queen, and these men were courtiers; she had the power to reward whichever one was in favor, which she did quite often.

I listened as she regaled us every morning with the considerable doings of the night before. The other women laughed. Occasionally an older woman would remonstrate with her, "You ought not to talk that way in front of that child" (meaning me); but she would be contradicted, "She's old enough to know what life is all about." I expected God to walk on the floor in person and strike Viola dead, but He didn't; I expected the other women to treat Viola with scorn and derision, but although some of the older church-going ladies disapproved, they didn't. Most of them had the attitude that it was her life and her business, and besides, they had problems of their own.

Across the aisle from me was Flora, a very black woman who looked like a "hard knot." She was short and skinny, and she looked as though she drank a lot. She did her work, but not with any enthusiasm. She didn't look up, not even when the floor boss came. The attitude she projected was, "Another day, another dollar, and I've got to work at something."

One day, in the morning, word came over the grapevine that the big boss was coming. We knew it was true because the floor boss, a big man whose stomach hung over his belt, started running all over the floor giving orders right and left. The line boss was running around like a chicken with its head cut off. Everybody was urging us "girls" to do more and more, to get the tobacco on the belt and not leave any empty spaces. Leaves to the "house" were canceled. It was going to be a trying time for everybody.

Every head on my line bobbed up and down, practically in unison. The men who supplied the barrels of tobacco had them lined up two deep behind us, so that when we were out of a barrel they could quickly shove another one in place. There would be no standing and talking while the men brought one down to us.

Soon, word drifted around the room. The big boss was on the floor. I was afraid to stop my work and try to spot him so I kept working, meanwhile watching the other women so that I could tell by the expressions on their faces if they saw him. That was when I noticed Flora. She was calmly putting tobacco on the belt, no slower and no faster than she had put it on all day. She didn't hurry one bit. I wondered what would happen if the boss came and she acted like that. She saw me looking at her, and she smiled a sort of hard, thin smile. I smiled back, for I saw in Flora's face that if the boss tried messing with her today, he was going to get it.

The whole factory hummed, and we bent and straightened, bent and straightened. Suddenly I looked up to see the big boss, and I nearly laughed out loud. He was about five feet six with a ruddy complexion that looked as if he were a hard drinker. He had a straw hat that came down too low on his forehead. But most startling to me was that he had on pants that were obviously too big for him, for they were held almost halfway up his chest by a pair of suspenders. With the hat down too low and the pants up too high, there was very little of the big boss to be seen.

He appeared on the other line, facing me but coming up behind Flora. He stood looking balefully around at the black women, all of whom were working their heads off. All except Flora. He was right behind her, and she didn't speed up one bit. She took the bunch of tobacco leaves from the pack and deliberately slapped them down on the belt; then took another bunch and slapped it down. Slap! Slap!

The big boss waited for his presence to be felt, but when it soon became clear to him and to the whole line and the line boss and the floor boss that Flora was going to ignore him the way she ignored the others the big boss spoke, "It looks like you're half-dead this morning."

Flora paused a minute with a bunch of tobacco leaves in her hands and looked dead at him. They looked at each other for a minute; then Flora turned her head and slapped the bunch down on the belt.

I nearly died. I was sure he was going to fire her on the spot, but he didn't. He moved on to another belt. I think that look told him she was another mean one like himself, and if he got started he was going to get a good cussing out. He didn't want to risk a scene right there in front of his subordinates.

Flora had won. In her way she had protested and was prepared to back it up.

People told me I would get used to the work but I never did. I stayed until there was a "laying off," and was glad when they got to me. Work at the American was hard and mind-numbing, and the factory wasn't doing anything to make it more human.

"God Don't Like Ugly"

Miss Angeline had worked for years for all of the Ransoms. She started working for Ransom Senior before his wife died; then, as the children married and established homes of their own, she went to work for them, too. During confinements, periods of illness, or other emergencies, one might call another and borrow Angeline for a day or two, a week, or a month. They swore by her: she was reliable, good, trustworthy. There was no one like Angeline.

She came often to see Nonnie on Sunday after church. She attended a church in another neighborhood, where she had originally belonged before she married and moved to Wildwood. One major topic of her conversation was the rhetorical ability of various ministers. "Didn't he preach!" she'd say. "My my my my *my*! That sure was a preaching man." And her yellowish-brown face would light up like the sun as she took her text right along with the minister and went over it verbatim, pausing to comment on the appropriateness of the illustrations he had used. "He's a preaching man," she would end, "as sure as you're born."

Then she would shift to her other main subject: the Ransoms. They were the devil, she declared, and God was going to punish every one of them. "Yes, He is. Just you wait and see. Take Mrs. Farrow." And Miss Angeline would tell about her latest escapades. Mrs. Farrow was the oldest Ransom daughter, and she had a severe drinking problem. According to Miss Angeline, she went for days on end without ever getting out of bed and coming downstairs. Her husband was a physician and had his practice to think about, and, with her inattention to details, a number of black maids came and went, trying to keep house and take care of the children. Miss Angeline went in several times a week to clean up, but the day-to-day running of the household eventually fell to Ethelene, the full-time maid, who was evidently something of an organizer and soon had everybody in line. Ethelene ordered the groceries, paid the bills, took the children to their private school in the family station wagon, picked them up after school, made dental appointments and took the children to keep them, and eventually started signing their report cards, for there was no one else to do it.

Mrs. Farrow, resentful that her household was running so smoothly without her, and resentful that Ethelene had assumed so much control, pulled herself together one day and came downstairs to set everything straight. Miss Angeline was there that day. Ethelene, unfazed by this intruder on the order she had established, firmly sent Mrs. Farrow back upstairs, whereupon Mrs. Farrow summoned her father, who came and fired Ethelene. When the children got home and found her gone they raised such a ruckus that their grandfather had to go get her. She came back—for a handsome raise in salary.

After telling about the sermon and the Ransoms, Miss Angeline frequently ended her visit with a story that she had evidently heard as a small child listening to older people talk about slavery. It had so impressed itself on her mind that she told it as if she had been there herself. I heard it so often, and her telling of it was so vivid, that I could see the story being enacted myself:

A woman, the mistress of the house, was very heavy, very cruel, and she sat and rocked in a rocking chair all day. When one of the black children displeased her about something she would call the child to her and force him to put his hands under her rocking chair. Then she would rock on them, as punishment. Later in life she contracted cancer and died a terrible death. Before her death the palms of her hands rotted and fell away. Over the years I must have heard that story a hundred times, and in my mind's eye I can still see Miss Angeline, her Sunday-afternoon hat on her head, extending her hands with the thumbs turned inward, illustrating how rotten flesh fell out.

"If You're Black Get Back"

"You wanted to see me, Miss Owens?"

I stood uncertainly in the office door. I was surprised when Miss Owens, an extremely close friend of the chairman of the English department and of his wife, had said to me after class, smiling a carefully molded smile, that I should stop by her office.

I knew that Miss Owens didn't like me, and I would have avoided her altogether if possible. Alas, it wasn't possible, for she taught one of the courses that I had to have in order to graduate.

Miss Owens, with the smooth brown face and the level eye, represented what I most hated and feared. I hated her because I was sure she wished me to fail. I had the feeling that when the prim, proper black bourgeoisie of Durham looked at me they wanted to wave a magic wand and make me disappear. For, you see, I was that dreaded thing that most of them tried to avoid if possible: the earth-black African peasant. (I often smiled to myself during the late 1960s when there was so much talk in the black community about getting back to "roots." I was part of those roots, had never left them, and thus felt no guilt about looking around for other ways of being and doing.) Miss Owens disliked me because I represented what she had come from, one generation removed, and what she evidently wanted to forget as completely as possible.

So with that knowledge and mutual hate between us we looked at each other that spring morning just before I was to be graduated. I feared her because I needed the course and the credit to graduate, but if Miss Owens crossed the invisible line that separated us, there would be a scene and I might not graduate. So I stood in the doorway and smiled while my eyes measured my opponent, and I wondered, merciful God, why did you let me be born and have to contend with horrible people like this?

"Yes, Miss Mebane," she answered.

I didn't make a move inside the room. Miss Owens wanted me to sit down voluntarily; then she wouldn't have to do the polite thing and ask me. But I waited. And I said nothing. This was another tactic I had learned. Say nothing and brace yourself for the worst. It was not long in coming.

"I've noticed your clothing," Miss Owens said, still smiling. I bared my teeth in a set smile but said nothing. "For example, today you are wearing a striped blouse, but your skirt is checked. Stripes and checks do not go together."

I felt pain in my chest, but I grimly hung on to my smile and said nothing. The conversation continued on the subject of my clothing and why didn't I buy some cute little blouses with Peter Pan collars and some nice solid-color skirts?

Nowhere in the conversation did Miss Owens ask me about my financial situation because she really didn't care. It was axiomatic in the black community of Durham that the less you had, the more "face" you had to put on. Twice a month, the women's weekly assembly at North Carolina College at Durham was devoted largely to how to dress—dress being defined as how to look as though you are affluent on very little money. After all, one had to make some distinction between the social classes. Why not start with one's clothing?

Miss Owens was anxious that I and the other black girls like me not present a picture to the outside world—the white world—that would make her ashamed. She would be ashamed of a look that said, "Yes, I've had a hard time in life and my mother works in a factory and sometimes there are things that go on at home that I don't want to talk about."

I fought down the hurt in my chest. When it appeared that that was all there was to be to the conversation and I started to take deep breaths again, Miss Owens continued. "Oh, yes. I read your article in the *Campus Echo* in which you express certain strong opinions." She was referring to a book review I had done; it wasn't the nature of the opinions that bothered her, but the fact that I had them. She said that she thought I should be more moderate in expressing my views, less forceful. I had plainly stated what I thought.

Underlying the whole interview, of course, was the official position of Miss Owens and her kind: be like us; that is the only way you can succeed in life. So far, I had resisted them; but what was more galling to them was that I had been successful in spite of resisting them. Evidently I had been successful in concealing from Miss Owens the absolute horror I felt at what the Miss Owenses of this world were, and I hoped to God I would never ever become one.

They thought that they had a system that would last forever. But it didn't. As soon as the college students finished fighting the racist whites and their system of segregation they turned their attention to the black campus and the class and color racists on it. The ensuing struggle of the 1960s was deep and bitter because it was a class struggle. The children of the black folk were tired of being spat on. And they rebelled. Though there were many excesses committed by the students during that period, they were in no way equal to the excesses that had been occurring on black campuses for a long time. The revolution was overdue.

MY AUNT ISADORA

❧ AMELIA DIAZ ETTINGER

"Remember to behave and give her thanks after your supper. Also remember to pick up and wash your plate." This is how it went, the memorized and tired message of my mother. Every day I had to go to the house of my aunt, and my mother to her work. The aunt, as my mother, was a widow. The aunt was much older and of great weight, which the disorderly street kids mocked by calling her *"culo grande."* But only when she wasn't present because, although she truly had an ample seat, everyone was afraid of her. She was so respectable and pious that even the priest of the church came to her home in search of advice. To me, my aunt was a different story. Never would I have asked for advice or even a clear direct question. Imagine if I ever looked at her in the face she would have landed such a resounding splat on my head! At the same time she would be saying, "Decent children do not look at their elders in the face; they lower their heads." It was because of this and other similar things that when I found myself in her house I tried to maintain myself out of her presence.

That was my life during the week. But I had my oasis during Saturdays and Sundays when at last I could sit in my house and dine with my mother. It happened that one day, and it is still unclear to my why, my good mother comes into my room early in the morning saying, "Wake up my child. It is ten to nine." Lying between the warm sheets I rubbed my eyes stretching from every which part until I slid right off the bed.

I dressed myself in my Sunday clothes ready to go to church in the company of my mother. But she tells me she is sorry that today she cannot go with me. She has already spoken to Aunt Isadora who is going to take me. "Damn be my pickle luck!" I thought without offending.

Before I had the opportunity to eat my breakfast the tremendous figure of my aunt appeared at the door. "Pickle luck," said I in my head. Well, there is no remedy. So in that way, hungry, disturbed, and even embarrassed, I walked the streets in the company of my Aunt Isadora. Here and there, one or another boy will pass us, turning his head to exclaim in admiration, "Holy Mass how big she has her . . . !"

Already in church, in the presence of the rector, the men taking their hats off would say to her, "Buenos dias señora," while their wives said, "¿Como esta usted, Doña Isadora?" To this my aunt only responded with a movement of her head. And I, standing by her shadow, felt like a fly on a crowded wall.

After such a long mass, and with my stomach empty, we began on foot back home. At least that is what I thought, when curiously I noticed that we made two turns opposite to our desired destination. We soon were in a neighborhood I had never seen before. We stopped at a house of very simple facade. No plants, no balcony, no windows. A house that looked more like a church. She was truly devoted, I thought.

We walked into the house, my aunt opening the door. My nostrils were assaulted with the smell of ginger, alcohol, incense, and who knows what else. A black woman dressed in a tunic and a turban appeared from behind a curtain. Such a sudden apparition she had been that my heart rode into my throat.

"Doña Isadora I have been waiting for you," the woman said as she cast an eye on me. "And who is she?"

"Forgive me mía Zoraida. But the wife of my late brother, God may keep him in his bosom, had today some business or another to attend, and you can see I had to look after the girl."

"Well, what can we do," Doña Zoraida said, lifting her shoulders as in resignation.

Opening again the curtain she made us step into another room. Here the smells were twice as strong and repugnant. When my eyes had settled in the dim light I noticed that the walls were covered with statues, stamps, and relics of saints. Even the legs of a hen (or a rooster) hung on Doña Zoraida's walls.

"Let us see, Doña Isadora, maybe today we will be able to see him."

"That God will grant, that God will grant, mía Zoraida," said my aunt with an unrecognizable voice.

Then Doña Zoraida, placing a smelly potion on the table in front of us, signaled us to sit facing her. She closed her eyes and began chanting this way:

"Legs of a goat . . . Escape!
Loves from Hell . . . Leave!
Come in Hearts of the Good Faith;
St. Lucas, St. Isidoro, and Benevolente."

This Doña Zoraida said while her body shook and trembled as if her mind had been diseased.

"Now . . . now I see . . . listen. Come here. Enter . . . here he is . . . here he is . . . Don Gregorio. Come here, enter my good man, we are good people here and your wife Isadora is present." And then rising from her chair she began to pant.

"Here I come . . . here I come," she said in a deep and distant voice. At that moment my aunt stood up, with surprising agility. Throwing herself on her knees, she exclaimed: "Ay! Mi Gregorio, mi Gregorio! Please let me see you."

I didn't have a chance to form a single thought when Doña Zoraida lit the lights of the establishment, speaking again; "I am sorry, Doña Isadora, but you know that screaming and losing nerve scare the dead away."

My aunt, who was still on her knees, placed her hand to her hair. Raising, she carefully arranged her dress. In the same fashion she calmly opened her purse, giving Doña Zoraida some pesos.

On our way back to the house, before my mother opened the door, my aunt looked at me straight in the eyes and said, "About Doña Zoraida, not a word to anyone."

The next day we were back to the same routine. Me trying to keep my body out of the way. And my aunt . . . well, as she had always been. But, after that Sunday, if by coincidence I found a shameless rascal mocking my aunt or screaming some insolence toward her, I stopped him in the street, giving him a word or two right at his face. After all, the lady of so much body was my aunt I-SA-DO-RA.

THE RAPE OF DONA

✌ LEE HOWARD

We had always lived
up Hogskin Holler
on the yon side of Skull Branch
laid our piece of land
and on the rise
our house in need of painting
but warm in the front room
at least during winter
and a breeze through the hallway
all summer long
In the morning always biscuits fresh made and gravy
and in good times a little fatback
I had six brothers, two sisters, a mammy and a dad
Pretty much the same as everyone had
It was my job to milk and of course the cleaning
and at harvest the picking was everybody's chore
I was happy with the life as a child of thirteen can be
with the knowledge that I hadn't much
but I had at least what everybody had

Then came what made me different
The story I'm a telling
is the tale that made me not the same
I was thirteen and long-legged
and not much meat a hanging on my bones

and feeling as much like my brothers
as ever a young girl will
It was August
and the picking was constant as the night
and all day till the moon rose
I bent over beans
like a bridge over water

Now everyone had done gone to supper
but me
for I had set myself a goal
and was only half a row from it
when Sam Copely who lived just down the road
came strolling through the summer heat
Now I had been knowing Sam
ever since I had been knowing anyone
since he lived just one farm over
and never did I pay any mind to him
coming over the ditch to say Howdy and it's sure hot
I said Yeah I'm tired I been picking since sunup
and I'm just near done
with what I am to do
And Sam says that's true
And I smelled whiskey on his breath
and then knew he'd been staggering not strolling
through the dust and the dew

And then he said You're thirteen now ain't you Dona
and I say thirteen and two months
And he says You're a woman now ain't ya
and I say Didn't figure I was
And Sam says he figures I'm looking like one
And I asked him how his garden came in this year
and he says Fair
and came close to me leaning like a branch over them beans
The whiskey as strong as sulfur on his words
and hurting my nose to smell them
He says Would you like a drink from this jar

and I say I don't reckon no gal my age
ought to be taking swigs
and he says he won't tell a soul
not mammy, pappy, nor the preacher
I say I'm done with the row
and reckon I'll go on in

He said Stay
I laughed and told him I had no time for his foolishness
Reckon I'd go
He said No
I went to go by him
laughing high and wide
and both his arms come strong down around me
I say Sam Copely what on earth do you think you're doing
and he said nothing
out of his mouth
but his hips pressed hard against me
said run
and I tried
I cried Now let go of me
and he says You're a woman now
You got to face the facts
and he unbuttoned the fly of his pants
Now you must understand
I had six brothers but not since I was a wee tot
had I seen one of them with his drawers dropped
and it not bigger than a finger
and not meaning more to me than my hand

The night was dark as the inside of a hat
with only a sliver of a moon making a tear in the sky
and Sam Copely fell upon me like a boulder rolling off
a mountainside
and I saw nothing but the black at the side of my eyes
and the brown streams of sweat running down his throat
My tongue was at the moment tied to my teeth
and my lips would not open
for fear of what would come inside

I hear nothing
but the tree frogs and Sam Copely's quick breath
and the rip of cotton underneath my dress
And then I felt fire molded into a knife
sear deep into my soul
stabbing me again and again
wishing to God I would die
somewhere
my voice remembered how to cry
and a loud "Mammy"
tore out of my throat

And Sam Copely never stopped
pushing his knife deep into my groin
but with one hand clapped tight over my mouth
he said Too late for your Mammy child
You got yourself a man now
You got yourself a man
Over and over he said the same thing
You got yourself a man now
and each time he said it
he rammed me hard as a stick
I was sure he would go straight through me
and you may well wonder
what I am doing during all this
I assure you I am trying to fight free of all this
but I weighed no more than a sack of flour at that time
and I had seen Sam Copely
carry more than four sacks easy on his back
So you may well imagine that it was no problem to him
to hold what amounted to one sack firm beneath his skin

Then suddenly the knife melts within me
and Sam becomes a dead weight upon me
and then like the world slipping off its own shoulders
I felt no lead pressed on me at all
only the iron is left between my legs
He jerks me upright
and tells me say nothing to no one

or they'll laugh and put you to shame for your lies
Remember you were here at night alone
Remember you are the one to blame
And I was thirteen and two months
and a child ain't noted for being wise
I thought for sure
I was for fault
and my pain was a sign making me see
that for sure no one but me was to blame
For sure no one but me.

A Woman's Work: Shoulder to Shoulder

❧ PART THREE

Working women, particularly in the rural areas, have always banded together to share responsibilities, not only in times of crisis but for the everyday chores of child care, meal preparation, household maintenance, and community improvement. "Public work," as farm and domestic workers call it, finds women building on that tradition to meet those needs, while at the same time adding to the list the need for solace for shared abuses on the job and for a hand when wages were scarce because of sickness or lay-offs. In an issue of *Southern Exposure* (vol X, no 4, winter 1981), devoted to working women, editor Tobi Lippin spoke of the "energetic building of networks, associations, organizations, and unions" of "Southern women fighting for personal dignity and collective justice." For despite objections to the increasing number of women in the workforce, women are managing to build such organizations.

The task is a formidable one. The South has a well-deserved and growing reputation for its strong antiunion stance, with special repercussions for women workers. Industries are lured here with the promise of a cheap labor supply and sex differentiation is a key element in the calculus, for women are still largely concentrated in the low-paying jobs. The state and local governments, civic and business leaders all have a stake in seeing to it that workers remain unorganized. But the workers—both men and women—continue to fight against these restraints. Battles for the right to bargain collectively and for safe working conditions have been waged in the factories, the mills, the shipyards, and even in the fields of the South. One of the major struggles that women have had to face has been overcoming their own racial biases in order to work with other women, as well as the sex bias reflected in the lack of women in union leadership roles. But as the selections in this section demonstrate, the process of uniting to reach a common goal or to overcome a common obstacle has helped women not only uncover new skills and strengths, but discover a surprising new kind of hero.

MILL VILLAGE

~ CLARA D. FORD

There's a big wheel
in this little town.
The spokes are paved,
narrow, and lined
with look-alike houses.
People troop in
and out of the hub,
working for The Mill
on the lifetime plan.

Look-alike houses
all in a row,
Act-alike people
with no better place
to go.

IT SEEMS TO HELP ME BEAR IT BETTER WHEN SHE KNOWS ABOUT IT

~ MARGARET JONES BOLSTERLI

One of the most destructive messages passed on to young girls is that the spirit of competition born of the quest for the "most desirable" boyfriend, and later husband, will remain with them all their lives; that they will, in fact, always see other women as the enemy. Furthermore, the myth of the Southern Belle coupled with the women-are-the-enemy myth accuses Southern women of having greater hostility toward each other than have our sisters in the North, East, and West. Southern history, when it deals with women at all, focuses on the accomplishments of unusual women or women in unusual times under the stress, say, of civil war; all but the more basic relationships are ignored. Southern literature, when it focuses on the lives of women, tends to further the myth of cutthroat competition and dislike.

So when the current phase of the women's movement in the 1960s and 1970s fostered support groups, it came as a surprise to many that Southern women found pleasure in such cooperation. Feminist influence has weakened the old cultural myths of competition among women to some degree, but young women are still being taught to distrust each other.

Southern women's private documents—letters and diaries that escape attention because they concern the humdrum of daily existence rather than the drama of history in the making—offer a new vision of relationships among Southern women: for most of their lives, their best friends are other women. And they know it. Nowhere does this seem more evident than among wives—the very group who should, according to the myth, be most reliant on men for their emotional support.

Nannie Stillwell Jackson lived in the late 1800s in Watson, a tiny town in the Arkansas-Mississippi delta region of Arkansas, and she kept a diary in which she recorded the details of just such a group of friends. Her diary records the dull and isolated life in a town whose only connection with the rest of the world was a dirt road so rough and muddy that each leg of the twenty-mile trip to the county seat and back required an overnight stay. Supplies came by steamboat to Red Fork, a port on the Arkansas River three miles away. There was no railroad or telegraph office, and no daily mail service until 1890. Most of Watson's residents were families of small farmers and the merchants who supplied them. Money was scarce, especially in the household of W. T. and Nannie Stillwell Jackson, whose 140 acres of land seem to have been either uncleared or under water too much of the time to be very profitable.

In 1889, Nannie Stillwell, a widow with two little girls and few financial resources, filled her desperate need for a breadwinner by marrying W. T. Jackson, a young man not only "beneath" her, but twenty years her junior. "Mr. Jackson," as she invariably called him, was practically illiterate. He worked the plot of land they owned, did odd jobs around the neighborhood, and butchered animals to sell for meat.

Nannie, on the other hand, was a woman of some education. Her handwriting is neat and clear and she frequently wrote letters for those who could not do it themselves. An avid reader, she even read aloud to her husband when she could get him to sit still.

Nannie's diary indicates that the relations between the Jacksons were strained and sometimes stormy. In fact, not one shred of affection or concern for his well-being is expressed in the entire diary. She shared a house, bed, and marriage with Mr. Jackson; emotionally, she lived in a world of females: her daughters, Lizzie and Sue, and a group of some twenty women who formed a network of friendship and support.

Setting aside the financial considerations that made a husband necessary, if all references to men were deleted from Nannie Jackson's diary, her life would not appear substantially different. But it is impossible to imagine it without women. Evidence like this suggests that contemporary women's support groups are but an attempt to recover a lost tradition in women's life-styles.

At the beginning of the diary Nannie is thirty-six years old. Her best friend, Fannie Morgan, is the nineteen-year-old wife of a man seventeen years her senior. Fannie has recently lost a baby and Nannie Jackson is most solicitous and caring toward her. They share a great many things: food, starch, household chores, and their troubles.

> Thursday, June 19, 1890: *I baked some chicken bread for Fannie & some for myself, & she gave me some dried apples & I baked 2 pies she gave me one & she took the other I made starch for her & me too, & starched my clothes & ironed the plain clothes & got dinner.*

This friendship threatened Mr. Jackson and he tried to curb it. But Nannie valued rewards of the relationship more than his approval.

> Friday, June 27, 1890: *I did some patching for Fannie today and took it to her she washed again yesterday & ironed up everything today I also took 2 boxes of moss & set out in a box for her, when I came back Mr. Jackson got mad at me for going there 3 times this evening said I went to talk about him & said I was working for nothing but to get him & Mr. Morgan in a row, & to make trouble between them & I just talk to Fannie and tell her my troubles because it seems to help me bear it better when she knows about it. I shall tell her whenever I feel like it.*

And tell her she does. When she feels sick and depressed, for example, she asks Fannie to make sure that all of her possessions go to Lizzie and Sue and that she be buried next to Mr. Stillwell, her first husband, if she should die.

Fannie and Nannie are as close as sisters. Nannie is as concerned about sickness in Fannie's household as in her own, and she seldom makes a special dish without taking some to Fannie; these are considered personal presents not meant to be shared by the family at mealtime but to be eaten on the spot.

Nannie Jackson's other close friends are Mrs. Chandler, Fannie's mother; Mrs. Nellie Smithee, a widow who works as a live-in domestic worker and field hand; and the Owen sisters, Miss Carrie and Miss Fannie, who board at the Jackson house during the school term while Miss Carrie presides as teacher of the one-room school. The Owen sisters are almost like sisters to Nannie, but are not as close as Fannie Morgan—the bond of wifehood is missing.

When one of Nannie's circle of friends is ill or has an unusually heavy load of work to do, they all pitch in to help:

> Thursday, June 19, 1890: *Clear and warm, very warm. Lizzie is a heap better. Today I went up and washed dishes for Fannie and helped her so she could get an early start to washing for she had such*

a big washing. Sue churned for her. Miss Nellie Smithee helped her wash and they got done by 2 o'clock.

The generosity of such acts of kindness should be measured by the heaviness of Nannie's own work load. She makes all the clothes, including underwear, for herself and two daughters, as well as shirts, nightshirts, and underclothes for Mr. Jackson. She also makes sheets, towels, and pillowcases from unbleached domestic cloth. All her cooking is done on a wood-fired stove for which she must carry wood daily.

Nannie washes all their clothes with water heated outside in an iron pot. They are scrubbed by hand on a rub board with homemade lye soap, rinsed through two tubs of cold water, then starched stiff as a board, hung on a line to dry, and later ironed with irons weighing from five to ten pounds each that have to be heated on the stove. The laundry suds are never thrown away; they are used to scour the kitchen floor. Her wash water must be carried from the bayou fifty feet away if there is not enough water in the rain barrels.

And, of course, three meals a day must be cooked. No packaged food is used, no bakery bread. There is a rare can of store-brought fruit only when somebody is sick and [needs] a special treat. The garden is Nannie's purlieu, as well as the milk cow and the chickens.

Since this is swamp country, people are frequently very ill. In these days of hospitals and undertakers it is hard to imagine the almost casual ways of handling the dying and dead before we had facilities to care for them—until we read Nannie's account of the death of a small boy in Watson, when Sue and young Lizzie ride to the graveyard in the wagon with the corpse because it is too far to walk. Then a friend dies during a period of high water in the bayou:

Tuesday, April 14, 1891: *Mrs. Archdale died this morning at 25 minutes to one she suffered a heap before she died and talked sensible up till about 4 or 5 hours before she died. Dove got there before she died but Mr. Jimmie and the doctor never did come. . . . Mrs. Morgan, Mrs. Newby, & Mr. Jackson, Kate McNeill & Fannie Totten all set up last night & we dressed her and laid her out. . . . The gentlemen have set up with the corpse tonight for Mrs. Gifford can't set up, Mrs. Morgan is sick and the rest of us set up last night. . . . Mr. Jackson went to Redfork today to see about getting the coffin made and it has come and Mrs. Archdale is in it.*

Wednesday, April 15, 1891: *Cloudy all morning the gentlemen took Mrs. Archdale away & not a lady could go on account of the water. It is falling but slow so slow.*

Miss Carrie Owen is the only financially independent woman in this network. She not only supports herself, and presumably her sister, but maintains her own horse, Denmark. Since the average pay for teachers in that county in 1890 was just $252 a year her independence was limited, but she received the respect due her as an educated woman. While living with the Jacksons she took part in community social life and joined in the sewing, but she did not perform household chores with the women. Mr. Jackson resented Miss Carrie and complained because Nannie wouldn't reveal their private conversations to him.

The amount of visiting that went on among Nannie and her friends is impressive. This was not a community where people lived close to each other; fields and pastures stretching at least a quarter mile separated their homes. The road was alternately dusty and muddy, and the bayou that runs through the area had to be crossed on a log. After heavy rains had swollen [the bayou], the only way across was by boat.

Nannie Jackson's network of friends included black as well as white women. The amount and quality of communication between blacks and whites in the South has always been a shadowy dimension of Southern history and culture; readers unacquainted with the rural South may be surprised at how much interaction actually existed between the races. Nannie expresses affection for several black women, and judging from their gifts and visits to her, the affection is returned. She wrote and received letters for them, traded poultry and dairy produce with them, and did sewing for them. In fact, without knowledge of the race of the women mentioned in this entry, one would have a difficult time sorting things out:

Wednesday, August 6, 1890: *I cut and made one of the aprons for Aunt Francis's grandchild & Lizzie & I partly made the basque Aunt Chaney came & washed the dinner dishes. . . . Mrs. Chandler, Fannie, Mrs. Watson & Myrtle McEncrow were here a little while this evening, Aunt Jane Osburn was here too, & Aunt Mary Williams she brought me a nice mess of squashes for dinner. Carolina Coalman is sick & sent Rosa to me to send her a piece of beef I sent her a bucket full of cold victuals . . . got no letters today wrote one for Aunt Francis to her mother & she took it to the post office, I* *gave her 50 cents for the 2 chickens she bought & a peck of meal for a dozen eggs.*

"Aunt," of course, is the Southern white form of address for an older black woman who deserves respect. Confusion reigns, though, when white women, who are really Nannie's aunts or are called aunt by the community, are mentioned. The quality of all the aunts' visits is so much the same that their races can only be told by checking the census rolls that categorized people, at least until 1880, as "white," "black," or "mulatto."

Women's culture in Watson was not hostile to that of men but separate from it and different, with its own center and order. It certainly does not appear to have been a culture of the oppressed but of those who simply share a common experience—an experience that they do not share with men, even their husbands.

It is easy to see how little girls in this community were enculturated to follow in their mothers' footsteps: Lizzie and Sue worked right along with their mother at household chores and spent their free time playing dolls and mimicking the roles of the adult women:

> Sunday, June 15, 1890: *Cloudy & warm sun a little, brisk south wind all day, Mr. Jackson went down to Mr. Howells this morning did not stay very long, he came back ate a lunch then went up on the ridge & helped Mr. Morgan to drive home Lilly & Redhead the 2 cows I am to have the milk of, Lilly is mine but Redhead is not she is in Mr. Morgans care and he lets me milk her, I sent Lizzie up to help Fannie clean up this morning & I baked 2 green apple pies & took one to her she sent me some clabber for Mr. Jackson's dinner Lizzie & Sue did not want to go anywhere today & they stayed home & played with their dolls & had Sunday school & a doll dinner out under the plum tree, I slept some read some & wrote Sister Bettie a long letter fixed up 7 journals to send her & cut a piece out of a paper that Mr. Jackson brought to send her, he has not stayed about the house but very little today, Lizzie & Sue & I have had a pleasant day.*

The daily lives of our foremothers shed some light on a question I have pondered for years. On the frontier and even years later, as in the time Nannie Jackson was keeping her diary, women and men did many of the same chores around the house and fields. Why did the women learn to cultivate an air of weakness and dependence so that a strong man would take care of them?

It is clear from reading Nannie Jackson's diary that women had no alternative. Since they did not have the employment options of men either in actuality or in their visions of themselves as workers, mothers conditioned their daughters to be weak. Women's and men's cultures were almost mutually exclusive. A woman's means to gaining a better life lay not in her competence but rather in her ability to attract a husband who could afford to hire some other woman to do the work for her that frontier women and poorer women had to do for themselves.

The conditioning process that nurtured this state of affairs is evident in the diary. Nannie's daughters share the housework, chop cotton, and carry water to the men in the fields, but it is obvious from the amount of time they spend playing dolls and washing dolls' clothes that, with Nannie's full encouragement, they are playing the games that lead to success in the women's world.

Yet rather than prompting us to decry the conformity and limitations in that world, Nannie Jackson's diary and other similar documents enable us to appreciate the practical side of women's culture. Looking back through her eyes, we see the strength and centrality of ongoing mutual support, both emotional and economic, as women shared goods, services, and feelings all at the same time. The varied facets of their networks gave the relationships between them a durability that may have been missing in simpler personal bonds.

Evidence like Nannie Jackson's diary belongs in the curriculum being taught to girls and women today, along with the texts of speeches and the dates of events. If we can bring into clearer focus in the very beginning of our education the now-hazy picture of our foremothers' daily lives, we might find in their shared experiences patterns to alleviate our own often lonely struggles today.

A fuller version of Nannie Stillwell's diaries, edited by Margaret Jones Bolsterli, appears in Vinegar Pie and Chicken Bread: A Woman's Diary of Life in the Rural South in 1890–91 (*University of Arkansas Press*).

OLE BLACK EMELDA

❧ LUISAH TEISH

Folks went to bed one night and when they woke up the next mornin, this strange woman, Emelda, had moved into Mabel Green's old shotgun house. She was so black that in the light of day neighbor-women, peepin from behind their Sears and Roebuck curtains, could see the blue highlights of her skin. Under the moonlight she looked purple. Her thick lips, stained scarlet in the center by alcohol burns, was movin, mumblin bout heaven knows what. People would point and identify her as a "Singalee" from Africa cause the heel of her foot seemed as long as the foot itself. She had several multicolored children, and in spite of her pregnant belly, no one ever saw or heard a man in her house. She was branded evil cause she sweat on her nose.

Nobody knew where she came from, but she was steadily goin down the road a piece to visit with that yallar gal, Desiree Rousell. A comely yallar woman; folks figured she was stuck-up cause she put a crude wooden fence around her three-room house and kept her children behind it; lettin them out only to go to school. And like a lot of the poor mixed-breed Negroes one could find sprinkled long the Bayou country, she didn't go to nobody's church, but could be caught, some berry-pickin mornins, standin in the woods talking to a tree. Some folks say she was a Hoodoo woman, others said it was the Indian blood that possess her to talk to sky and trees. Anyways, the good Christian men of Cut-Off, Luzanna, forbid their wives to have any dealings with her.

One mornin, bout dawn, just fore he went to work on the pipeline with the other men, Jed Mason took a mind to beat his wife, Cora Sue. It was a common thing in this neck of the woods, where men who worked from sunrise to way past sunset suspected their women of messin with pissy-tailed boys while they were away. Truth of it was, between the children and the laundryn nobody had no time to be messin. But Cora Sue was pretty and preferred to tend her okra garden, aided, sometimes, by Joe Willie Bland's boy, Pete. So nobody even twitched an eyelid that morning as Cora Sue come runnin down the mud road, screaming for dear life. Ole Lottie Price saw Cora Sue jump over Desiree's fence, clutchin her only son in her arms.

Jed come after her, pantin and grittin his teeth. But this time he stopped dead in his tracks. Desiree come to the front yard with a warnin, "You git on way from here, Mr. Mason." Jed Mason realized where he was. "Meanin no disrespect, Miz Rousell, but this here is a family matter." He moved to open the gate. Desiree stepped back. "I say there ain't gon be no beatin here, Mr. Mason." The thick of Jed's neck got thicker and he busted out, "How you gon stop me? That's my wife." Desiree reached behind her porch rail and aimed her shotgun barrel at his heart. "And it's my property you standin on, if I kill you on it, law won't hold me to blame." Emelda come walkin to the front and picked Cora Sue up off the ground. Now all the neighbors come out to look, mumblin bout the crazy Creole lady and how she turn Big Jed Mason round. Cora Sue took to havin coffee with her and ole black Emelda after that and Jed lost his taste for beatin his wife.

Summer rolled lazily down the muddy Mississippi. Funeral parlor fans and iced tea fought the Bayou heat and mosquitoes while Desiree and Cora mopped pipin-hot sauce on bar-b-que meat and Emelda moaned of her condition to a bowl of yellow potato salad. It was always quiet in summer, when everybody was too hot to bother bout other people's business. So without warnin humid summer days drifted into breezy autumn evenins.

One evenin Desiree went off somewhere, leavin her children in the house alone. Now some folks say she left one of them candles burnin and the devil tipped it over, others say her oldest daughter had took to smokin. But, some mysterious how that yallar woman's house caught fire! First a thin stream of smoke gotta botherin Miz Adams' chickens; then old man Carter's dogs commence to howlin; after while every house in runnin distance knew Desiree Rousell had caught a blaze.

A crowd of women gathered. Ole black Emelda, heavy-pregnant now, was just returning from work that evenin. With the stench of shrimp all over her she pushed her way through the cluster of gapin women and ran into the burnin house. She came out and laid four screamin children beyond the fence. "Don't just stand there, you dumb heifers!" she shouted at the petrified women, then disappeared into the flames.

Miz Anderson ran to the market to call the fire station . . . two towns away. After nine rings the chief answered tellin her his men wasn't comin way out there to water no nigger's house! She almost cussed him but remembered who and what she was and hung up instead.

Now old black Emelda salvaged some food and clothes, but when she headed for the door her skirt tail swished and caught fire. Lottie Price wrapped her shawl round her arm and reached for Emelda while Cora Sue hacked away at one burnin wall. Suddenly young women was runnin for their hoses, old women come with shovels and buckets, and neighbor-girls tended the cryin children. Emelda looked round her, wiped the sweat from her nose, and fainted in Lottie Price's arms.

That night, when Desiree Rousell come home, she found a one-room boarded-up shanty, no bigger than a chicken coop, stocked with food. Her children were tucked asleep in one corner of the room. Miz Bishop's oldest girl, Marylou, was there with them and she told Miz Rousell to go on up to the house and have coffee with her mama and the other women tendin to ole black Emelda.

WOMEN IN THE TEXAS
ILGWU, 1933–50

❧ MELISSA HIELD

First Dressmaker: "Have you ever wondered what you would do if you had Morgan's income?"
Second Dressmaker: "No, but I have wondered what he would do if he had mine."

THE BOSSES PRAYER
Now I lay me down to sleep, I pray I can low wages keep. If workers should strike action take, I pray the finks their heads to break.

These two labor jokes may not seem humorous today, but in 1937 they underscored one very real fact in the lives of Texas garment workers, three fourths of whom were women. Wages were bad, at least 50 percent lower than those of garment workers in the Eastern states, and efforts to organize International Ladies' Garment Workers Union locals provoked carefully organized, brutal tactics by manufacturers. Working women in the Texas garment industry fought back using legal or, if necessary, violent actions to secure union contracts.

Whether they won or lost, in terms of numbers of contracts signed and members gained, is not the most significant point about the history of the International Ladies' Garment Workers Union (ILGWU or ILG) in Texas. Rather, the fact that hundreds of individual women garment workers participated in strike after strike, despite repressive measures taken against them, indicates, in the words of Olivia Rawlston, former Dallas ILG local president, "union-mindedness" was strong in Texas, a state known for its indifference and even hostility to organized labor.

In Texas and throughout the country, 1933–50 was a key transitional period in terms of women's work, and many women who were active then in Texas garment unions are still alive. Hundreds of women in Dallas, San Antonio, and Laredo participated in militant strikes lasting weeks. They were neither difficult to organize nor passive union members.

More important, most of the labor supply for garment factories in San Antonio and Laredo was composed of Chicanas throughout this period, and black women entered the Dallas garment factories in significant numbers during World War II. Black and Chicana women were paid less than Anglo women for the same jobs and were usually limited to the most undesirable, low-paying work. They had the most to gain from unions and enthusiastically supported the ILGWU's efforts. Cultural differences between the union organizers and these women, together with the union's refusal to hire them as organizers, however, were significant factors that prevented the ILGWU from becoming firmly established in San Antonio and Laredo.

The period 1933–50 saw major changes in the profile of the typical American working woman. About 24 percent of all women over age fourteen were in the labor force. The median age of women workers rose to over thirty, while the number of married women in the labor force increased to 35 percent in 1940. More families depended on a second income for financial security.

A crucial fact about women workers is that they have been concentrated in a few, low-paying areas of the economy. In 1930, domestic and personal service, clerical work, and the manufacture of textiles and clothing were the industries employing most women. Not only were women paid less for unskilled work, but they were also paid less than men for skilled work in the same industry or occupation. This fact has, for the most part, not changed.

World War II brought some relief from these conditions. Wages increased and for the first time women in some occupations experienced job mobility. Two million women entered war-related manufacturing industries; the clerical work force doubled; business and professional fields opened to women. For the first time, black women were not limited to jobs as domestics, laundry workers, or farm workers. In Dallas, in 1942, the first group of black women were trained to operate sewing machines.

These national trends in women's employment hold true for

Texas as well. In 1930 about 20 percent of all Texas women over age ten were employed outside the home, primarily in factories, laundries, and department stores. A 1932 survey by the Department of Labor showed that 36 percent of them were married and that half of the women worked at least fifty-four hours a week. White women earned between $6.50 and $12.90 *a week,* but black and Chicana women were paid a median wage of $5.85; they earned less working in the same jobs as white women and more often worked in jobs that were seasonal, marginal, and less desirable.

The garment industry in Texas boomed during the thirties as manufacturers fled the unionized East in search of cheap labor. Texas showed a 40 percent increase in clothing manufacturing firms from 1930 to 1936, primarily due to the supply of cheap, skilled, Chicana labor in south Texas.

The nature of the women and infants' wear industry in the thirties and forties promoted the exploitation of the garment worker. Women's wear was highly seasonal, with hectic rushes followed by slack periods with no work available. Workers were paid by piece rate, a highly unstable system based on factors such as tradition, personal opinion, and employer's discretion; hence, rates varied widely from factory to factory. Employers lowered the piece rate if costs had risen or if workers seemed to be making too much money.

The garment industry, to a greater extent than other industries, relied on home work—the parceling out of sewing to be done on a contract basis at home. Home work allowed the contractor to avoid any legal responsibility for his workers. Hundreds of Chicanas in San Antonio and Laredo, skilled in fine needlework, a cultural skill learned by women in Mexican schools and convents, *earned 2¢ to 5¢ an hour.* These women were paid *less per dozen* garments than each single garment was sold at retail. These women worked ten to fifteen hours a day, sewing handkerchiefs or infants' clothes involving intricate embroidery, smocking, and tucks —highly skilled but tedious, time-consuming work. They received no pay for work rejected as unsatisfactory by the contractor, and often they were not paid for weeks. These Chicanas bore heavy financial responsibilities for their families, and home work was often the only source of family income.

Working conditions in many shops were deplorable. Charlotte Graham describes the Justin-McCarty shop in Dallas as a hot and dirty place with no fans, and where lint and dust hung from the ceiling. The machines were in long rows on one floor of the shop. Workers were not allowed to leave their seats, and bundle girls brought the work when a worker called for it. Those who were pets of the foreladies received "good work" and bigger bundles, cutting down on the waits between bundles and the time changing thread, so earnings went up per hour. Graham said that a ten to fifteen minute wait meant a loaf of bread to her.

Further, Graham states plainly that the management cared more for the machines than for the workers and that workers were treated as less than human. Once, when Graham ran a needle through her finger, breaking it off inside, she waited an hour and a half to see a doctor with thread hanging out either side of her finger. She was not given either time off or compensation for the accident. Workers were not allowed to use the bathroom except during the thirty-minute lunch period and fifteen-minute break. This rule infuriated Graham and others because there were only facilities for a few, and there were 400 employees in the shop. She and other workers generally put up with these abuses because "Not working meant not having bread in your mouth."

Under the National Recovery Administration (1933–35) wages increased, though women still received lower wages than men for the same work under the provisions of 159 of the codes. In addition, hours were reduced, particularly in the textile industry. Manufacturers, however, found ways to get around the codes. Under the provisions of the garment industry code, workers were to receive $9 per week during a training period lasting a certain number of weeks, and $12 per week thereafter. According to Charlotte Graham, workers at Justin-McCarty were fired just before the end of the training period and then rehired as apprentices. They were never paid $12 per week. The thirty-six-hour workweek established by the garment-industry code was circumvented by having the workers punch out at five P.M., leave by the back door (their usual entrance), then return by the front door and work until eleven P.M. without punching the clock.

The NRA also guaranteed laborers the right to bargain collectively. As a result, leaders of the ILGWU, such as David Dubinsky and Meyer Perlstein, were able to lead successful union drives throughout the East and Midwest. Dubinsky was determined to organize the markets outside of New York, and in July 1934 assigned Perlstein to the Southwestern region, extending from Minnesota to Texas. Perlstein was particularly interested in Texas, not only because Dallas was a sizable garment center at that time, but also because of the hundreds of skilled Chicanas in San Antonio and Laredo working in clothing factories and doing home work for starvation wages.

From 1933 to 1940 a strong commitment to the ILG on the part of the rank and file, together with strong leadership by Meyer Perlstein and ILG organizers, such as Rebecca Taylor and Myrle Zappone of San Antonio and Mary Jane Miller of Houston, initially promoted the rapid growth of the ILG in these cities. For example, Dallas garment workers' persistent efforts to organize a union throughout 1937, despite the tactics of the Texas Dress Manufacturers Association, indicated a strong desire to establish unionism there. Women garment workers participated in strike after strike, some of which involved violence and repeated trips to jail for many women. Furthermore, the ILG attracted many members through its social and educational programs.

"Union-mindedness" continued on the part of some members of the rank and file throughout the period 1940–50 despite the fact that ILG organizers led no significant union drives in any of the four major garment centers. Though many Anglo women moved out of the garment industry into war industries, black women and more Chicanas, potentially strong sources of union support, entered the shops.

The problem with union organizing during this period lay with the unspoken attitudes, on the part of both the union and the workers themselves, toward the workers as women. Labor unions, particularly those affiliated with the AFL, as was the ILGWU in the forties, traditionally viewed women as difficult to organize because of their lack of skills and high turnover rate. More important, even in a union composed of 75 percent women, women were leaders at the local level only, as business managers, presidents of locals, and organizers. Few women were elected to national office or allowed to make policy. No black women or Chicanas were made ILG organizers in Texas, and few organizers spoke Spanish or understood the important cultural differences among these ethnic groups, making the task of organizing even more difficult. Though most women organizers were paid less than men—and knew it—they still expected to be treated differently from men even in the labor market and didn't argue.

These attitudes, together with the union's failure to win any new contracts in the forties, led to a growing lack of commitment to the

ILGWU. The passage of the state's "right to work" law in 1947, which prohibited the closed, or all-union, shop was a psychological as well as practical defeat for the union. Victory in the thirties was followed by stagnancy in the forties, a pattern revealed through the history of the Texas ILGWU strikes and organizational drives.

In terms of successful union drives, San Antonio was the most significant of the four major garment centers in Texas. Organizational efforts began in 1933, and two locals were chartered by the ILGWU in 1934. Workers asked the local Labor Temple to request the ILG to come in and organize the hundreds of skilled Chicana dressmakers being exploited by the city's manufacturers.

The first three union drives in San Antonio were unsuccessful in winning contracts from dress manufacturers. A B. Frank's plant closed down after it was organized. The Halff factory switched to the manufacture of shirts to escape the jurisdiction of the ILG. The first strike against Dorothy Frocks in 1936 lasted six months, until the company moved to Dallas. But the strike was resumed by the Dallas ILG local, and Dorothy Frocks finally signed a union contract in November.

In May 1937, Myrle Zappone, a machine operator who had worked with Meyer Perlstein in the Dallas strike (1935), organized a strike against Shirlee Frock Company, which proved to be the first real victory for the ILGWU in San Antonio. Shirlee Frock manufactured infant and children's wear and depended heavily on home workers. These Chicana home workers proved to be the strength of the union because they served as pickets. The owner claimed that because they worked at home and not in the shop, they were not his employees and therefore their picket was illegal and no strike was in fact taking place. Over eighty pickets were arrested during two weeks in July and charged with blocking the sidewalk, unlawful assembly, and vagrancy. The owner had enlisted the support of the police commissioner and the mayor in an effort to break the strike through the use of arbitrary arrests and other forms of harassment.

The National Labor Relations Board promised to investigate and began to prepare evidence to prove the home workers were employees, but the commissioner refused to back down. Even a restraining order against the mayor, commissioner, and police obtained by the ILG did not stop arrests and harassment until August 4 when the owner finally agreed to sign a contract. The union won a wage increase to 20¢ per hour and a five-day, forty-hour workweek, which doubled their former pay with a five-hour decrease in their workweek.

Eight months later, in March 1938, twenty-two workers at the Texas Infants' Dress Company in San Antonio went out on strike. The majority were Chicanas. They demanded a discontinuance of piece work, an increase in minimum pay, and a reduction in the workweek. Because the workers already belonged to a company union, which they had been forced to join, the plant manager denied that there was a strike. Also, since much of the work was done by home workers, and they were on the picket line, officials claimed there was no strike. Work continued at the factory because Mexican citizens were hired as scabs. The ILG finally obtained a partial agreement from the plant manager on March 31, permitting the ILG to organize workers and banning organizing activities by the company union.

These two successful strikes helped to secure a contract in late 1938 with Juvenile Manufacturing Company, an infant and children's wear firm employing about 400 workers. By 1940, membership in the three San Antonio ILG locals had climbed to over a thousand. This two-year union drive was the first successful one by a CIA-affiliated union in Texas. The fact that the majority of garment workers in San Antonio were under union contract meant better wages, a shorter workweek, and an end to some of the abuses of the piece rate and home work systems. The ILG provided complete support for the strikes: the best attorneys, bail money, and experienced organizers.

The ILGWU scored its biggest success in Texas in San Antonio, but low wages, long hours, and bad working conditions were the rule in garment shops in Dallas, Laredo, and Houston as well. Organizing in the first two of these cities in the early to mid-thirties benefited Houston garment workers, as manufacturers in those towns realized the union was there to stay. The fact that rank and file women actively participated in early union drives, some of which involved violent strikes, indicates that they knew they had to organize because it was the only way to improve working conditions and wages.

Membership declined, however, in the forties until, by the early fifties, only about 600 workers belonged to the ILG. Rebecca Taylor noted that this was because workers were tired of fighting the antiunion "machine" composed of city officials and dress manufacturers. Problems between Chicana workers and Anglo organizers made union drives difficult, particularly because the union refused to hire Chicana organizers. Also, the "right to work" law, symbolizing Texas's antiunionism, demoralized everybody in the labor movement.

There may have been several other reasons for the stagnation. Since the Texas membership never totaled more than about 0.6 percent (1940) of the ILGWU's total, the lack of attention to Texas may have reflected a lack of interest in such a small market on the part of the union's leadership. Elizabeth Kimmel, ILG organizer in Houston from 1947 through the fifties, stressed that the ILG made many mistakes in Dallas. In 1935, when they were forced to use militant tactics that had worked in the East, the people of Dallas were not ready for them. Also, the national pulled out after the strike, leaving the locals cold, because the effort had cost too much money and won no results. This caused disillusionment among the workers. According to George Green, labor historian, the decline in the Houston ILG seemed to be related more to the fact that the garment industry there could not compete with other cities. Finally, if more organizers in San Antonio and South Texas had come from the rank and file, the ILG might have sustained its earlier strength through the forties.

For many women garment workers during the thirties and forties, a commitment to the philosophy of the ILG and labor unionism in general was the most significant reason for joining the union. Charlotte Graham, whose grandfather was a minister, referred to her union activities as "missionary work at home." Mary Jane Miller revealed that, for her, the union was a "cause" through which she became aware of racial and social injustice. She found union work to be the most effective way she as an individual could deal with injustice. Garcia's father, a Baptist minister, had taught her that she should think of others first. Labor leaders supported free education, civil rights, and the abolition of the poll tax, which indicated to her that they shared her father's philosophy. Another key factor for union involvement was having a union background, with union work in one's family. The appeal of union activity as a good job for women in the thirties and forties drew many into organizing.

Several issues were significant in the lives of Texas women garment workers as they were affected by the union. Though the majority of women in the shops were married, there were few protests about child-care problems. Many women had relatives who cared for their children during the day. Andrea Martinez said that employing a maid from across the border was a common practice in Laredo among working women. The maids could not come on Mondays, however, so either she or her husband stayed home from work.

A more complex issue than child care or husband's reactions to union activity was the problem of discrimination on the basis of race and sex. Women held positions of only limited authority: they were the officers of locals, business managers, directors of educational programs, secretaries of labor councils or organizers. They attended national conventions as delegates, but were rarely union policymakers, and few were promoted to higher-paying positions within the union. Everyone accepted the fact that the union was run by men, though some women were more cynical about it. Latane Lambert, a longtime labor organizer in Texas, noted that the only difference between then and now on the issue of sex discrimination is that people talk about it more now.

Andrea Martinez was highly aware of the racial-cultural problems in the Laredo ILG. She always had to translate for the Chicanas who attended district ILG meetings with her, since the union officials did not speak Spanish. The union's business manager, who handled grievances, was Anglo also and translating complaints was often difficult. Though *Justice,* an ILG publication, was available in Spanish, it often arrived late. Martinez stated that she knew Anglos got better jobs in the union then, and they still do.

Olivia Rawlston and Bernice Garcia emphasized, on the other hand, that there was comparatively little racial discrimination within the ILG. Though Rawlston was president of the Dallas "B," or segregated, local, she stressed white and black women worked well together in the shop. Bernice Garcia's Houston local was made up of whites, Chicanas, and Puerto Ricans. (Blacks were not brought in as operators until the early fifties.) Discrimination was just not an issue there, according to Garcia.

Today the ILG is the most racially balanced union in Texas, built on progress made in the thirties and forties. Yet the fact remains that black and Chicana women had even less access to high-level union positions than the little afforded to white women. Black women and Chicanas were welcomed as members, but not as organizers or leaders above the local level.

The ILGWU's commitment to education had a positive impact on members in both San Antonio and Houston. Elizabeth Kimmel and Rebecca Taylor both explained that the ILG was concerned not just with what happened in the shop, but with "culture." Through its educational programs the ILG provided more than a day's work, Taylor stressed. The union served as the educational and social center of the members' lives.

In San Antonio, Rebecca Taylor coordinated an extensive program that included painting classes, summer camps, weekend outings, and English classes. Myrle Zappone emphasized that the Chicanas in the local were enthusiastic participants, as few had had any formal education or spoke English. A psychologist gave lectures and answered questions on child care. Plays, pageants, and dances, including instruction in both the Susie Q and Mexican dances, were popular social activities sponsored by the ILG. As a result, Taylor noted that many Chicanas became more self-reliant and independent, particularly those who received special training as officials of the local.

Mary Jane Miller directed an educational program in Houston that offered social activities such as choral and drama clubs, as well as English classes. Entertainment at the local Labor Temple usually included programs of such songs as "Solidarity Forever" or "Mammy's Little Baby Loves a Union Shop." All these activities built up a sense of sisterhood that was beneficial in creating a spirit of unionism, Miller explained.

At the ILG summer schools held throughout the U.S., rank and file members learned the economics of labor, labor history, and parliamentary procedure along with songs and dramatics. Lectures on birth control and sexuality were part of one program in 1937.

Without such tangible signs of commitment as successful union drives, good contracts, and strong leadership, workers' "union-mindedness" diminished in the forties. The potential for a strong union was outweighed by the force of traditional attitudes and expectations that made organizing women seem too difficult, and cultural differences that kept the ILG from total success in organizing the hundreds of Chicanas in the garment industry. But among those women who did participate, memories of their experiences are still strong, as is their sense that the union had been an influential force in their lives; many are still committed to the ideas and goals of "union-mindedness." Bernice Garcia and Olivia Rawlston, leaders in their locals, still work in garment shops. Elizabeth Kimmel is a union organizer in Texas, and Latane Lambert continues to do union support work. Andrea Martinez summarized her feelings about the union this way:

> Through the union we were always paid a little more than minimum wage; we got vacation paid, medical benefits, and could not get fired unjustly. When we are organized we pay dues to get help. . . . If we cannot clear our differences [with management] we have someone to help us. If you go alone nobody will listen, but if you go as a group . . . they will hear.

SHOULDER TO SHOULDER

∞ ANNE BRADEN

In 1978, workers in the gigantic Newport News, Virginia, shipyard owned by Tenneco Corporation voted to be represented by the United Steelworkers of America. In 1979, after the company stalled negotiations, the workers struck for eighty-three days. In a major breakthrough for organized labor in the South, Local 8888 won a contract covering the yard's 16,000 workers.

Because of laws won by the civil rights movement, the shipyard began hiring women in traditionally male jobs in 1973. By the late seventies, one third of the production and maintenance workers were women, and they have played an important role in the union. In the process, they have watched their lives and personalities change. Of the women quoted here, six are white—Paula Axsom, Nancy Crosby, Jan Hooks, Judy Mullins, Sandra Tanner, Ann Warren. Three are black—Cynthia (Cindy) Boyd, Peggy Carpenter, Gloria Council. "We got to know each other on the picket line," said Peggy Carpenter. "Oh, we may get mad now and then, but we say what we have to say, and we work together. We know who the enemy is. We stuck together, and it paid off."

Ann Warren, mother of two sons, now grown, steelworker delegate to Newport News Central Labor Council: I was one of the first women ever to work on a ship. I hired in on October 4, 1973. I was separated from my husband; my sons were still little boys, and I knew I could not support them on a minimum-wage job. Then I saw a newspaper ad that the shipyard was going to hire a thousand women, so the next morning I was there. The government had told them that they had to hire a certain number of women to comply with EEOC [Equal Employment Opportunity Commission].

I hired in as a tack welder; now I'm classified as a mechanic in the shipfitters. We do very heavy work. I've worked with steel foundations that are bigger than a couch. I'll never forget that first day in the shipyard. They put me underneath a ship, held up by the big pillars. A young man was going to teach me; ten minutes later he leaves and for a half hour I sit there looking at that huge ship over my head, thinking, "God, don't let it fall."

At first I got a lot of static from the men. "This is no place for a woman, you ought to be outside taking care of your kids." I got angry one day, and I told one of the guys that I had to feed my damn kids just like he did, that's why I was there, and I never had too much trouble after that.

Sandra Tanner, a painter and member of Local 8888's safety and health committee: I went to work in 1976, and there still weren't many women in the paint department where they put me. I'd never done anything like this before. I grew up in North Carolina; my father worked in a textile mill; my mother never worked outside the home. I did clerical work for W. T. Grant, worked up to management. They went out of business, and I came to the shipyard. I've always been the prissy type, and my brother said, "You'll never make it through the winter." It was cold, no heat anywhere on the ship; you had to eat outside or in the bottom of the ship because you had only twenty minutes, and you never knew whether your lunch would be there because a big rat might come and take it right out of your tool box. But I made it through the winter. Then my brother said, "You'll never make it through the summer, it's worse, it's so hot." But I made it through the summer, and I'm still there.

Jan Hooks, twin sister of Ann Warren, mother of two daughters, editor of Local 8888's newspaper, The Voyager: I'm a crane operator. The cranes fascinated me from the day I went in the shipyard. I had two daughters, no job, and had separated from my husband. I'm trained as a secretary, but I enjoy being outside. Ann was already working there and said come to the shipyard. My department is grunt-and-groan work; it's classified as an unskilled department— primarily uneducated black men. And I'll tell you those uneducated black men accepted me a whole lot quicker than anybody and went out of their way to help me. The white men in the age bracket from thirty to forty-five were the ones I had the biggest problem with. They seemed to feel the most threatened.

My first day in the yard I was sent to the bottom of a ship. They put me in a little hole, with no lights, and gave me a two-inch paint brush and a metal shovel and told me to clean this hole out. I was scared to death; it was hot as all get-out. But one woman working with me pulled me out, and she jumped all over the supervisor, told him no woman, no *worker*, was going in a tank by themselves without a light, or ventilation.

WARREN: When I first went there, they had only one bathroom for women in a six-block area. We raised Cain; six women fighting the whole shipyard. So they brought us two portable johns, and the men used them at night, and they stayed filthy. We got a padlock and locked them. One day it was real hot, and one of the girls was angry because the stench in the john made her gag. A construction supervisor—one of the biggest men in the shipyard—was down on the shipyards; she grabbed him by the hand, put him inside the toilet, and locked the door. She made him stay in there about ten mintues, and when he came out, he was heaving, he was so sick. Two days later we had the prettiest and brightest brand new toilet you've ever seen.

In 1976 five men formed a committee and asked the Steelworkers to help them organize. Women soon joined.

Peggy Carpenter, mother of a nine-year-old girl, a welding inspector, and financial secretary of Local 8888: Before we had the union the supervisors felt they could talk to you any kind of way. And they would promote their girlfriends or women they liked; there was no seniority.

WARREN: Jan's and my father worked in the shipyard before he retired, and he was so proud of us both. He took us both out and bought us our work clothes when we first went in. He's always been ahead of his time—brought us up to show no partiality to anybody, black, white, man, woman. And he knew about unions because I remember walking a picket line with him when we were four years old. That was in the North Carolina mountains in the forties, at a big laundry. Jan and I went and asked our father what he thought about the union. He said yes, a union was probably the best thing that could happen at the shipyard, and if we wanted it to go after it. So we both did.

Judy Mullins, a machinist and a leader in Local 8888's work for passage of the Equal Rights Amendment: It was different with me. Union is something I did not grow up with at all. My dad worked in the shipyard, but he said don't join the PSA [Peninsula Shipbuilders

Association, the company-controlled union that then represented the workers]. He still considers the Steelworkers crime and corruption. But in the yard I listened to the men complain—I mean from day one, I heard them—about working conditions, low pay, lack of benefits, management pushing people around, unsafe conditions. And I knew a union was needed, here was a chance to change things a hundred percent.

Gloria Council, a welder and recording secretary of Local 8888: My sister was in the union before I was. The company made up things to fire her. But the union fought and got her her job back. So I saw what a union could do.

Local 8888 includes about as many office workers as production workers. Women who were pioneering in the heavy work on the shipways soon found allies among the women who worked in the offices, many of them on the highly technical computer jobs.

Paula Axsom, mother of two grown children, now Tidewater coordinator for ratification of ERA: I'm a materials supply clerk; I monitor books for spare parts, a bookkeeping job. Those of us in the office were lowest on the totem pole in salary. Before we got our contract they were hiring clerical employees at minimum wage. I had been at the shipyard fifteen years, but production workers who had been there just a few years made more than I did, and I was topped out as to where I could go. All that has changed with the union.

Cindy Boyd, mother of two young children, now co-chair of Local 8888's compensation committee: I work in the office, and actually I was doing pretty well before the strike. I'd been there seven years; my father was in service, and I worked summers during high school for the government, hoping I could someday be a clerk-typist. When I got the job at the shipyard, they trained us on computers, and I thought it was marvelous. The reason I went out on strike is that my husband works in the yard, and I knew what he was going through, being a black male in that shipyard. Not just him, but the women, too, with unsafe working conditions, no benefits. So we both came out on strike, and I was scared. We have two kids, and we didn't know if we would have a job again, but we decided to make that stand.

The computer operators put the company through a trick when we went out. We knew our jobs, we trained other workers, but we never wrote down procedures. We took that information out with us in our brains, and the supervisors didn't know how to get the work out; they really messed up the computer system.

When we got back, it was terrible. Harassment like I'd never heard of before. I had to go to a doctor and get medication. And they took away all the interesting duties we had, gave us menial tasks, and I finally asked for a transfer. Now I'm a materials supply clerk. I learned I had to fight because they weren't giving me anything. I used to cry when supervisors would harass me, but no more, I fight now just as hard as they fight me.

Nancy Crosby, who, before the union, worked on a highly skilled job in the yard's computer center: We all learned to be fighters. I worked in a highly secured area, very interesting work. Then my husband, Wayne, got active in the union and became president, and they took many of my duties away from me and finally transferred me, supposedly temporarily, to another job. They didn't trust me. I was in a salaried position and was not eligible for the union, but when the strike came, I went out, too—stayed out with the others, walked the picket line. After the strike I asked if I'd be put back in the computer center, but they said the job was no longer available. So now I have a clerical-type job in the design unit, where I belong to a different Steelworkers local, 8417. We've all given up some things for the union, but we've gained more. I learned about unions in Georgia where I grew up. I was one of eight children; my dad died when I was eleven, and we were very poor. I got a job as a store clerk to put myself through high school. But after I was married, Wayne and I worked together in a small Georgia can plant, and we helped organize a Steelworkers local there. Whether you are in an office job or on the shipways—I know that shipyard management has a lot more respect for those people they know will stand up to them.

WARREN: So we were all together. I'm an old shipyard worker, I stay dirty, and Cindy and Nancy and Paula, they're nice, working up there in the office. But there we were, working side by side, in the union hall, on the picket line, during the strike.

Local 8888's strike in 1979 was rough. Many strikers were arrested. State and local police attacked the strikers brutally on several occasions.

AXSOM: When the strike began the union organizer said he didn't want women on the picket line; he was afraid we'd get hurt. But the women went anyway.

WARREN: One of the first ones who got arrested was a woman. Police arrested her husband, and she made a flying leap and tackled the lieutenant to the ground. It took four of them to put her in the cop car. And we had a policeman with a camera; he'd harass the devil out of people, so we ganged up and covered one gate with fifty women, and every time that cop brought the camera up, we posed for him; we harassed him until they finally took him off the gates. Even the wives came out, mothers pushed babies in carriages on the line.

TANNER: Since the strike we've learned so much about our rights, about safety. That yard is a dangerous place. When I first went there, working in the paint department, they put me to busting rust—grinding rust off the ships' hulls so they can be painted. My supervisor never even showed me how to hook up my grinder. It has no guard, so not knowing how to use one you could cut your hand off. I busted rust for three days before I even knew what a respirator was. They had respirators, but they didn't educate the people. When we came off the ships you couldn't tell who was white or black, we were covered with rust.

But with the union we started having safety meetings once a week, and they educated us so much. I got to arguing with my supervisor all the time about how we needed ventilation and more safety equipment. I stayed in a lot of trouble, but I figured my lungs were worth it. I got so interested in safety that I've gone back to school part-time. I only finished high school before, but now I'm at the community college, studying occupational safety and health.

WARREN: None of us knew the rights we had under federal law. The state is not that much, but federal laws like EEOC, the Civil Rights Act, labor laws, our rights under OSHA, we learned all that.

COUNCIL: You always had the right to refuse to do dangerous work, but before the union there was no one to guarantee that right. Now there is. The main thing is that the company knows now that we are not afraid of them.

CARPENTER: I come from a struggling family of women. My mother and father separated; my mother worked in a chicken plant, plucking chickens, and went to school at night. She was a strong woman. I think I'm naturally like her, and the union brought out the real me. It gave me a chance to use my abilities. I didn't go to college, but math was my favorite subject, so when I first went to the yard, I tried to get into clerical work. I'm glad now I didn't because I'm using my math as financial secretary for the union.

WARREN: That shipyard has always made the women, and the men, too, feel like they were stupid, ignorant. But they found out through the Steelworkers and our learning process that we are not ignorant people. For example, Jan had never worked with social services in her life, but she handled food stamps for the whole strike. She got to know everybody within a 200-mile radius who dealt with social services. Cindy is now one of our leaders, co-chair of workers' compensation. One of them, head of the compensation committee, went to Washington recently to testify on that. The shipyard has found out that we are not as stupid as they thought we were.

Women are fighting back against sexual harassment on the job now. One woman took a supervisor to court, and he was fired. She had asked for a raise and he said, all right, if you'll sleep with me, only he used cruder words. Now this was a white supervisor and a black woman—and she went back and asked him again, and he said the same thing. And she taped him.

CROSBY: So now they bar all tape recorders from the yard area.

TANNER: But the company is also turning it around and trying to use the sexual harassment thing to turn worker against worker. They're now telling our co-workers they'll get fired for sexual harassment.

HOOKS: The discrimination is still so rampant. In my department you see so many white guys that are supervisors, or specialists, and there's not a single woman above third-class mechanic. The work force in my department is 80 percent black, and I bet not two percent are above mechanic.

WARREN: As far as this company is concerned the people in that shipyard are either white men, or they are Southern white gentlewomen that don't have any business working, or they are niggers. And I mean they actually call them that, sometimes to their faces. Some women, white and black, have been made supervisors, but they are tokens. The government told the company to comply with EEOC, so they found women who scabbed. A decent supervisor who treats people right, man or woman, gets shafted. They want supervisors who will stay on people's backs all the time.

The women—along with union men—have gone into politics. In 1981, Local 8888 representatives, in coalition with several other unions, took over local Democratic conventions in Hampton and Newport News and elected most of the delegates to the state convention.

WARREN: We don't have anybody in office around here who will stand up for working people. Whether it be on the city council, in the House of Representatives, senators. And we figure we have to start here and put the people in that we need. The only way you can do that is to register to vote, and you'd be surprised how many people on the Steelworker rolls were not registered to vote.

AXSOM: So we ran a telephone bank. It's estimated that at least 2,500 people registered through those phone banks. Soon we'll be gearing them up again.

WARREN: Tenneco put on a campaign in the community for four years saying the Steelworkers were trouble with a capital *T*. So the whole area got against us, first because we were women in the shipyard, then because we were Steelworkers.

AXSOM: But I think we are turning that around now. Not totally, but people are coming around, people who were scared of us, they are knocking on the door, they are calling.

CARPENTER: This is something new for the South. And I think more unions, more working people, are going to get together, statewide, nationwide. We know what we want; we want a fair shake. We don't need to be rich or have a big Cadillac. We just want to be able to live and raise our children and not have to struggle every minute. I saw my mother struggle so, working in the poultry plant, and never have anything for it. Oh, we never went to bed hungry, she saw to that, but it was such a struggle for her.

WARREN: We've got to fight together, or we'll have nothing. One person can't do anything, but when you've got people behind you, you can accomplish things.

MULLINS: And for the betterment of everyone. Not just for us, but for everybody, try to make things better in our workplace and in our community. Because we are not going to make any changes in what's going on in this country until we can make changes in our own community. And that's what we're trying to do, make things better for everybody.

HARD TIMES
COTTON MILL GIRLS

❧ VICTORIA MORRIS BYERLY

In nineteen fifteen we heard it said
Go to town and get ahead
It's hard times cotton mill girls
It's hard times everywhere

Country folks they ought to be killed
For leaving their homes and coming to the mill
It's hard times cotton mill girls
It's hard times everywhere

I've worked in a cotton mill all of my life
And I ain't got nothing but a Barlow knife
It's hard times cotton mill girls
It's hard times everywhere

Us girls work twelve hours a day
For fourteen cents of measly pay
It's hard times cotton mill girls
It's hard times everywhere

They raised our wages up half a cent
But the poor old hands didn't know what it meant
It's hard times cotton mill girls
It's hard times everywhere

They raised our wages up half a cent more
But they went up a dime at the company store

It's hard times cotton mill girls
It's hard times everywhere

When I die don't bury me at all
Just pickle my bones in alcohol
Hang me up on the spinning room wall
It's hard times everywhere
—ANONYMOUS

At the turn of the century my great-grandmother, Mary Frances, was middle-aged with eleven children. My great-grandfather, Cicero, was earning a living as a sharecropper and with odd jobs. In 1910 he was hired by the Cannon Company to help dig the foundation for the Amazon Cotton Mill in Thomasville, North Carolina. That same year Cicero and Mary Frances were separated. She took the children, moved to a small four-room house near town, and went to work in the cotton mill. The oldest child soon followed her there as did, eventually, all eleven children, some beginning work as young as eight years old.

My grandmother, Florence Iola Mae, started spinning at the Amazon when she was eleven. She was married at fourteen, had five children, and was widowed by the time she was forty. My mother, Clara Mae, was eighteen and the single parent of a one-year-old daughter when she was taught to spin. I was also eighteen when I went to work in the mill. These four generations of women and their children have, together, worked around 400 years in the cotton mills so far.

I didn't stay in the mill long. My family encouraged me to get out and stay out. Being the first one of us all to get an education, they thought I ought to be able to do a little better. But to do so, I concluded, I had to leave Thomasville.

Ten years later I went back to the Amazon Cotton Mill village. I visited dozens of mill women who were grown when my grandmother, now 74, was learning to spin, others who grew up with my mother and their now-grown mill-working daughters with whom I used to play. I began to find a legacy rich in history and folklore, and thus was born the Southern Textile Workers' Oral History Project, an effort to lay claim to a history largely omitted in the official annals. It is the new kind of history written in living rooms and on front porches, not libraries, which is changing the way in which Americans think of their past, and themselves.

BERTHA MILLER: I was born in Randolph County eighty-six years ago. I wanted to be a farmer, yeah, but I didn't get to be one. I was raised on a farm and I like a farm. I'd rather plow than do any other kind of work I've ever done in my life. My Grandpap Hunt use to live with us. He made coffins. My daddy was a good man and a hard worker. We rented our land, we didn't own it, but we had all we wanted to tend. That was the best living I ever did. We'd go possum hunting, rabbit hunting, cut wood together, work on the farm, and me and my daddy we'd plow. I remember he got sick after we come to town. He worked down at the cotton mill for several years until he got down, plumb down, and wanted to go back home to the farm. That's where he died.

My mother was a little old bitty thing, weighed about ninety pounds. She was a good Christian woman. When we moved here from the country she went out there to the cotton mill and went to work. I was eleven years old when I went to work in the mill. They learnt me to knit. Well, I was so little they had to build me a box to get up on to put the sock in the machine. But then I always was short. When I was three years old I didn't weigh but fourteen pounds. When I went to work in the mill just about all the women there dipped snuff. They dipped to keep the lint out of their throats. You never saw a woman smoking cigarettes back then. The most awful-looking sight I ever saw was a woman smoking a cigarette. I thought, lord help.

I worked in the hosiery mill for a long time and, well, then we moved back to the country. But me and my sister, Molly, finally went back up there and went to work in the silk mill. I come over here and boarded with Green Davis and Lou. They kept four other mill girls besides me. I worked twelve hours a day for fifty cents. When paydays come I just drawed three dollars. That was for six days a week. I lacked fifty cents having enough to pay my board.

ALIENE WALSER: I didn't have no family before I was married. My mother died when I was five; my father died when I was six. I was switched here and yonder and everywhere. My mother's sister kept me until I was ten. Then she said she couldn't keep me no more so they brought me over here to the Baptist orphanage and tried to put me in that orphanage home. But they wouldn't take me because they said my mother and father had died of tuberculosis. Then my brother got married and I came to live with them in Thomasville. That's where I met my husband. My brother's wife and him separated when I was fourteen years old so I quit school and went to housekeeping for this family who had four children. Two dollars a week for cooking and scrubbing. I went with my husband for about eight months before we decided to go to Virginia to get married. Got one of my friends to go with me. He was seventeen and I was fourteen, but we told them in Virginia that he was twenty and I was eighteen. I remember that I had on my first pair of high-heeled shoes. I never will forget trying to walk up them courthouse steps. And, honey, I could stand under your arm, I didn't weigh but seventy-four pounds. The magistrate took one look at us and said you younguns go home. So we come back here. Finally, we got his mother and one of his aunts to go sign for us and we were married in Lexington. We lived with his parents in a six-room mill house. When my first baby was born I remember I was sitting there sewing with my mother-in-law one night and I said, "I wouldn't mind having this baby if I didn't have to have my stomach cut open." She looked at me and said, "Honey, you mean that you don't know no better than that and fixin to have a baby?" I said, "What do you mean?" And when she told me I said, "Ain't no way I'm going to go through that." That like to have scared me to death. See I didn't understand anything about my body. If I had I wouldn't have had so many children.

I was fifteen when I had that first baby and thirty-two when I had my eighth. The first time I ever started my period I was going to the spring to get a bucket of water. I was living with my brother and his wife. All at once I looked and blood was running down my leg and it scared me to death; I didn't know what to do, so I ran in the house and told my brother's wife. She told me to go in there and get a rag and put it on and to not say nothing about it to my brother and grandfather. And that was all there ever was to it. That's all I ever knowed. She told me it would happen again. And I said, "What for?" She never explained nothing to me about it. Didn't nobody. I didn't know nothing about birth control. I wish I had back then. Maybe I wouldn't have been so tired.

My first day of work I was terrified of my bossman, but I got use to him and stayed at that job until my last baby was born. My husband worked on the second shift at the mill and I worked on the third. He'd leave work in time to get home to the children so I could get to the mill in time to start work. After work, I'd come in of an evening and clean up the house, make the beds and such, not only that but my children back then they were small and I'd come in and I'd have to wash their school clothes, lay them all out, go to bed sometimes about two or three o'clock in the morning. Then I'd get up a few hours later to fix breakfast and do some more housework before I went to work. I got my nerves so bad that time that my bossman told me I was going to have to go on another shift.

Then I worked on that shift until I was seven months pregnant with my last child. My bossman came and told me I was going to have to quit because they didn't want nobody in there after they were six months pregnant. They were scared something would happen to me and it would be on their hands. So I got a leave of absence for six months, but I didn't go back to work for six years. I just couldn't go back.

BESSIE HENSLEY: The first mill house we lived in was a little three-room house that set there next to the mill. Right beside the mill. You could look out the bedroom window, the kitchen window, the front room window, from anywhere you wanted, you could just look out, the mill was always there. It was just a plain old wooden house. We heated with a coal heater and a wood stove in the kitchen. Back then in the thirties if you had a house at all you were lucky.

It was after World War II when Earl and me joined the union. We sure did. We went to meetings and paid our dues. The had got the union during the war, but after the war was over they told the hands the gold rush was over, and they never would sign another contract. Well, we went on strike and stayed out for months and months. I remember that day I didn't walk off my job, I just went to the mill gate and when they said they was going to strike I just didn't go no further. Nobody did. There wasn't but two or three that went in that day. After that didn't nobody go in. I expect we stayed on strike for a year or more. The reason we went on strike was to keep the mill from treating the hands just any old way. See a union is a good thing if it's carried out. If they were good people that owned the plant and would work with the people they wouldn't need a union. Now you take a plant, sometimes the bossman thinks he's better than the help. But it's like this: if the help wasn't there, the bossman wouldn't have a job. And if the bossman wasn't there, the overseers and the people who owned it wouldn't have nothing. That's the way I look at public work. It takes the floor sweeper on up to keep a plant running.

During the strike we had what we called a commissary and the union would buy food and give it to us. I worked in the commissary every week that it was open. You know, they'd have three-member, four-member families and so on, and we'd have so much we'd put in a box for each family. Most of it was canned stuff, dried beans, potatoes, and stuff like that. On the picket line we'd just laugh and have a big time. It was cold but we did it. That lasted down there a long time. We'd cook and eat down there in a tent. We'd take dried beans and stuff down there and cook them. Either that or cook them here at home and take it down there. Everybody would get together and eat and then we'd feed the kids when they come home from school. I felt like we did good at surviving.

Then them that was running it went back to work. I told them that they went coward and left us in the wide open. And then we had nothing. I remember some of the women went into work one day and some of the women on the picket line jumped on them and beat the hell out of 'em. Well, I didn't care one bit cause they had no business crossing the picket line. If those yeller people had stayed out of there we'd have got our contract. And it would have been a good place to work.

ARE YOU LOOKING, COUSIN DELL?

✍ REGINA M. K. MANDRELL

Sue was dead and Cousin Dell was making her shroud. The days of my staying in bed with my sister, so that people would not think she was really sick, were over. For Sue had always wanted me to stay in bed, too, on those days when her "poor little mortally wounded heart," as our old doctor had told Mama, was so bad. I always did, for my big, lovely fourteen-year-old sister had been my idol as far back as I could remember

Now Cousin Dell was busily stitching in and out on the soft, creamy cashmere. Cousin Dell was an institution in our family at such times. As soon as word got around among our big family connections that the Death Angel had paid his visit (and it seemed often—epidemics and disease took a heavy toll) she moved in. Her tiny, dark figure domiciled itself inconspicuously in the corner of Mama's bedroom, where amidst the quiet comings and goings and soft weeping and chattering of bereaved relatives and friends her needle plied its sorrowful task. But when I saw my sister, for the last time, the terrible, deep hurt was gentler—for the creamy cashmere and the lacy ruching made her look just like an angel, and I had the feeling that what Mama had told me about meeting her in heaven was now really true.

As far back as I can remember Cousin Dell had figured as an important branch in our family tree. On Sunday afternoons, whether hot and sultry of a summer or brisk and invigorating of a fall when the wind whipped in from the Gulf, Papa would always summon the younger of the clan to go for a walk with him. Often we would visit with Cousin Dell in her lower flat of a once-beautiful old antebellum home. Here, in the far corner of what was the former grandeur of the dining room, was Cousin Dell's hemstitching machine with its surrounding tables piled high with bits and packs of materials.

The machine was never opened on Sunday, but we all sat around while Papa and Cousin Dell discussed the comings and goings, marriages and offspring of our big connections. Restlessly I would pull off my Sunday patent leather baby doll slippers and wiggle my cramped, hot toes. But as I grew older, I learned Cousin Dell's true story.

She was sixteen that summer when Meredith Cassel came south to regain his health after a bout with tuberculosis that he contracted while in medical school. After their marriage life moved swiftly and tragically for Cousin Dell. The two babies who came were not strong, and Cousin Dell grew up very quickly, with the responsibility of the babies and Cousin Meredith, too. Disappointed at having to abandon his medical career he hated the bookwork that chained him to the mill-supply house every weekday. And when Meredith was accidentally killed while duck-hunting, her cup of sorrow was running over.

Gradually, however, there came new strength to ease the situation.

"Wayne," Cousin Dell confided to Papa, "I'm going to have my own business." She found the flat in the old Salsworth Place and moved in with what lock, stock, and barrel remained, and her new hemstitching machine.

And so began her business. In the shadow of the imposing old columns of the cathedral, Cousin Dell lived for half a century. She kept her finger on the pulse of the city's heartbeat as surely as she did on her hemstitching machine. Histories and happenings of the families for whom she worked were hers to know and enjoy as she deftly adorned layettes and bridal outfits and graduation frocks —and time and again the shrouds for her infinitely large family connections.

One day, long after her little boys were grown, they came and closed the hemstitching machine, and took down the sign. Cousin Dell had finished her last trousseau.

There were services at the cathedral, and then at old Magnolia Cemetery. Kith and kin from far and near gathered there, for the valley of the shadows has a way of thickening bloodlines.

And I remember how heavy my heart felt, as for the last time I looked at Cousin Dell: not so much because she was gone—for she had earned this sweet rest—but because the Industrial Age had moved in and made Cousin Dell's "going-away" gown.

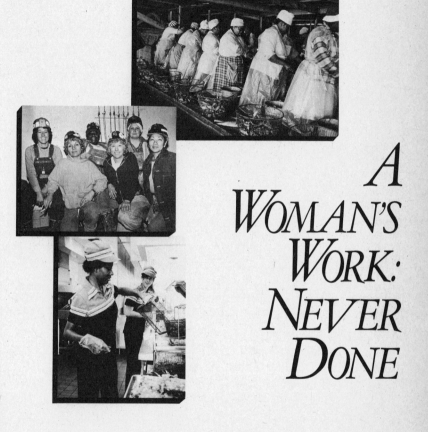

A WOMAN'S WORK: NEVER DONE

❧ PART FOUR

As boundaries that once defined and limited women's work become more flexible, popular attention has focused on women who enter previously male-predominated preserves, both in the corporate world and in blue collar and other professions. There are often dramatic stories to tell. Although the last 15 years have seen many changes in the distribution of women in the workforce, the majority of women are still concentrated in the service and clerical fields where the pay is relatively lower. They too have stories to tell that are often far removed from the popular assumptions about the nature of their lives and work.

Most women work because they must. They work at what is available and they see clearly the drawbacks and limitations of their jobs. Some have successfully seized the opportunity to improve or gain greater control over their working conditions.

The women who speak here share a sense of self-worth, and each strives in her own way for dignity in her working life. From the coalminer whose husband does the housework to the prostitute who tailors her working schedule to earn more money and spend more time with her son, these women defy their assumed powerlessness by taking control of their choices.

Elsie Reddick and Anna Mae Dickson, are women who directly confront the potentially devastating barriers of sexism and racism by entering public service in lifelong efforts to break out of the limiting positions society had assigned to them. Their sense of history and community cannot be defined by their job descriptions alone, nor will they be revealed in statistics that show how many women of which race work at what type of job. Only their own words can give life to such facts. They also force us to think about our own biases and our own potential impact on the future.

It is certain that the coming decades will place a heavy burden on us to assimilate rapid changes in the workplace as well as in social values. We have a strong foundation to build on that extends back to generations of women—most of them, in fact—who have always had to work for a living.

WHAT SHE AIMS TO BE

❧ SUE MASSEK

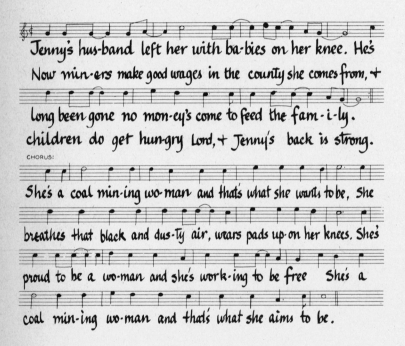

Jenny's hus-band left her with ba-bies on her knee. He's
Now min-ers make good wages in the county she comes from, +

long been gone no mon-ey's come to feed the fam-i-ly.
children do get hun-gry Lord, + Jenny's back is strong.

CHORUS:

She's a coal min-ing wo-man and that's what she wants to be, She

breathes that black and dus-ty air, wears pads up-on her knees. She's

proud to be a wo-man and she's work-ing to be free   She's a

coal min-ing wo-man and that's what she aims to be.

Second Verse

Robin's learned it's hard to find a job that satisfies
A woman needs to use the strength that in her body lies
It's a rough and rocky journey from the kitchen to the mine
But strength is gained from struggle and now Robin's doin'
   fine.

Third Verse

It's dark and cold and dangerous down in that dusty mine
And the fear of fire and cave-in are hard to leave behind
But the life that woman faces down in that lonely hole
Would be brighter now if you'd respect that woman loadin'
   coal.

COAL-MINING WOMEN

✧ MARAT MOORE

It is late afternoon in the Rebel Queen café in the crossroads coal and cotton town of Cordova, Alabama. Elizabeth Laird spends much of her free time here since her children have grown and gone. The jukebox blares as two teenaged boys feed quarters into the blinking lights, but she continues talking, slowly, deliberately. The contours of her face, like those of her speech, are plain but gentle and belie her fifty-nine years. Just a half hour before lines of fatigue creased the layer of coal dust on her face as she sat down heavily in the bathhouse, drawing solace from a cigarette. Now she has recovered.

ELIZABETH LAIRD: My father worked in the mines in Aldridge, Alabama, just a few miles down the road. He dug coal with a pick and shovel. He worked from can to can't, you know—before daylight to after dark. I never thought about it then, but now I wish I had went in the mines earlier, younger. I started keeping house after my father died, at fifteen. I'm fifty-nine now. I've been working nearly forty-five years.

I went in the mines when I was fifty-four. Been there five years. Five years more and I'll get a ten-year pension. That's what I'm planning on. Then I'm going to write my book and buy a kiln and do ceramics.

When I was twenty I was working in the cotton mill. That's textiles, here in Cordova. I worked twenty-three years as a weaver. When I first went to work I made $14 for five days, eight hours a day. Before that I kept house for people. Three dollars a week.

Monday morning till Saturday morning, taking care of two children.

I would have loved to stay home with the children when they were small. But I think once you work, you're used to your own money and get too independent. It's not a bad thing. When I married I was making more money than he was.

The ten months I worked as a spinner like to got the best of me. It was the hardest work I've ever done. Each spool had a brake on it, chair level off the floor. You had to brake them with your feet. So if your work's done bad, you hopped around on one foot all night.

The divorce was eleven years ago. I picked up a moonlight job in a café and did two jobs a day. I had three kids, two in college. My husband paid child support for the youngest, but child support in Walker County is just not that much, about $20 a week. The mines was the only place I could work on one job and have time with my youngest son. He was about fourteen or fifteen. He was so proud. He was the first kid in school who had a mother as a miner.

When I went in the mines I no longer had to work sixteen hours a day, which is what I was working when I went in. Six days a week at the factory and seven days a week at the diner right down the street. The other eight hours I slept.

If I had a daughter I would give her an education, but it wouldn't be that bad if she wanted to go in the mines. I would agree to it. I want my children to do what they're best at. Two of my sons are in white-collar jobs. I couldn't stand that. I can't tolerate being dressed up, with my face fixed and my hair fixed. I like to feel free, and when you've got on hose and high heels and makeup, you can't feel free.

Long before women were listed as miners on company payrolls they worked alongside brothers, fathers, and husbands when the need for their labor outweighed the taboo against their presence underground. Ethel McCuiston was among the largely uncounted numbers of women in this century who hand-loaded coal in contract or small, family mines. Women were employed under the care of some male relation; their contribution acknowledged as a bonus in the male's paycheck.

· · ·

ETHEL MCCUISTON: I was always told that it was bad luck for a woman to enter the mines. My grandmother told me that when I was a small child. When I got married, that was in 1937, my husband was a timberman. Times was very hard back then. We'd been married about two years when the mining started booming, and he got a job in the mines. That's where it all started.

I didn't start work regularly until about 1941. When I first went in, my oldest was two years old, and my other was one. I was twenty-one. I borrowed one of our boarder's belts. I had long hair, and I stuffed it all up in the cap. The boarders would laugh. They got a kick out of seeing me dressed up like that.

I just couldn't stand the thought of Arthur working over there by himself. During the war there were about half the miners there as were there before. About all the miners were drafted into service. Arthur knew how desperate they were for coal. He would go in there and undertake to do the whole job himself. The other wives called me a fool. I told them Arthur's life is just as sweet and precious to me as it is to him.

I'd come over there and help my husband make the dynamite dummies to put in the holes so we could shoot the coal down. I would be in the back shoveling dust and watching those big steel poles holding the top up, and if I seen them a-giving, I'd always holler. That way he had a buddy to tell him to cut the machine off and jump. When we were cutting coal I got down on my knees and I shoveled that coal just like any man. I really helped him.

Some of the men would come out in the morning and find out I'd been in there that night, and they'd be a-cursing and going on. But the boss, he was a wonderful man. He said, "If Ethel didn't help Arthur cut coal last night, there wouldn't be no work today. What would you think if your payday came up small?" Some of them said, "I'd just quit." And he said, "Go ahead. I'm not going to tell her not to. She can work anytime she wants to." He told them he'd call it a great honor that a woman would come into the mines to work so they could work and make bread for their families. After a while they didn't mind my being there a bit. Some of them would quit, and then think better of it and come back in two or three months' time.

When I was working regularly I worked about three nights a week. I would work all night from about seven in the evening until about five in the morning. I would go home and build a fire in the coal cookstove and boil me a big kettle of water and take a bath and clean up. When I washed my things out they'd be just as black as that dust I shoveled. Then, quick as I got cleaned, I'd start cooking breakfast for the day shift [boarders] and the school kids. I'd get the day shift off to the mines and the kids off to school, then I'd get the beds made and the dishes washed and the cows fed, then cook breakfast for my husband about nine o'clock. Then I'd go to the field or do whatever I had to do. I never did need much sleep.

One thing I'm bothered with a lot [now] is smothering. I call it sinuses. There has been a lot to suggest it was black lung. They've kidded me and told me I should go get x-rays. But there's no record of me working. They just put a bonus in Arthur's pay. So I wouldn't have anything to show.

When these [new] women went to working in the mines, it was terrible what people would say. I don't blame women a bit for going where they can make the most, if they have to get out and work for a living.

See, I know what it's all about. I've been back in there, and I know. I just say, "Lord bless em! Help em! Don't let them get hurt."

Women miners with experience have moved up from shoveling the belt to becoming equipment operators, foremen, and safety inspectors. One of the most coveted positions is with the federal Mine Safety and Health Administration (MSHA) as a federal mine inspector.

Thirty-three-year-old Sandra Bailey of Mayking, Kentucky, was one of six women hired nationwide in the agency's coal mine inspection program. The other five were part of an "upward mobility" program that allows clerical workers to gain inspection training. With nearly six years' underground experience, Bailey is the only woman with mining experience training to become an inspector.

SANDRA BAILEY: I have been a waitress, a school bus driver, and I've worked in a shoe factory and a school lunchroom. There's very little work here other than the mines. I put in applications for a year, just on a lark. In the meantime, I found a CETA job with senior citizens, driving a van. I really enjoyed the work, but it didn't pay anything at all.

At first I was afraid of the grueling work, afraid I couldn't do it, although I'd always felt that I was emotionally and physically strong. But I did it. After the first week I felt pretty confident that I was going to make it.

At first I was so ignorant about the mines that I didn't know the danger. It took a while, maybe three weeks or a month, and then one night I was sitting there thinking while on a break that there must be a thousand ways to kill yourself in a coal mine. To get killed. Just by touching the trolley wire, just by putting your hand in a belt roller. Just by so many things that you had to constantly be on your guard against. I was lucky that people tried to teach me the safe way to do things. I became more and more interested in safety, and I started studying up at home on pamphlets that the federal inspector would leave around.

I'd see people run through unbolted breaks sometimes, for short cuts, and I would try to tease them into realizing the seriousness of it. I'd say, "You sure did save yourself a lot of steps. We could have been off work tomorrow for your funeral."

I used to take those very same chances. I really did. And I didn't realize the seriousness of it until one night when I was running the scoop and went through an unbolted break, and just as I went through it, it fell in. That really made an impression. So I became more and more safety-conscious and was on the safety committee at our local, the first female officeholder in the local.

When a man quit the safety committee to become a federal inspector he suggested to the president that I be appointed to fill his unexpired term. The president was a little bit leery of such a radical move, and he asked the membership to speak up if they had feelings against it. No one spoke up. It was carried by the majority.

Being on the safety committee was really frustrating because you have all kinds of responsibility and no authority. You have no authority to enforce the law. You have to convince people to do what you would like to be done. Sometimes I felt I was in the middle with everybody against me. It was a good education.

I had been working real hard to get a district safety inspector job, like a woman in District 17. But then, very unexpectedly, after three years of applying and struggling and begging, the federal people finally hired me. Now I work in the lab with dust samples and only get out in the field occasionally. That's been a big change and a big disappointment. I just couldn't settle in to working with the government at first. I had achieved this apple pie in the sky that I had been working for for so many years, and suddenly I was without goals. But I definitely won't stay where I'm at.

I've never ever done office work before. You have so much independence as a miner, to do the job, not necessarily at your own pace, but to choose what to do first with very little supervision. You can see the fruits of your labor, it's visible. Whereas answering the phone all day you can't see anything visible that you've done.

And I miss watching the coal being cut. It is really beautiful. I really miss seeing production. And I began to realize how many, many women there were out there who would like to have the same opportunity that I was having, but the opportunity was just not there without a little encouragement. One night at work it just hit me that if this hadn't come along, I would probably still be a waitress, or working in a school lunchroom.

I will never ever be the same person I was before I went underground, never in a thousand years. I feel now that whatever life has to thrust upon me, I can handle it. I'll just never be the same again.

In Ermine, Kentucky, Bonnie Howard was raised with the old ways, by grandparents who cared for her until she was of age to go to work and care for them. It was a mutual relationship that has continued into her marriage, and Bonnie sees nothing unusual in the fact that her husband, Dan, does all the housework and child care for their daughter, Martha, while she puts in her eight hours underground on the "hoot owl" shift.

"When one gets sick, the other works," she explains, and points out that Dan, also a miner, worked until illness forced him to leave work. Martha is accustomed to seeing her father wash the dishes, sweep the floors, and work the garden, while her mother leaves the house for the mines and a union paycheck.

Bonnie was still sleeping the afternoon I arrived, unannounced, on their doorstep, but Dan ushered me into the bedroom and we began talking. Dan and Martha shared in the conversation the way they shared the workload because, as Bonnie put it, "That's just the way we do things."

BONNIE HOWARD: As far as working, I've done a little bit of everything. I've been a waitress, cook, secretary, school bus driver, butcher, nurse's aid, house cleaner. Now a coal miner. I started work when I was a freshman in high school; I worked on the weekends and after school.

I never imagined me a-goin into the mines. What got me into it,

I was working as a butcher, and came up from being a trainee, but my pay didn't raise none. Right there, that killed me ever being a butcher.

At the first mine I worked at they asked me why did I want to start working at the mines. And I told them I was a butcher, and my work went up but my pay didn't get any higher. My husband was sick, and I had a child in school, and I needed a job that paid good money.

I guess it was about a week later, they told me, we have to hire a woman, and your work record is good. They hired me on a Friday, and I went to work that Sunday night. I'd never been in a mine before. I was nervous and scared. I kept watching the top and the sides so hard I got a crook in my neck. Going in on the mantrips, I kept my head way down below my knees. I was really scared, to tell you the truth. Still am scared.

I never told Dan I was going into the mines until after I took my physical. He about swallowed his tongue. He thought I was kidding. But he told me, if you can be a butcher, I know you can be a coal miner.

They worked me real hard at first, to see if I was man enough to take it, as the old saying goes. The first thirty days they about bruted me to death. I didn't think I could stand it. I worked everyday. I'd be so tired that I'd come home and could hardly put one foot in front of the other.

If it wasn't for my husband, I don't think I would have made it. That's the truth. He done all the housework. He took care of the kid. He did all the cooking, all of it. All I did was come home and bathe and go to bed. I'd hit that bed and they wouldn't wake me up because I'd be so grouchy they couldn't stand me.

DAN: It's a shame, the way the men talk about a woman going into the mines around here. A shame.

BONNIE: They start lies on you. The women were jealous. I knew one woman, made her husband move on day shift. She didn't want him to work with women. They had day shift full of men whose wives were jealous.

DAN: The way I see it, you're buddies. She's my buddy if we work side by side. I don't care what she wears, whether it's a two-piece bathing suit. When she does her job and I do my job, that's it. We get the same pay.

BONNIE: After I got laid off from the first mine I picked rock right beside Dan. There was one other woman. Dan was the one helped to get her on. A lot of the other men were against women.

DAN: My boss said if he had five men like Bonnie he could run 500 tons of coal a day.

MARTHA: I thought it was a new experience for Mom. I thought it was neat. When she told me, I said, "Hey, my mom's a miner!" But I was really scared the first two weeks.

BONNIE: She still has nightmares, afraid I'll get hurt. Most people, they don't explain mine safety to their kids. I tell her, if you do your job cautiously and right, you are not likely to get hurt. But I ain't saying you won't. . . . The reason I'm in there working is to keep her out. I want her to have the education that I didn't have. I'd like to see her make a doctor, if it's possible. And as long as I'm working, I'm going to see that it's possible.

Lord, if I didn't have Dan I don't think I could survive it. I'd just have to let everything go until the weekend. I'd be so tired. I never worry about my kid, whether she's hurt or anything, because I know Dan will take care of her. He does all the housework. When I go to bed the house is clean. Even if he works, he comes in, and we do it together. You may think it's fantasy, but it's the truth.

DAN: I think a husband should help his wife. I don't give a heck what that woman does. If a man comes in after working all day and the woman's been there at the house, she's got more work there than the man who's gone out to a job. If I come in from work I still help her. I grew up under my mommy's coattails. She taught me how to do it. I can bake anything I want to, cook anything, sew anything, mop, wax, clean windows, anything.

BONNIE: It's fifty-fifty in a marriage, if it is a marriage. I'm in there to make a living for my young'un and my husband if he's sick. If I was sickly he'd take care of me, so what's the difference in me taking care of him?

IF YOU GOT TIME TO LEAN, YOU GOT TIME TO CLEAN

ALMA BLOUNT

The ads feature a young, conventionally good-looking race car driver called Runner. He catches a date by phoning a young lady to ask if she'd like to join him for "some homemade biscuits" at Hardee's—after they've danced the night away. In another episode Runner and a friend charm their dates into believing they have grilled their own fabulous burgers when in fact their "secret recipe is four blocks down the road," and they've really serving Hardee's Big Deluxe charbroiled hamburgers with "that special Hardee's sauce."

Biscuits made "from scratch" and chicken filet sandwiches "good as Sunday morning at Grandma's"—the accent and appeal of the ads aim to be distinctively Southern. "And we consider ourselves a Southern operation although you'll find us in thirty-four states," a spokesperson from Hardee's headquarters said. "Because North Carolina is our heartland. That's where we began."

It started over twenty years ago in Greenville, North Carolina, where Wilbur Hardee ran a restaurant that was known for its hamburgers. Jim Gardner and Leonard Rawls, two business entrepreneurs, purchased the first franchise from Hardee in the late 1950s and built a Hardee's Restaurant in Rocky Mount, North Carolina.

There were five restaurants in Hardee's Food Systems (HFS) by 1961. Today there are about 1,300 Hardee's Restaurants throughout the Southeast and Midwest, and several in Japan, the Philippines, and Europe.

Hardee's is the fourth largest food chain in the U.S. after McDonald's, Burger King, and Wendy's (in number of units and volume of annual sales). In January 1981, Hardee's Food Systems became a subsidiary of Imasco, Ltd., a Canadian investment organization. Among the ranks of the employees, no one seems to be particularly concerned about any changes in business practices or image that the new ownership might bring in the future. One regional supervisor thought the new owner's name was Tabasco.

Hardee's Food Systems still maintains its corporate headquarters in Rocky Mount. There it coordinates the management of 500 company units and keeps tabs on 800 units owned by several franchises. (Company units are owned and opearted by HFS, whereas franchises are managed by individuals or private companies who pay royalties to HFS for the Hardee's name and logo, sell Hardee's products, and agree to adhere to Hardee's food preparation and business procedure guidelines.)

The restaurant where these interviews were conducted is owned by Boddie-Noell Enterprises, the largest privately owned company in the HFS chain, with 160 franchises in North and South Carolina and Virginia. The manager stated openly that he didn't have women working the grill because he likes to have them up front. There are at least twice as many female as male employees and most are seventeen to twenty-two years old. All benefits—such as health insurance, sick leave, life insurance, and paid vacation—become effective only after one year of full-time employment, but most employees work part-time and usually don't stay for longer than six to eight months.

A number of middle-aged homemakers work for Hardee's, a spokesperson from the company's public relations department claimed. "Many housewives find the part-time hours, especially the 11:00 A.M. to noon peak business hours, to be ideal for their schedules, and the split is really about fifty-fifty between the number of middle-aged and the number of teenaged workers among the approximately 20,000 Hardee's [Food Systems] employees nationwide," he added.

Wouldn't these thousands of adult, mostly female, fast-food workers be the first ones displaced if a subminimum wage measure for youths sixteen to twenty-one years old, sponsored by Senator Orrin Hatch (Republican, Utah) were approved by Congress?

According to Hardee's public relations person, no. The homemakers' hours and the teenagers' hours vary anyway, he asserted, and the older people usually opt for working during the business day while the teenagers are more interested in the after-school hours.

But according to AFL-CIO economist Clara Schloss: "I have yet

129·

to meet anyone who can prove that lower wages will generate additional jobs and won't result in the substitution of younger for older workers. Women moving into the work force—single heads of families—would be especially vulnerable."

If Clara Schloss is proven right and the assurances of Hardee's proven wrong, what recourse will Hardee's employees have? Very little at this point: the Hardee's chain, like other fast-food chains across the country, has no unions.

(*Editor's note*: The names of the two women interviewed here have been changed at their request. They feared they might lose their jobs. The public relations person who spoke with us also requested anonymity.)

MARY SMITH: I'm seventeen. I go to high school. I've worked here a year. This was my first job. I wanted to work so I just came up here and started. I usually work about thirty hours a week, in the summer and the school year, too.

What I do here is take the customer's order, bag it, take the money, make sure things are stocked up for the next order, and keep the store kind of looking nice from the customer's viewpoint, right?

The girls usually cashier, but the guys don't. We have one guy here who cashiers some, but they don't have girls work the back line. You know like we might go back there if it's slow or if they need help, but they don't put us on the schedule for work like that.

Most of the time the girls batter the chicken and stuff like that and the guys clean the grill; we don't do stuff like that. They don't know, much, how it is being a cashier, and we don't know, much, how it is working that back line. Like they don't know some of the stuff we get from the customers, the pressure and all. I think we should switch off sometimes so they'd known how hard it is. Everybody gets paid the same at first and then we get raises by how long we've worked here. [Although the women were not aware of any salary difference between counter workers (mostly women) and grill workers (mostly male), the pattern in fast-food chains is that grill workers are more frequently granted full-time status, making them eligible for benefits and overtime. The Hardee's manager refused to discuss salaries, referring us to the corporate public relations office.]

I still get minimum wage, but they say I'll get a raise in September.

There's more black women than white. Three white women and the rest black. The white women just don't apply here. We've talked about it and there've been several to come here, but they end up getting fired or they quit or they think the work is too hard—most of the time that's what it is. They get fed up with it or something and say it's not worth the money.

I'd say most of the white women who worked here are high school dropouts, but like I'm still in school and some of the black women are in college. Most of the rest of the black women are in their twenties and they got another job plus this one.

You meet a lot of people here. That's one thing I like about the job.

It might be slow here sometimes, but we always have to keep doing something.

Drive-thru is hard. Cause you know you got to get all the people their orders, right, and you run over there for something and you got to get back cause your beeper is going and then somebody else is at the window. You got to really keep your pace up.

Like between 12:00 and 1:00—lunchtime—it's packed. Daytime probably thinks that nighttime doesn't work as hard, but at nighttime you have to really clean. And I think we should get more money for as hard as we work, not less!

I know about the subminimum wage thing and I mean it doesn't even make any sense, as much as we clean. There's too much work in here to be getting paid a *minimum wage.*

If I could do whatever I wanted, probably I'd do my own business somewhere. No food involved! If I can help it I'm never working in another fast-food. When I first got the job doing this, people that have worked in it before told me I wasn't going to like it. And they were right. It is hard. You know, you get fussed at and chewed out by the customers and you can't say nothing to em.

JANE BROWN: I started working here because I got fired from McDonald's. I talked to the manager here. I told him I wanted to be a crew chief or a manager. He said, "Would you mind working your way up?" I said no, and I started.

The women are cashiers because when people come into a fast-food place they want to see feminine qualities. They don't want some husky man with a big voice waiting on them. They want something pleasing. And most people think the feminine is the most pleasing.

131·

What's it like here? Let's say you come in early in the morning. You get people who want to order this. So you order it and all of a sudden, often you've totaled the machine and you can't change it and they say, "Wait a minute! I want to change my order!" And the people expect you to be smiling all the time they're doing this. But I don't smile all the time. I have this very bad habit of cutting people short. I show my anger sometimes by the way I speak. I get in trouble for it. I've been writ up once or twice for it.

But I'm very open about my feelings. Except when it comes to the managers and then I shut up real quick. Cause I don't want to lose this job. Not yet.

The black girls have mostly lived in one area all their life, and I've been a few places—like I've lived in Europe. I freak em out sometimes because of my straightforwardness. But, in fact, I get along with the black girls better than the white girls.

It does pose a problem that I'm one of only three white girls here. There aren't many white women who live in this area. But I think there's more black women working in fast-foods anyway. I really don't know why.

I think people who work in fast-foods ought to get at least $4 an hour because we're the ones who keep everyone else going. I mean, if people had to take an hour off for lunch and go to some restaurant, then they wouldn't get the work done at their job. But here they can come and get waited on, and get back to their job. We're practically the backbone.

If I had my choice to work at any fast-food I'd work at Hardee's. Even though they have a lot of pressure here because there's so much food preparation like with the biscuits and the chicken sandwich and the roast beef, people seem like they're more down to earth here than anywhere else. You know, like at McDonald's they have the rank structure. And if I'd a wanted to go into the military, I would have gone.

And at McDonald's, you've got all this machinery around you. Here, you've got a little bit of humanism. You don't hear a lot of people talking good about Hardee's sometimes, but that's because you've got to wait for good material and people don't like to wait.

I plan to work here until I either get higher status or a better job. But I plan to keep this job because it will be hard to find a job.

IT'S SOMETHING INSIDE YOU

~ WENDY WATRISS

Throughout the long history of racial and sexual discrimination in the South, women have found ways to survive with a sense of purpose and self-worth. For most women the struggle has been private rather than public, set amidst the commonplace circumstances of our lives and overshadowed by the more dramatic episodes of social change. This is the story of one such woman: Anna Mae Dickson, a black woman, a maid born in a rural East Texas county sixty-one years ago.

To put her story in perspective, one must understand the world in which she lives. Seventy miles northwest of Houston, between the piney woods and the rich bottom lands of the Brazos River, lie the small towns and farms of Grimes County. Nineteenth-century planters found the county's blacklands ideal for large-scale cotton farming and many brought slaves with them from the old South. From pre–Civil War days to the early 1900s blacks were a majority of the county's population. The Reconstruction era brought about the emergence of strong and vocal black leaders, and the Populist movement attracted strong support in the county. At the end of the century, however, five months of terrorism and the murder of two prominent black politicians ended black voting and no black took part in county politics until the election of a black school board member in 1972.

The exodus that started in 1900 was only the beginning of a long out-migration that decimated black leadership and left blacks a minority of the county's 12,000 people. Few whites or blacks living today remember that blacks once held public office or were important in the political life of the county.

Sixty years of political rule by the White Man's Union also insulated the county against social and economic change. A corn, cotton, and cattle economy prevailed through the 1950s. Large farming and mercantile interests, often linked by family connections, succeeded in keeping industry out of the county until 1960. Social relations remained static as well. Only in the last fifteen years, for example, have Polish and German families, brought in as sharecroppers in the 1870s and 1880s, started to mix socially with the old Anglo-American families.

After the imposition of New Deal farm policies, it became almost impossible for most blacks to escape the sharecropping system. Even those who had been able to buy land earlier found themselves unable to make a living as small independent farmers. Although nearby oil fields and the growing industries in Houston became an escape valve for many blacks after the depression, the move was not always easy for those who had grown up in close-knit rural family groups. Roads were bad and communications difficult in most farm areas through the 1940s. Unless relatives or friends lived in the city, finding work and a place to stay became a deterrent to moving.

For a black woman growing up in the thirties and forties, it was particularly difficult to break out. As late as 1960 a young woman raised in Grimes County with only a few years of formal schooling could look forward to little other than farming or working in white homes. Industrial jobs in Houston were open primarily to men, and competition was tough for the better paying urban jobs in hotels, boarding houses, and affluent private homes. Farming itself was limited because landowners were reluctant to rent land to families headed by women. The only women who escaped the economic bind in Grimes County were teachers and the black, home demonstration agent. Most of them were daughters of the small landowning and professional class who could afford the cost of education and the necessity of paying off local school trustees for a job.

Domestic work was plentiful in the county; it frequently meant steady employment but rarely paid a living wage. Even with the various fringe benefits that went with working in white homes, most women could not make as much as a man. In 1960, for example, the average income was $1,445 for a working man in the county and $620 for a woman.

With the rise of the civil rights movement and the integration of schools and public agencies in the county, however, a number of black women, such as Anna Mae Dickson, have emerged as community leaders. Now a grandmother and in her early sixties, Mrs. Dickson has worked as a cook, baby-sitter, and housemaid since she was thirteen years old. In recent years she has become president of a newly integrated PTA and a spokesperson for the black community. In the small brick home she and her husband recently built, constant activity marks the day: there are several families to feed, meetings to plan, and two grandchildren demanding attention. The phone rings all day—women seeking aid on home demonstration programs for underprivileged children, a school benefit, an immunization clinic, a church project. Between meetings Mrs. Dickson caters weddings, sometimes for as many as a thousand guests, and cleans other people's homes.

As she tells her story there are no dramatic climaxes, no acts of heroic grandeur—just the day-to-day effort to survive and maintain her sense of self-respect in a world that consigned her to a position of servitude. In the search for maneuvering room for herself she found she could step out and help others in the struggle for respect in a white-controlled world.

"After more than forty years of working in other people's homes, you learn that you never know what's in a person's mind. It's true for them. It's true for us. They may keep you from speaking out, but they can't keep you from thinking. It's something on the inside of you, that's what keeps you going. And you learn to be two persons to live through it all."

Growing up during the thirties and forties, Mrs. Dickson chopped and picked cotton for seventy-five cents a day and helped her grandmother wash and iron for a living as well as raise hogs and vegetables. The grandmother who raised her had never been more than twenty miles from home and applied strict standards to the young Anna Mae.

"In those days, you know, a lot of our people didn't let the girls get out much. I got many a whipping for slipping off and easing on into town to the ballgames on Sunday afternoons when we had nowhere else to go. When we got basketball, and I wanted to play on the team, Mama didn't want me to. She didn't even like girls to wear those short-sleeved dresses that would show the pits of your arms. And you better not be caught with a dress above your knees! The closest I got to a dance was when she'd take me to Saturday night suppers. There was dancing and gambling all right, but she put us where we couldn't see it.

"I look back and say what an awful way to grow up. But we

didn't know it then. Now I know that people had a hard time, but as children we didn't think about it. A half-gallon syrup bucket was as good for us as lunch boxes are for children today. And we didn't think anything of walking three miles back and forth to school."

But when the chance came it didn't take long for her to learn there were other things to do. Anna Mae was seventeen when she finished the ninth grade at the three-room country school and went to Navasota to the county's only colored high school. By her own admission she was "green as a pea"—a girl who had never danced and never seen a Victrola.

Halfway through the tenth grade finishing school became secondary to other concerns. "I didn't have clothes like the other children at school because Mama wasn't really able to give them to me. I felt that if I went out and worked I could get some of the things I wanted. I wanted to get out in the world! It was an adventure to get away.

"I had wanted to be a secretary for a long time because once I saw the secretary to the high school principal and that seemed to be the most important job I saw a black woman have. But if you lived where I did you did domestic work or farming, even if you finished high school. If you married you worked for a chance to get on somebody's place that had real good land that you could farm and make good crops. For a black girl there wasn't anything like working at the stores. They weren't open to us at that time, in the late thirties. And I don't remember any registered nurses that was colored working in the hospital then. The only nursing that you did was taking care of people's children. It was easy to find a job baby-sitting, or somebody to cook for and houseclean. So that's what I did. And I didn't leave Navasota because I was scared to go to a big place like Houston. I worked for $2.50 and $3 a week back then in 1938. And by the end of the 1950s I was making $10 to $12 a week.

"I learned to take what opportunities I had. For a long time, for example, I wouldn't work for families that didn't have children because I found out there was more opportunity working in homes where there were children. If you were real good to the children and took care of them well you could do more things and the people would help you. I first got to know Houston because I worked for a family that had a little boy that took sick. They carried him to Houston to stay with his relatives and that little boy didn't want to leave me. So I went, too. The relatives saw how well I looked after that boy, and one day, to my surprise—because I wasn't getting very much from them—they took me to a big store and bought me some real fine underwear. It was the first time I ever had good underclothes.

"You could learn a lot about cooking in some homes. I'll never forget the first time I had to cook and serve a dinner by myself. I was thirteen. It was my first steady job—working summers between school. The lady was having fifteen people for Sunday dinner. She was having these little birds they call quail. I had never seen them before. Well, she showed me the recipe book, explained it to me, and said to have it ready when they came back from church. I was so scared I must have cried the whole time I cooked those birds! But I served them. And that lady didn't let anyone say anything bad about the food or the way I was serving it. I'll never forget that day. That lady taught me everything I know about cooking for white people.

"I felt like this in my work; I felt like if I were trustworthy and were kind to the people I was working for they would allow me more opportunity and help me. I found out it worked to the good. Like another family I worked for, they had a store. Now I always like to know what happens on the inside of things. And stores were important in those days because we got our credit and everything there. So I got this family to let me go and work in the store Saturday afternoons when I finished the meal at home. I'd hang up the garments that customers tried on so the clerk would be free to wait on them. They didn't hire colored girls as clerks then. But I'd watch how they did things, and I learned how those stores operate on the inside.

"Conditions changed from family to family. I've worked for people I would go back and work for anytime because they treated me as a member of the family. They didn't treat me like a servant. You'd try to find the people who seemed like they'd help you get ahead. But actually people chose us most of the time rather than we choosing them. You'd get jobs by somebody recommending you. So I've had to work for people that treated you like they didn't have any feelings for you. Some people, I don't care what you did, it was never right.

"Like this banker's wife, one day I was serving a lunch for her. She had all the bankers there, and she was the only woman. She had her meals served in courses. We had got to the dessert and coffee. I came in with the coffee cups—I used to be able to tote twelve cups of coffee on one hand and serve with the other. Well, I went in this day and it's a wonder I didn't scald two of those men and scald them good! When I set the first cup of coffee down, Mrs. Thompson hollered, 'Anna Mae, goddamnit, you're serving that coffee on the wrong side!' Boy, I just started to shake. One of the men just caught the tray and set it on the table.

"I went back in her kitchen, and I looked at the dishes stacked from one end of that room to the other. I took off her dainty little apron and her dainty little hat piece and folded them up in the drawer. Then I put on my old straw hat, and I walked out.

"When I went into a family I'd tell them the children had to obey me. One family I worked for had a little boy, and I guess he just hated black folks. He would spit on us and do things like that. I said to the lady, 'Now I want to tell you there's one thing I cannot tolerate: I cannot stand for anybody to spit on me. If he does that you may hate me for the rest of your life, but I will whip him good.'

"Well, one day I went to work, and I was wearing one of those blue uniforms. And, girl, when I ironed one I thought it shouldn't have a wrinkle in it anywhere! So I thought I was looking pretty cool that day. The lady was sick when I got to work, and she asked me to dress the little boy for school. I dressed him and brushed his hair. When I turned around he spit on the back of my dress. I grabbed him down in that bathtub and whipped him good with a rough towel he had there. His mother started yelling, 'Are you whipping him?' I said, 'I sure am!' She started to say something, and I said, 'Don't bother, I'm leaving anyway.' I left and never went back.

"Another time I was called a thief. You know that is something you never want on your record. Stealing is one thing I never did. I never even wanted to break anything.

"Well, I was working for this schoolteacher, Mrs. Reagon, and she had some beautiful pocket handkerchiefs. One Sunday she went to church and later on she couldn't find the handkerchief she took with her. She said, 'I know I came home with that handkerchief, Anna Mae. I know you got it.'

"Oh, my God, I just flipped! I started yelling at her, telling her what I thought, and you could hear me down the road! 'If I were stealing and I had to take a pocket handkerchief, I'd be a pretty poor thief,' I told her. 'What in the world would I do with one of your pretty little handkerchiefs, other than wipe my sweat with it? If I were stealing I certainly wouldn't take something that you'd miss right away.' I quit right then and there and walked out.

"Her daughter came up to the house before I left and said she would look for it because she didn't believe I took it. Sure enough they found it the next day in Mrs. Reagon's coat sleeve. Mrs. Reagon called me at home and said she and her husband would like me to come back to work. I said, 'I'm glad you have cleared my record, but you'll have to find yourself another Anna Mae, because this one won't be back.'

"When you grow up into something all your life, you don't always think about the negative side. Like coming in the door—all our lives we'd been going to the back door, so I never fretted much about it. But some things did bother me. Why could I go out the front door to sweep the porch but couldn't go through that front door for any other reason?

"Or you would go in the kitchen and make biscuits and rolls for people because they weren't buying bread in those days. Now you know you got to put your hands in it to make it. All right you'd make the bread and then after it would get brown and ready to eat, but they wouldn't want you to put your hands on it. And it was the same thing with meat. You could touch the meat before it was cooked, but after it was done, don't touch it! Oh, that would get me mad!

"But you'd go on because you needed the work. There were mornings I hated to go to work. I'd be saying to myself, 'Why don't they do their own work? I do mine, why don't they do theirs?' Then I'd get angry with myself—thinking about dropping out of school, thinking if I had gone on to school maybe I wouldn't have to be doing this kind of work. Wouldn't have to be going to the back doors to work.

"You did what you had to and didn't feel sorry for yourself. We just had to make a living and that was the only way to do it."

In 1942 Mrs. Dickson left Grimes County to spend three years working in a Houston boarding house, cooking and waiting on tables for $13 a week. But when she separated from her husband, after becoming pregnant with her second child, her employer wouldn't keep her on. So she went home to have the baby.

During the time she'd been away the county's population had shifted dramatically with many of the poorer farming families— both white and black—leaving for jobs in the city. But from the late forties to the mid-sixties local economic opportunities were even more restricted than they had been two decades earlier, especially for poorer people. Industrial representatives looking for new places to locate factories during World War II were allegedly turned away by the bigger landowners around Navasota. At the same time government support programs helped drive tenant farmers off the land while technological changes and the distribution of cotton allotments made it almost impossible for a small independent farmer to make a living. It was not until the late sixties and early seventies that black people in the county began to see the economic benefits of the civil rights struggle.

The return home and the coming of a second child were the beginnings of a change in Anna Mae Dickson's life.

"I used to be a devil. I didn't bother anybody because it was my life when I was off work but I used to drink heavily. I did that for almost ten years—after I dropped out of school, while I worked in Houston, and when I came back. Right up to when I had my second baby about 1947.

"One night I got so sick, and when I stopped and looked back on what I was doing I dreaded the life I was living. I was ashamed. From that day to this I haven't drunk anything."

In 1950 she joined the church again. Through her work in the Baptist missionary society Mrs. Dickson discovered her own organizing skills. When she spoke people listened. This experience strengthened her sense of responsibility and from the church she went on to other community activities. She directed home demonstration programs for black girls and helped establish one of the county's first clubs to raise funds to support school athletics, and has organized numerous social service programs, including a volunteer fire department.

"Now it looks like the more I do the happier I am and the better I feel. My children, they worry about my health and tell me to slow down. I tell them I ain't ready to die yet."

In a county where there was little black activism during the fifties and sixties and where many black people are still reluctant to work with whites in community activities, Mrs. Dickson is regarded as a leader by both groups. She thinks it is important to maintain links with the white community and to have the black representation in community organizations. She is the first to say that conditions have improved for women and for blacks, but she has no illusions. She sees a need for blacks to stand up for their rights, but she has no patience with those she sees as an embarrassment or an impediment to long-term progress.

"We abuse the opportunities we have gotten. Since we have got integration we don't want to take our time to come up anymore, to do the little jobs that need to be done. We just want to zoom to the top. And then when you get to the top you don't know what to do to stay there. I don't mind starting up from the bottom. That's what my life has been about. I take time to learn. Before I jump into something I get all the information I can. Whatever I do, I want to show progress. I tell people all the time, 'I'd rather be asked up anyday than have to be asked down.'

"Too many of us do not understand what this integration means. Take when our schools in a northern part of the county integrated in 1968. The colored people—most of them—were only interested in their children getting over to the white school where they could get hot lunches and all. They weren't thinking about what would happen to our teachers, how many colored teachers was going to be out of work.

"We had a meeting with the supervisor and none of the other colored would say anything. I got so tired of getting up and down that I asked the superintendent would he please let me talk sitting down. I sat there and fought for our teachers all night! And our bus drivers. And, girl, I fought alone. Then when school started, and they didn't have a job, they were wondering why. Out of nine or ten of our teachers, three was hired back. You've got to watch, and you've got to learn.

"I'll tell you this. I don't care whether I'm with them (the whites) or not. I don't care about sitting in the classrooms with them and being around them. That's the only thing I would like to have, equal opportunity. And then we will have to learn to cope with it.

"I have tried honestly to teach my children to get whatever in life they can that will help them benefit themselves, to make them be better citizens. I have taught them what I know, and I have asked that they help me. I made them finish high school. The two oldest girls did finish and started college but they got married and quit. The youngest two are both in college now.

"With both my children and my grandchildren I have encouraged them to reach high—not to think about what somebody else is doing but about what should be done. And I have always told them that the only way to do it is to start within yourself first. And then your family. And then just spread out!

"Sometimes people don't know what they are doing. What did I know when I went to Navasota from the countryside? You go along and it's like sometimes when you're driving and thinking about other things and then come back to yourself suddenly and look at the speedometer and you're way over the speed limit. You weren't doing it intentionally; it's just that your mind was drifting somewhere else. That's what I think we do with our lives. We let our lives go. We follow the gang. We don't think about how precious our life is or what we can do with it.

"Like the old slave woman said when she was being whipped for praying. 'I may not be speaking it out, but you don't know what my heart is doing.' You have something inside of you. They can never take it away from you."

PROSTITUTION I: TRYING
TO MAKE A LIVING

✒ ADAPTED BY **PHAYE POLIAKOFF**

"I know the name of the game is survival and money."
—an Atlanta prostitute

Harlot. Hooker. Trollop. Whore. These words evoke either nervous laughter or serious social condemnation—but always images of the "bad" woman.

Public attitudes toward prostitutes and prostitution have been shaped by a combination of myth and history. And history has given us all the extremes upon which the myths and images are based. The notion of the prostitute in America as a downtrodden victim of oppression comes to us from earliest colonial times when women were imported from the streets of Europe and kidnapped from the villages of Africa. Throughout the history of this country, women have seldom had control over their bodies or their labor. In the South, a social structure evolved that added the dimension of race to the traditional bad/good woman dichotomy as black women became the legally and socially designated "bad" women necessary to perpetuate the double standard. The use of black women as chattel included the sale of their female offspring to serve as sexual slaves.

At the other end of the spectrum is the popular notion of the pampered, glamorous queens of the night. These women, too, have their historical counterparts in the select few who became celebrated as whores and madams in the boom towns and cities of America during periods of rapid growth. Many women went into the business for themselves, using their bodies as commodities. Some even got rich.

Regardless of the favorable or unfavorable circumstances under which these women labored, the underlying assumption was that women's bodies could be bought and sold for the pleasure and convenience of men. Practicing prostitutes are aware of this assumption, and for thousands of American women, prostitution is work. Yet, due to social and legal sanctions, listings of jobs held by women seldom include prostitution.

The idea of prostitution as some sort of sleazy fun—rather than work—is encouraged by laws classifying prostitutes as criminals and by media images of prostitutes as happy hookers lounging in luxury apartments or walking the streets in expensive furs. Prostitutes have been looked upon as fallen women, lacking in moral upbringing and in need of decent employment. In fact, most prostitutes see their line of work as better-paying and no more demeaning than welfare or the low-paying jobs usually available to women.

The women whose words follow here were interviewed in Atlanta in 1980 by Adina Back, Marianne Connolly, Phaye Poliakoff, and Barbara Solow for WRFG radio in Atlanta, Georgia. The series on prostitution was funded by the Georgia Endowment for the Humanities. The names of the women quoted have been changed.

WENDY: I live in a whole lot less fear of a lot of things. Little fears like can I afford milk this week, or can I come up with the twenty-two bucks for my son to go to school? Can I pay the phone bill? I'm a single woman and a mother, too. If I were living on what I could make as a waitress I'd be frightened a lot of the time. I'd feel a great deal more pressure because I remember what it was like to live from one paycheck to the next.

LOU: I'm not advocating that women should be prostitutes, but we want alternatives. Unfortunately, more women are going into prostitution because the economic situation is getting worse. You got two little kids. Welfare isn't really enough to survive, and it's humiliating besides.

WENDY: The way I became a prostitute was by finding my back against the wall and very little else to do but come up with a lot of money any way I could do it. I feel like there are an awful lot of women in America whose backs are against the wall. Battered wives who can't escape because they do not have the money to walk out the door with two or three kids—and where are they going to go? And when they get there what are they going to live on till she can get a job and an apartment and some money? So they get to watch their kids beaten or get to be beaten in front of their kids every day. Women in America have their backs against the wall more often than not.

LISA: Why work so hard that when you come home, you just fall out because you're so tired? All right, for a woman to bring home $200 a week—and that's a good-paying job for a woman—it's nothing for a woman in a bathhouse or on the street to make $200 in an hour. It's hard to say, "I'm gonna take this $200 just cause I need it and I'm not gonna do it anymore," so you quit that little job that took you all week to make $200, if you were lucky. If you had a college degree. But you got to have money to live. You got to have money to pay your rent, to buy your groceries.

Women's roles at work often reflect their roles in the family as social and sexual providers. Just as the vital services performed by a woman in the home are often not recognized or valued in the same way as the work her husband does, the public job market places a lesser value on her services as well.

SALLY JO: What is prostitution? Selling of the body? To me, every woman is a prostitute in one way or another. I've been a housewife for fifteen years. If I would be good to my husband during the week, like extra sex, I'd get extra money at the end of the week to buy a pair of shoes or a blouse.

PHOEBE: It's just as bad behind the bar [working as a barmaid]. Sometimes you get regular customers who come to the bar and they want to tell you all their problems at home and everything else. I have some customers who come in every day who don't have the slightest idea I do anything else besides tend bar. But it's just as bad with them as it is with some of my dates. They want to sit there for hours and buy you drinks, and they don't feel you should have to wait on anyone else. "Pay attention to me. I've got this problem I want you to solve." And you really don't want to be bothered.

ANNIE: I worked at Steak 'N Eggs for a while, and there's a lot of guys come up there regularly, just to sit and drink coffee. And when they want to pinch you on the ass, I thought, "Hey now. Wait a minute. I'm not getting paid for somebody to pinch me on the ass up here. You leave me a $50 tip for that cup of coffee or you keep your hands off.*

---

*From "The Pebble Lounge: Oral Histories of Go-Go Dancers," by Phaye Poliakoff in *Frontiers* (Summer 1983).

Almost anyone will tell you, "A prostitute is a bad woman." But why is she bad? One reason often given is that she makes herself available to more than one man. She oversteps the sexual boundaries surrounding women. She also commits the final offense, she demands money in exchange for sex. She says, "I'm not doing this for love or enjoyment. I'm just trying to make a living." The separation of women into "good girls" and "bad girls" has allowed women's sexuality to be defined for men's needs.

LISA: Sex gets to be just like working in a factory or being in an assembly plant. It's just something you do. You close your eyes and do it. It gets to be an everyday thing that doesn't bother you anymore. And if it does, after you look at the money it doesn't bother you anymore.

GINA: I never thought I'd do it. I'd always been a prude. You had to go with me two months before you could touch me. But finally I did. I started working in the hotels at first, but I got barred from all of them. I thought it was cheap to walk the streets. But there's a way to do things. You can have some class about yourself no matter where you work. So from the hotels I went to the bathhouses, and then I finally went to the street. I work from my car. But even now, I have to get high to go to work cause I don't like to deal with the fact of giving my body to everybody. I don't mind blow jobs that much. I'm very good at it. But I can't stand to have somebody jumping up and down on top of me all the time.

MARY: They're buying your time. They're not really buying you. Most of the women I met were fairly proud. They felt like they were doing a job, and they knew what they were doing.

Another occupational hazard facing prostitutes is arrest. Clean-up campaigns, crackdowns, and street-sweeps occur with periodic regularity around the country. But streetwalkers and black prostitutes often act as buffers for police action, absorbing the fervor of clean-up campaigns, while other forms of prostitution continue to flourish. This kind of selective enforcement, in some cases, helps to prevent women from moving out of the business.

SALLY JO: There is always a risk, but when it happens they treat you like a criminal. You're fingerprinted and mugged and all, and it's humiliating. They have all the power. As I was working I got a case [busted]. A prostitution case. And I'm thinking, ain't no big thing.

I'll get out of it, first offender, you know, $150, I can pay that now. But it's not like that. The bond is so ridiculous. They give you a $6,000 bond. That's why we never have a win. Most of the time we're trying to get the bond lowered. How much do they think prostitutes make? Are they crazy? If we made that we wouldn't be out there but once a week. And in most cases it is entrapment. The police have entrapped you. In my incident he took his clothes off, he laid on top of me. He went through all of that. That was unnecessary. Do black girls get locked up more than white girls? The answer is *yes*. Go down to Decatur Street [Atlanta's city jail] and see for yourself. See how many of them are black and how many are white. *Yes!*

MAE: If you get a case, you say I'm just going to go straight after this. But by the time you get the money to pay the lawyer you get another case. It's a vicious circle. So you can't stop. They fine you so much money—working in a straight job, you could never pay it. A $300 fine *today*. A $500 fine *today*. Or thirty, sixty, ninety days in the stockade. And the judge isn't going to believe you instead of an officer. There is no such thing as innocent until proven guilty when you go before the judge that first day. It's whatever he says you did, that's what you did.

Because of their illegal status, a prostitute usually has no legal recourse if she is raped, robbed, beaten, or if a client refuses to pay. Angela Romagnoli of the National Task Force on Prostitution sums it up this way; "When a man wants to hurt a woman, who's easy pickings? Prostitutes. They are throwaways. They are not protected." An Atlanta prostitute agrees, and describes her own experience looking for police protection:

MAE: Do you think I could get any protection? *Hell no!* We're streetwalkers. We don't have no rights. We shouldn't be out there. I met a man last night, driving a Mercedes-Benz, money all over the place. He almost killed me. I blacked out three times—he strangled me. He kept screaming, "I have so much money, what could anybody do to me? I could buy my way out of anything. The headlines would read: 'Another Prostitute Killed by Wealthy Man. Good Riddance.'" When I finally got away and told a policeman, he says, "Lady, I'll tell you what. Go to that Chevron station, and I'll radio for another car so you can file a report." I said, "A report? That man just turned the corner. You could catch him. I'll tell you what. Forget it. You go after your jaywalkers and your traffic violations, cause you're not going to do a damn thing about it anyway."

Pimps of one kind or another have long preyed upon the illegal and dangerous status of the prostitute, offering a type of protection for a large financial cut. The brothel and the madam have been replaced by the street pimp, who is in turn being replaced by "legitimate" businessmen running escort services. Some of these are part of escort service chains, headquartered in major Southern cities.

MARY: It consisted of an apartment where a bunch of girls would sit around the telephone. And there were a couple of guys who backed the thing with money. The people I worked for did certainly make a lot of money. They had the income of maybe five or ten girls, maybe more, coming into them every night. Even after their expenses they made enough to make it worthwhile to them. Definitely more than any of us made.

It's safer working for the escort service. And it's better money. And it's probably more socially acceptable in the eyes of the person who is picking you up. Which means it's safer and more money.

LISA: A lot of the girls on the street would love to work in the bathhouses. There just wasn't ever any room for them. Then you're out of the cold in the winter, you have showers, all of the comforts of home. Plus you don't have to run from the cops on the street. You don't have to worry about being taken in for loitering. True enough, the man that owns the place, he did make a lot of money. But the girls took a lot less chance of being hurt.

SALLY JO: I've made up my mind. The security is worth it. I don't know anything about the escort services except for what I hear. Now I'd never work for one on Peachtree Street, that's out, cause I know they don't do nothing for you. But in Buckhead or Sandy Springs [wealthy Atlanta neighborhoods] or somewhere where they've got a lot of money, I wouldn't have to worry about catching no case, cause you know they're paying the police off. Ain't no way in hell they're gonna bust nobody in Sandy Springs.

Concrete options exist to eliminate the current legal double standards for prostitution. Legalization is a misnomer since the name implies that it would help women. Actually, legalization has come to mean heavy regula-

tion, keeping men in control of prostitution and able to benefit even more from it. Decriminalization would repeal the present prostitution laws and would allow women to control their own means and methods of work. Most prostitutes favor decriminalization. Angela Romagnoli explains why:

"We need it decriminalized, not legalized like it is in Nevada. The situation in Nevada is good for the capitalists, the person that owns the business and the customer, but not good for the women, unless that particular house-owner happens to be nice. Women aren't allowed to go into town. They are stigmatized. They work long shifts; it's like slavery or something. But it's legal, and it's for the convenience of men. They're making big bucks off it. But they tell you how much you charge, and they take a cut on your tips. We want to work out something where it's decriminalized, where the regulations and the licensings are worked out for the women's interests.

"If women are going to be prostitutes, we want to make the job better, with things like protection against rape, assault, and robbery. They need a place to go, a hot line, they need supportive services. We want services for women who want to get out of it. We're working for jobs to be upgraded all the way around, for all women, including prostitutes. If you decriminalize prostitution and raise women's economic status in legitimate work, you will see less prostitution. If women continue to earn 59¢ for every dollar, you will not see a diminution of prostitution. If I go and do a workshop on prostitution, mostly people just want information. They don't want to talk about strategizing. If you start talking about support systems for prostitutes, a lot of women get real nervous. It sounds like you are supporting prostitution. Not all women start to freak inside, but some do because prostitution is an issue that borders on everything in a woman's life.

"For women there's always been a lot of negative stuff surrounding sex because we definitely haven't had power over our bodies and our sexuality. I just don't want it to be dumped on prostitutes. I think it's really ridiculous, like the prostitute is responsible for perpetuating the sex roles. Any woman who is participating in the system in any way, you could say the same thing to. It's really bad that women are divided. This division keeps women from being powerful. If men can turn around and scare you by calling you a whore or a lesbian, then they can keep you doing what they want.

149 ·

It would be very bad for men if women got together and stopped feeling like they were separate from each other, if women who were living straight lives saw that prostitution was not that much different from what any woman has to do in order to survive. A prostitute is looked at by other women as though she is the scum of the earth. It keeps us from being powerful."

PROSTITUTION II:
NOT NO EASY BUSINESS

✌ SARAH WILKERSON

When Ronnie Turner moved back to Norfolk from Pennsylvania she was running from a bad marriage and a husband she realized might kill her. Turner was then in her early twenties, without a high school education, and already the mother of three children. In Norfolk she hoped to find a job and make enough money to support herself and the child she brought with her. Under great economic pressure she took a job in a massage parlor. The following year the city closed the massage parlors and Turner lost her job. Within a year of arriving in Norfolk she entered the business of prostitution. When interviewed in October 1982, Turner was the only white woman among more than forty regular streetwalkers working in the downtown area of this Virginia city.

As Turner talked, the difficulties and dangers of prostitution became apparent. Turner's son is not aware that his mother supplements her welfare check by prostitution, but keeping this knowledge from her child is a minor problem considering the major hazards of the business: robberies, rapes, arrests, beatings, and drug abuse.

The most telling evidence of these hazards is the gradual disappearance of female streetwalkers from the streets of Norfolk. The number and variety of streetwalkers in the downtown area changes depending on the season, the day of the week, and when the navy men get their paychecks.

What's surprising is that of the forty regular "working girls," only eight are women. The rest are male transsexuals and homosexual transvestites, known on the streets as "he-shes."

The growing number of he-shes has undercut the business of the female streetwalkers, partly because the he-shes generally charge less than the women. This increased competition has made it harder for women to justify the risks they take working the street.

Despite the dangers, many women like Turner continue to engage in this line of work. She and the other prostitutes are members of the community and rely on it for the success of their business. This is how they make a living, and regardless of moral judgments and laws, it is a business.

This is not no easy business. It's not like people think. A lot of men say, "Oh boy! If I could be a woman, I'd be rich!" It's not easy at all. It's not easy on your psyche. It's not easy on your self-esteem. It's not easy with being arrested. It's not easy getting bad customers. It's not the kind of money people think it is. Maybe you'll see one person a night, that's fifty bucks. What the hell.

I'll tell you this, when you're losing your home and you're about to lose your child and your child don't have shoes or you're hungry, you learn you can do anything. You'll learn that you can do anything, even if it had to be robbery. You'd do anything to eat. People have to survive and that's the way it is.

In my hometown, there was no kind of work there. I worked in soap plants, chemical camps, textile mills, shoe factories. That's the type of work. I've worked hard in my life. I've worked real hard.

[At the massage parlor] I was being paid a wage by the owner. You put it in your mind it was a part of the massage. You didn't just . . . you massaged the whole body. And I got $10 for topless.

I remember the first time I did it [went with a man as a prostitute]. The massage parlors were getting ready to close down and this man offered me $300 and I needed the money *so* bad. We went over to this building and he was undecided whether I should do it, too. We got there and I said, "I can't do it. I can't do it!" We drove away and he said, "I don't want you to do anything that you don't want to do." I said, "$300 . . . take me back." Then I said, "No, I can't do it." We must have drove around four times before I got the guts to even go up there. And it was very simple. Here I had been with the man. I'd massaged him. I had seen him nude and everything. It just seemed . . . well, you know how society makes it seem.

It's hard to put a line on what is prostitution, you know? Everybody prostitutes theirself. Now, this is what I say to the men that say, "I never paid for sex in my life." I say, "Oh, yes you have. You take a girl to dinner. You take her to movies, and you buy her drinks. You've spent $40, $50 on her. You take her home and then you still don't know. Maybe she still won't jump in the sack with you anyway. You're just playing on the odds." I say, "I don't want you to pay for my dinner. I don't want you to pay for the drinks. Give me the money, let me spend it the way I need to. I don't *need* dinner and drinks. I need to pay my bills." In the long shot it's the same way. A man is paying for it. But they got a phobia about paying for it as putting cash in a woman's hand for sex. They'd rather do it the underground way.

My prices are more expensive than the other girls. One night maybe I'll make $200 and some nights . . . I won't sell myself short. I don't know, something about that, I just won't do it. I guess it's keeping up my self-esteem, like I'm worth it. If I've got to do this, I've at least got to prove I'm worth something.

When you're with a customer it's a job. First of all you've got to figure his mind out. Where he's coming from. Is he doing it for loneliness or what? Every customer's something different, you know. So all the time your mind is thinking, "I've got to do this this way or got to do that that way." And trying to find their little, you know, things that turn them on. And it's so much thinking, keeping your wits about you that you're not really involved. It's very few times, I don't think maybe two, three times in my life, that I've had an orgasm with a customer and it's one I've known for a long, long time.

If they're nice guys, if I've known them for a long time and we get along good, talk, you know, talk and friendship, it isn't offensive to me. Sometimes it's very offensive to me. Sometimes I'll get somebody who I wouldn't even speak to normally. I don't mean to sound like a snob, but I wouldn't give them the time of day, and yet I got to give them my *body*. It's something you got to really steel your mind to.

But if it's a *good* customer, let's say it's a stranger, you tell him the price, he don't try to gyp you down first of all saying, "I ain't got that kind of money." He just goes ahead and accepts that. Then, you always have to get your money first hand. You always, you *always* have to be in control. *Never* let them get in control because then you're in trouble.

Never go without getting the money first. They try to steal the money back. Oh, it's just so much crap. You got to hide it good. And sometimes they'll beat you to get it back. And there's ones that lay out there and take you out and they'll give you the money and then they rob you of everything you made the whole evening. I remember when I used to make $300 and $400 and get robbed of it. You know there's no worse feeling: you've worked hard all night and you're tired and then have some idiot come and rob you of your money. That's why I bring everything home right away. I don't keep it on me when I'm working out there.

We're all okay to each other [on the street]. It's a code just like anything else. If I stand there and offer $50, the girl next to me would never, *should* never say, "Well, I'll take you for $40." She won't be on the street long. Somebody will do something to her.

We also look out for each other. Let's say I see a customer in a car eyeing me, a girl will come up, poke me, "He ain't got no money." Or they'll come up and say, "He's trouble. Don't mess with him." Same way with me, if I see one of the girls looking at a customer I've been with that's been trouble. You give warnings to each other. If you feel like it's gonna get trouble, you tell a girl to take the license number down, "If I'm not back in an hour, yeah, call the police." But we very seldom do that. We just try to let the person know ahead of time that we got the other girls looking out for us. If one of the girls don't show back up and something might be wrong . . . you know. It's a system of lookout. It's sisterhood.

We call each other friends, but we don't socialize with each other, really. A lot of them are roommates and everything, but I'm a lot of a different case. Most of the black girls that work out there, their kids stay with their mother. They're on their own. They can operate when they want to or not. They don't have to cover their back like I do with my family, with my kid and everything.

A lot of them are drug addicts. The drug and prostitution businesses almost always run together. They got to make money just like me to keep their habit, but they're *freer*. If I was free and didn't have my kid here I could make a lot of money. But the kid'll be home this evening and I won't be able to work probably all week again.

With the recent economic hard times, crimes against women downtown have become more frequent and violent. There are no big-time pimps in Norfolk, and although some women have boyfriends or husbands controlling business and providing protection, most of the women are on their own. In July the body of one known streetwalker, Joyce Bilups, was found mutilated in a Norfolk alley. The murder is still unsolved.

Honey, you're always a bit scared. If you're not, you're stupid. If you're not scared, you'll let your guard down and that's when you're gonna get hurt. And you're gonna get hurt out here. I don't have any teeth.

[Joyce Bilups] was turning $10 tricks in the alley and also she used to rob people, but her mistake was just getting the wrong customer. All of us will get the wrong customer one time or the other. I have spurts. I've had a weekend when I've had three troublemakers. I'll think I'm not *ever* going out there again. I'm so glad to get away. You know, I had a Yellow Cab driver rape me on the way home from work one night. Guy picked me up at Steak 'N Eggs at four in the morning. I haven't been out there for about a year and a half. I'm just starting to go back.

What I'd like somebody to really do, study on, is why it's wrong; why the women are looked down on and degraded for being a prostitute, but it's all right for the man with the money.

Once in a while they'll put a girl [police undercover agent] on the street and if a guy propositions her they'll arrest him and he'll get a small fine. But not like us, we can go to jail so long. They can bury us.

I don't really want to see nobody go to jail no more than I want to see me go to jail. But I don't like their techniques; they catch you with a john, making him talk against you. And sometimes you haven't even talked about money yet and they'll say, especially if the guy's married, "If you don't say she did this and that, we're gonna run you in." Most of them are scared to death and that's how the cops can get them to say anything they want against you. So they get a statement from him that incriminates you immediately. He's gonna say whatever he can to get away from them and not have his family know what he's done.

I wouldn't like to see the johns arrested. I'd like to see them have different prostitution laws or have a different way of doing it. But we're not Paris, and I guess we never will be. It's just like Prohibition. It's something you're not going to be able to stop so why don't you try to deal with it in a different way. If you can't stop people from drinking, you're not going to be able to stop sex. A person who says you can is out of their mind.

TESSA

VIVIAN M. LOKEN

The one standing by the window
profile beveled out of
   sunlight through glass
hair spinning in sheer spirals
   to earth-round coiffure.
Yeah, the one supple-busted
   filling tight an embroidered blouse.
The one with eager stance
whose high heels arch her feet upward
giving her the slim sleek likeness
   of a gazelle.
She that is drawn naked through the eye
of the needle called desire
by seven young men half-circling
   the water cooler
who fondle her presence to the
   coffee break ending
who treat her extra cool and lofty later
their fantasies set away.
She is only a typist—and black at that.

MISS ELSIE RIDDICK

~ CARMINE PRIOLI

This generation does not know how suffrage was obtained. They know nothing of the pleading, the talking, writing, speaking, etc. etc. our women did—not many were the[ir] mothers or grand-mothers—a small [?] fought, bled, and some died to obtain it. It has just been laid in your laps—I wonder how many women of to-day have ever stopped to think and wonder how we got the vote. It was no easy job, but a few determined women held on until Victory was won. It took years.

When Elsie Riddick came to work in Raleigh in 1897, North Carolina state government employed two female stenographers. Mindful from the start that she was confronting a man's world, she was nevertheless deter-mined to become a "pioneer businesswoman" and embarked on an admin-istrative career that exceeded fifty-two years. At the outset she gave no thought to the cause of women's equality. Although the "mean and dirty" business of politics had interested her even as a girl, she agreed with the prevailing notion that on election day the roisterous polls were "no place for a woman." But one of the young stenographer's responsibilities in the North Carolina Department of Agriculture was to write the paychecks, and the discrepancies between her own meager earnings and those of her male superiors fired her resentment: "I did the work," she crisply declares in her Autobiography, *"and they drew the pay." Through her associa-tion with state government she learned that her predicament was common to all working women. Further, she reckoned instinctively that the higher pay scales for men issued less from physical or intellectual advantage than from the exercise of political strength.*

By early 1920, Elsie Riddick was thoroughly immersed in the drive for female suffrage. As president of the Wake County Suffrage League she helped engineer the secret mobilization of scores of Raleigh women who, anticipating their legal and political coming of age, arrived at several precinct headquarters on March 27, 1920, demanding equal representation. The next morning, in a front-page article, the News and Observer reported on the "coup" that left the men in some precincts "too dumbfounded to remember their manners and [they] stood by speechless."

After the successful fight for suffrage Riddick turned her influence and energies toward organizing North Carolina's working women. During the next several years, as president of the North Carolina Federation of Business and Professional Women, she traversed the state helping to establish new local chapters and delivered many encomiums to the abundant possibilities that awaited their members. To further solidify newly won gains, Riddick called for a platform of political action favoring reclassification of the federal civil service merit system, the establishment of a women's bureau charged with improving benefits and working conditions, and the prohibition of hotel discrimination against unaccompanied traveling women.

In 1923, Elsie Riddick was promoted from secretary to assistant chief clerk in the North Carolina Corporations Commission (later the Utilities Commission), and in succeeding years became active in a score of political and humanitarian organizations. Her service to North Carolina continued for nearly three more decades, and in 1949 she reached the height of her professional career by being the first woman appointed as chief clerk. This was an interim assignment, lasting only three months until her retirement, but it opened the way for the next four women chief clerks who have maintained that position up to the present time.

For six years after retiring Riddick continued her work as secretary of the Raleigh Civil Service Commission, a part-time position she had held since her appointment in 1934. When her health began to falter in 1955, she reluctantly left Raleigh for her childhood home of Gatesville, North Carolina, where she died of a heart attack on December 23, 1959. She left behind an unfinished autobiography recalling for her "nieces" a half-century of service in the cause of women's rights. Substantial portions of the work are in nearly finished typescript. Other sections, however, are rough, handwritten drafts, some of which are here transcribed to illustrate the early experiences, idealism, and humanity of one of North Carolina's most accomplished women.

In those days when [a woman] said she was a stenographer you could see noses turn up, sneers on the face—in fact, no real nice girl had any business in an office all day with no one but a man, so they said. All who did were considered cheap and not proper ladies. At the time there were only three women in the government departments: the one in the governor's office, an elderly lady whom he took to Raleigh with him, then one in the chemistry department . . . [then me].

My career began when I walked into the [commissioner of agriculture's] office in July 1897. I went in the office with this old man who was a Republican, but at heart he was the kindest and most considerate human being possible. The secretary was a stout, red-haired, freckle-faced gentleman. I have forgotten, but I believe he was a bachelor. After the introduction he took me to the office of the stenographer next to the commissioner's office and introduced me to the files.

The secretary sat back in his swivel chair, with a cigar, to meet the visitors. Of course, he opened the mail, and more and more of it was turned over to me each day to answer. As I sat every day and watched him in his big chair I began to think I knew just as much about the office, and, in addition, there were things I could do that he could not. It seemed I was there to do the work, as in all offices, and he was there to meet and shake hands with the people (but I cannot say to look pretty because he was anything but that). Then when "payday" came I grew more restless and dissatisfied as I wrote my paycheck for $30, the secretary's for $125, and the commissioner's for around $200. I did the work and they drew the pay. This went on for several months, and I was allowed $40 and finally $50 from the budget.

The motto of the Riddick coat of arms is *Fac et Spera*, meaning "Work and Hope," so I rolled up my sleeves and began to work. I was not too busy to realize the injustices and wonder why a man was paid a much larger salary than a woman if she was as capable as the man. This was happening to all women in every type of business and profession. A little flame of resentment began to flicker within me, and I felt that there must be some way to make conditions more attractive for women to enter the business world.

I was always most interested in the "doings" of the legislature, the various bills that were introduced, the pros and cons relating to each one, and the budgets for the various departments. I could realize the increases for the men were always much larger in comparison to those for women—an increase of $10 per month for a woman and several hundred dollars a year for men. Legislatures in other states were in session usually at the same time, and I always noted that women "got the little end of the stick" in other states. So I realized it was not just in North Carolina but in every state of the Union, and my eyes were opened to the fact it was true in every nation—I was more impressed with the fact that it was a "man's world," [but] it should be changed.

Although just a girl, through contact with my father I had caught on to many things and thought I could join in the [political] conversations. During the sessions of the legislature I kept up with what was going on. . . . So many bills came up that I did not agree with, but although I thought very strongly and would express my opinion I had no "say" [i.e., vote] as to how they should be decided.

When I left my little hometown I did not give any thought to women not having a vote. All that was left to the men. In fact, politics was considered so mean and dirty. Why, the idea of a woman going to the polls never entered my mind. All dreaded an election day. So many went to the polls drunk. There was so much argument and fussing, and later on in the day the candidates and their supporters were mad enough to fight—and often did—it was no place for a woman. Month after month this little check for $30 was mine and the men were still swiveling, smoking a pipe or chewing tobacco (it was the day of the spittoons), with their big checks, and more and more work and responsibility was coming to me.

Elsie Riddick's dissatisfaction flowered into political action when she came under the influence of the writings of the women's suffrage leader, Carrie Chapman Catt. In the comments that follow she gives us some firsthand recollections of what it was like to be in the vanguard of the suffrage movement in Raleigh in the early part of this century.

We found about as many women opposed to suffrage as men. Many had property in their own name but spent as the men said—that was a man's job, they said, not theirs. A few of us in Raleigh would get together—not all unmarried women either; many were wives and mothers, but the men called us "cats" and "old maids," and said we couldn't get a husband to rule, etc., etc. Many of the married women would not take part because they said it would hurt their husband's business, but many worked "under cover," so to speak. We talked about it to women all over the state and one by one the larger towns organized a league. This active work went on and on; a bill being introduced at every session of the legislature until we won in 1920. The session of 1919 turned down our bill but the next election was quite important to the Democrats, and a large majority of the women were Democrats, so we immediately began a fight to have the governor call a special session so we would be in a position to register in order that we might vote in the coming election. [We] put our heads together and talked over with our leading men the legality of going to the precincts and demanding registration, just as a young boy would on becoming of age during the period between precinct meeting and time for voting. We would be twenty-one, so to speak, and able to vote.

Five of us went from my precinct. It was all secretly planned so the men would not be waiting for us with bats in their hands. Just as the men arrived we women stepped up and were they surprised when we told them why we were there! They were so surprised they could not turn us down—they held their breaths while we held ours. [Finally,] we were not only recognized, I was made chairman of my precinct, the *first* woman in Raleigh to hold this position.

January 1920 brought five ratifications in addition to the states we already had . . . February rolled up six more. . . . With ratification by the state of West Virginia and the state of Washington by a unanimous vote, there were thirty-five states and only one more was needed. North Carolina and Tennessee were anxiously waiting [for their legislative decisions]. We still were tense about North Carolina, [but with Tennessee's ratification] we did win. What a celebration!

Many honors came to me through my fight for suffrage for women. I say "fight," it really was just that—not with my fists but with words and maneuvering. We found very few women who wanted to take the time or responsibility of going to the polls to vote, and really women did not try to think the matter over, how necessary and serious it was. Always we would get the reply: "Let the men do it, that is their job." But many of us felt it was also a woman's job to think about the laws under which her children had to live. But it affected not only the women of that period but every woman thereafter.

The replies we would get from the men! Many, many of the members of the legislature hid behind the women's petticoats. One said, "Miss Elsie my heart is with you, but my stummick is agin you." Another said, "I was just raised against it; my mother would not vote and she would not want to vote." We had to plead with them; they had the power in their hands. It took lots of nerve for me, a young woman, a stenographer, to approach a lawyer, an outstanding businessman, and many, many old men who had been sent to the legislature by their counties to vote.

I have lived to see so many changes everywhere women are concerned. God created Adam and Eve for each other. It is true she persuaded him to eat the apple, and much has been accomplished through persuasion, but as I advanced in years I realized that it took more than persuasion. Men were not supposed to dominate in everything and in every way. God gave women sense, ability, and intuition; they should live in a more equal state. I was not a mother, but I [did work] in a business office. I had nieces coming after me. I wanted to be able to think as I wished and I wanted them to do the same thing.

Elsie Riddick's autobiographical papers are in the Southern Historical Collection of the Wilson Library, University of North Carolina at Chapel Hill. Excerpts from them appear here with the permission of the editorial committee of the collection.

KEEPING MIND, BODY, AND SOUL TOGETHER

Keeping it all together is no easy task when faced with the contradictions between real conditions and the perceived values of Southern life and work that confront all classes, colors, and ages of Southern women. Laboring under generations of myth and stereotype that recognize at any one moment only a single dimension of their existence, Southern women have used a variety of measures to move beyond their assigned roles: caring nurturer, glamorous belle, loyal helpmate, or red hot mama. Rebelliousness, resourcefulness, and creativity have allowed women to transcend the restrictions that these labels imply and establish their own definitions of self that allow them to survive and in some instances to escape them.

While defiance may lead to rebellion and to action, as in the case of the mother who defies the requirement of loyalty intrinsic to the Southern view of "sacred motherhood" by placing limits on the self-sacrifice she will endure for the sake of her son, it can also lead to total inaction, as in the case of the Southern belle who simply shuts down—and shuts out the world entirely—rather than accept the role assigned to her by class and kin.

There are seeds of rebellion buried in the letters from lonely and isolated women who look for help from a stranger on a TV advice program and may be questioning their very right to change their prescribed lot.

All have much in common with the ordinary women whose lives of hard work and simple possessions appear to the undiscerning eye to be no more than drudgery—but who have developed and sustained one of the South's most enduring art forms, quilting. When they are able to make a beautiful whole out of scraps and discards, they demonstrate the craft of "making do" on a grand and artistic scale.

DEAR MARY CATHERINE

❧ CONTRIBUTED BY **MARILYN SEWELL**

"Dear Mary Catherine" is a television advice feature on a station in Kentucky. These letters, received from 1980 through 1981, reveal a learned dependence coupled with the insistence on protecting their men, a lifetime of giving without receiving and of yearning for love, the trap of respectability, financial deprivation, and a sense of isolation—from people as well as resources. Yet there is an underlying tone of rebelliousness that indicates a growing need to question, to seek one's due; and a restless need to be assured that it is right to do so. These are the voices of Southern women and, in particular, women of rural Kentucky. But look more closely. They are the voices of women everywhere.

Dear Mary Catherine,

I'm twenty-eight years old and I have six children. I'm Fat. I've tryed to diet every way I know how my husband gets worried about me being Fat but seem's to never give me any constalations of helping me or taking me out to make me feel better—lot's of time's I don't even feel like living. Everything seems to be a mess. Please tell me something to do. I'll be listening tuesday morning don't tell my name on TV. Just call me

OVERWEIGHT & SAD

Dear Mary Catherine,

I think your program is very helpful for women who don't know what to do when something bad is happening to them. Whenever my husband says he'd like to make love to me I feel sick and when he touches me I think I'll actually throw up. I have to stop myself from shuddering by thinking about something. I daren't have the light on in case it shows. He doesn't hold an erection for very long and he always wants me to help and he doesn't even have an emission now except rarely and I feel hateful. His apologies set my teeth on edge. I wait to be alone to masterbate to a climax. When I think about our children and our good times I feel a remembered love. But he hasn't been attractive to me sexually for years. I've thought of leaving him but I can't hurt his pride and the family would never forgive.

Help me please.

Dear Mary Catherine,

I'm a wife and mother of four children been married twenty years. We went to a picnic one Sunday afternoon, we came home and out of the blue he says he is going to leave, he packs his clothes and leaves. He'll tell us the reason sometimes. He works away from home a lot so I guess there is another woman. But he won't admit it. He comes in and out all the time. We see him almost everyday. We don't want for anything; he pays the bills and keeps us in money. We don't even have to ask for it. I'd say we see him more now than we did when he lived with us. He's been gone five months now. What I want to know is do you think he will ever return. Or should I just give up?

Dear Mary Catherine,

I am forty-two years of age; have been married twelve years; and have two children, a girl eight and a boy six. We have had an ideal marriage except for finances; however, both of us work and we enjoy the simple things of life and stretch our combined checks from one payday to the next.

Yesterday I became ill at work and returned home about 10:30 to find my husband in *my* bed with a mentally retarded girl who is twenty or twenty-one years of age. My love, respect, and admiration for my husband died on the spot. I want out. The only trouble is the joint bank account has a total of $8.73. I have no mother, father, brother, or sister to whom I can go. My friends are casual acquaintances with their own problems. What can a forty-two-year-old woman with two children do under the circumstances. Please help me.

Sincerely,
LONESOME TOOTS

P.S. Don't suggest seeing a psychiatrist or psychologist please. There is no money. Don't suggest going back to school as I have two children and no money. I was never very good at school anyway.

PERSONAL

Dear Mary Catherine,

I have a very personal problem that I would like a personal answer to.

I have been married for nearly eight years and have a daughter five years old. I love them both dearly, more than I think is humanly possible. Two years ago I went to work on a part-time basis and really enjoy my job. I work five hours a day.

This is my problem. There is this man I do not work with directly but see several times a day. He is a very dear friend. My husband had met him and likes him. The problem is the man has told me that he would like more than friendship and all I have to do is say the word. He does not pressure me, but he has told me that if I ever need him he'll be there. I would like to keep him as a friend, but I am afraid, also, that if the right mood hits me at the wrong time this relationship is going to go farther than friendship. He is a person that is very easy to talk to and is really an understanding person. I think that is why he is so appealing to me. He understands me, I think, more than my husband does. I'm not falling in love with him, but I am very attracted to him and I feel very guilty about it. He is fifteen years my senior but he is not old, if you know what I mean.

My husband and I went together for about two years before we were married, and I did not have any other relations with men other than my husband before we were married, but have always wondered what it would have been like to have had other lovers. . . .

Am I alone in the way I feel? Am I crazy to wonder about myself and this guilty feeling I have? Please help me understand myself if you can. Write me soon, if possible, at this address.

. . .

Dear Mary Catherine,

I thought I would write to you, I got your address when I was over there. I just loved to hear John ever morning on town and country. But I had to come back over here on the 27th, because I was layed off, and my rent was High, I couldn't pay it. But I sure Hated to leve my apt. But now this old man is sick, and I am very funny, I hate to move off. But if things don't change, and he won't even speak to me or ask me how I feel, but soon as I get breakfast on the table, comes in eats, walks back in, gets in his chair, sits there until lunch is on the table, but I am lonely and depressed, all I have to talk to is my little dogs. And my cousins are gone now they both died with cancer. One was buried at Lex. Ky. Cemetry, and one here at Dayton.

I guess you think I am nuts or crazy, but I can't have *no love* here *or peace* and no happiest, so I want you to write me a letter and give me a little advice. I am coming back to Lexington in July. Send me your phone number I will call you one morning. But tell me something I can't stand for to be mistreated.

Dear Mary Catherine,

I am a fifty-three-year-old woman mother wife and Grandmaw. I am young-looking for my age but I have lived and had children without *Love.* I still am. My children were borned thru desire not love. All I know is work and clean houses for money as my Husband no longer desires me as a woman or wife. I have done everything I know like having talks discusions my feelings but he doesn't care, only for my chores. But to seek another person would be disgracing my children and grandchildren but I am depressed. I am lonely. I keep my house clean cook wash and do for other people. I got to church but I never have love not even a kiss or goodbye. I have a fifteen-year-old boy still at home but my Happies are writting Songs.

PARALYZED

~ LEE SMITH

This is a short story and it is not about me either. It's about my first
cousin Mary Lou Stoles. I'm the one writing it since she can't lift a
muscle; she is lying over there next door just as paralyzed as she
can be and still be breathing. It's the most pitiful thing.

From where I am sitting on my back porch I can look out
through my clematis vine and see my backyard with my clean
clothes all hanging out neat and straight on my clothesline, and I
can see the Levisa River (Levisa means Pretty Pictures in Indian)
right out beyond that, and the railroad track where the coal trains
go, and then the mountains starting straight up just as green as you
please behind the railroad. Dew is on everything because the sun
won't come up here until about ten o'clock. I mean it will *come up,*
but it can't get over the mountains and hit the yard before ten, the
mountains are so high. Looking up I can see the sky, bright blue,
and tell it's going to be another sunny day. Another scorcher.

I've lived here in Grundy, Virginia, for nearly forty years, and I
wouldn't live anywhere else if you paid me. I like it. There is some
that don't, but I do. I know all the sewers run into the Levisa,
which looks so pretty, and I know that mountain I'm looking at has
got strip mines all over the top of it and all over the other side of it
too like a honeycomb. But that's progress. You can't tell me anything about it I don't know. I was born right here in this house in
the front bedroom, the one with the window looking out on Route
460. Right now my mother and my uncle Louis are sleeping upstairs, Uncle Louis breathing real heavy due to his black lung, and
over there next door, not but about thirty feet away from my back
steps, my cousin Mary Lou Stoles is stretched out in *her* bedroom

that she has always had. She hasn't been out of that room since she paralyzed herself nearly two years ago.

That was the setting and now I will go on into the plot: as much plot as there is to it, I mean. The big trouble is that this is real life and so the plot is hard to pin down. Things just happened, the way they will, and when you look back you think, "Oh, if I hadn't closed the door just *then*," or, "What if I had gone over to Knoxville for the summer when Aunt Louise asked me that time, what *then*?" But you didn't do it, you didn't go, and so you never know, and looking back it's hard to say when the important things happened or even what they were because all the days went along so smooth back then, like water under the bridge. But there's no point in throwing the baby out with the bath water. I always say you've got to salvage what you can and keep ahold of what you've got and not be looking off in the clouds somewhere. If my daddy hadn't gotten so bad off I never would have taken over the hardware store, for instance. I didn't know a two-by-four from a hole in the wall that day I started. I didn't know I was starting it either; I thought I was just going in to see how everybody was getting along with Daddy sick.

But my cousin Mary Lou Stoles was the prettiest girl you ever saw, and I'll be the first to say it. When we were girls, she was so pretty that people—women, too—would just stop still in the street to get a good look at her. She had real long black hair, real curly, and these dark, dark brown eyes and dead white skin with the pinkest cheeks, all natural. It used to make me sick, somebody born looking like that right next door, related and all. But there wasn't any way to get around it. That's the way she looked *all* the time, and after a while you had to get used to it. Mary Lou herself never did get used to it, she thought there had to be something else all the time when the way she looked would have been aplenty for anybody else.

I remember the night she won the Miss Grundy High Contest: she wore a strapless white ballerina-length evening gown covered all over in seed pearls with rows of net ruffles going all the way down its skirt, bright red patent leather high heel shoes, and a red velvet ribbon around her waist and another around her neck. Mary Lou had a flair all right. Nobody else would have thought to have put a ribbon around their neck. She stood up there all by herself on the stage holding some red roses while the Grundy Golden Wave rhythm band played "America" and the yellow tile walls of the senior high auditorium shook and shook with the noise. Buford

Garber, who was a disc jockey in the daytime and was the emcee that night, went out and put this little bitty tiara on her head and it flashed in the spotlights like real diamonds, and he put a sequin banner across her that said "Miss Grundy High." She stood up there by the ornamental potted palms and smiled, and flashbulbs were going off everywhere like fireworks.

"How do you feel?" Buford Garber asked in his big disc jockey voice. "What are you thinking right now?"

"This is the happiest moment of my life!" Mary Lou blurted and burst into tears. It was the best thing she could have done. The crowd went crazy, clapping and whistling and yelling and carrying on. They loved it for her to cry. It was all right to be that pretty if you cried about it, and so everybody was running out onto the stage and kissing her and hugging her.

I went, too. I had been in the beauty contest myself, as a matter of fact, mainly because Mary Lou's mother had told Mama it would give me some poise, but I went off in the second round. I knew I would, and I was glad Mary Lou won it. So I hugged her, too, and it was like hugging a doll or something, like she didn't even know me. Offstage, by the Coke machine, my Aunt Helen, Mary Lou's mother, was just about to have a fit she was so excited. She had two boys, too, but it was Mary Lou that she really set store by. She had dressed Mary Lou up like a doll all her life, and now it looked like it was about to pay off. Aunt Helen had big plans for Mary Lou: the Miss Buchanan County Contest, the Miss Claytor Lake Contest, the Miss Virginia Contest. Who knew what might happen after that?

Mary Lou got all the way to runner-up in the Miss Virginia Contest, and she won everything in between. Now that she is paralyzed Aunt Helen has put all her trophies and ribbons right up where she can see them, on top of her bureau dresser and on the wall. Aunt Helen is the kind that ignores everything she doesn't like. She just plays like it doesn't exist, and it doesn't as far as she is concerned, and she acts like nothing ever happened to Mary Lou between winning the beauty contests and now.

After the contest I remember I went on home with Mama and Daddy. Loretta Belcher was having a party and I wasn't invited, but I didn't care anyway. I had to get up early for Sunday School the next day. Anyway, I was sitting at the kitchen table drinking a Coke, still wearing my formal, when the telephone rang and it was Mary Lou.

"Will you come back over here and get me?" she said. She

sounded like she was crying. I had my driver's license, but Mary Lou was still too young to get hers.

So I got up and got the car keys and put on a sweater and told Mama where I was going. The auditorium was a mess, paper cups and stuff everywhere. Some people were cleaning it up. The doors were open but the curtain inside was closed. She was sitting back there on the stage all by herself in the middle of her seven-piece set of white Samsonite luggage that she had won for being Miss Grundy High.

"I thought you were going to the party," I said.

"Jerry wouldn't take me," she said. Jerry was this boy that Mary Lou was dating then; his family was just trash and I never could see it, her dating him, with all the boys she had her pick of. You should have seen them driving by her house on Sunday afternoons. But Aunt Helen never would let Mary Lou go out with the same boy two nights in a row. Aunt Helen wanted her to be real popular.

"Why wouldn't Jerry take you?" I said.

"He said I'd be too popular now, he said I'd be stuck up. I'm not stuck up, am I?"

"Well, whether you are or whether you're not is not any of my business," I said, "but I wouldn't go out with that Jerry anymore if I was you."

She said something.

"What?" I said.

"He plays the guitar," she said. "He wrote a song about me last week, now he won't even take me home."

"Well, come on," I said, and I had to load all seven pieces of that Samsonite luggage into the car myself because Mary Lou had to carry her roses and her trophy and her makeup case. All the way home she was sitting real still on the seat and her hoop stuck out over the gears.

"Don't you tell Mama I didn't go to that party," Mary Lou said when we got there, and she got out of the car and ran across the yard to her house as quick as she could, leaving all that luggage in the car, and I watched her go until the white of her dress was gone. "Thank you," she called back. Then she closed her door. Thank you, my foot, I thought, but I know when to keep my mouth shut and I never did tell Aunt Helen a thing.

The boys Mary Lou liked were always weird. Mary Lou had a weird streak in her that she got from her father. Harold Stoles was a failure, everybody said so, I don't even know what he ever did for a living besides that. They lived on Aunt Helen's money, which was considerable, her being an only child and her father had a patent on some special kind of rivet that people use everywhere in coal mining, even in South America.

When I think of Uncle Harold, I think of him in their living room of a summer with the drapes pulled, just sitting in there in the dark. He never would answer the door. Mary Lou was in there with him most times when I came over to ask her to play. She was the only one in that family that ever paid any attention to Harold Stoles at all, and God knows what they talked about. Mary Lou's brothers had already gotten out of that house as quick as they could though, I'll tell you that, and they never did come back. One of them is in Alaska on a pipeline and the other in Ohio, right today, and they don't send anything but Christmas cards to their mother.

Mary Lou and her daddy used to stay in that room all the time. Sometimes they would have me come in there with them, and then Harold Stoles would read us "The Little Tin Soldier is Covered with Dust" and "The Spider and the Fly." Mary Lou used to always get real wrought up and start crying, but he went right on anyway. She liked to get upset and cry and he knew that; it took me longer to figure it out.

I think that's what she liked about religion: all the carrying on. In spite of all Aunt Helen's efforts, Mary Lou never darkened the church door until her daddy died. Then she went to the funeral, of course, which was real simple and real short. There wasn't much you could read out of the Bible that would apply to Harold Stoles. Mary Lou took on so at the cemetery that two men had to help get her back in the car. Nobody else carried on like that, of course. It was bound to be a relief for Aunt Helen. Now she could open the drapes and air out that room where he'd been for so long.

Mary Lou started going to church after that, which tickled Aunt Helen to death until Mary Lou started going too much, when Fred Lee Sampson, Evangelist, and the Singing Triplets came to town. Fred Lee Sampson set up a big tent and then he set up a little tent behind that one, but you couldn't go in the little tent unless you were saved at the revival. I don't know what all they had in the little tent besides a plastic pool for baptizing, and Mary Lou never would say. I wasn't about to find out for myself. I don't hold much with electric guitars and singing triplets and microphones and that sort of thing. I've been saved since I was ten years old.

The second week of the revival Fred Lee Sampson had somebody build him a big plyboard cross to put in the big tent and he drilled all these holes in it and screwed little colored Christmas lights in every hole and put up everybody's name under one of the holes. If you got saved or rededicated your life, you got to screw in your little light everytime you went to the revival after that. Naturally Mary Lou loved it. She loved to go up and screw in her little light. Mary Lou was real religious from then on, especially in the summers, until she went to college. Aunt Helen said Mary Lou was making a spectacle of herself. She used to make Mary Lou promise not to rededicate her life anymore or she wouldn't let her go to the revival, but Mary Lou did it anyway.

Well, it came time for college. I went over to Radford and majored in home ec. To tell the truth, I didn't much mind when Daddy developed emphysema in the fall of my sophomore year and I had to come on home to take care of him. Somebody had to look after Granddaddy and Uncle Louis, too, and it was just too much for Mama. I had learned enough by then anyway. But Mary Lou kept on going to college. Radford wasn't good enough for her either. Oh, no. Not even East Tennessee State University was good enough for her! Aunt Helen took that rivet money and sent Mary Lou off to some fancy school on it.

In college Mary Lou majored in English and started looking like some kind of beatnik. She never came home if she could help it. Aunt Helen didn't like the way things were going, but there wasn't much she could do about it after she had sent Mary Lou there. Whenever anybody asked Aunt Helen if Mary Lou was in a sorority where she was, Aunt Helen's eyes would just glaze over and she'd say something about the weather. By that time Mary Lou wouldn't have touched a sorority or a beauty contest with a ten-foot pole. She always had to be one way or the other, Mary Lou. She never could be in between. When she did come home, she dated Hubert Blair who was out of law school by then and was starting to go into the coal business on the side, but she wouldn't go out with him much even though Aunt Helen was really pushing it and he was just crazy about her.

Hubert used to talk to me about it. "I just can't understand that girl," he would say, shaking his head. "She's the craziest thing I ever saw," but he was smiling about it. Hubert was the best catch in town, if you were interested in that sort of thing, until Mary Lou ruined him. He wouldn't look at anybody else, and she treated him so mean. I used to bake him some gingerbread and take it by every now and then to try and pep him up. Because Mary Lou was *morally loose,* that was the plain truth about it, and everybody knew it. It just killed Hubert. That's how she wrapped him around her little finger, and that's why she got those long distance telephone calls all the time when she was home. To talk to her, though, you wouldn't have known it; she tried to pull the wool over everybody's eyes by acting so sweet.

I asked her straight out one time if she was ever going to marry Hubert or just keep stringing him along, and she laughed and said she was going back to school to get a master's degree so she couldn't very well marry anybody right now, could she? She had let her hair grow out then and it was hanging all the way down her back. Of course she didn't need anymore education. She just wanted to hang around with those weird people you find in places like that, and sure enough she got tangled up with one of them and started living with him in New York City without the benefit of clergy.

Hubert was the one who told me that. He went up there to try to talk some sense into Mary Lou and there they were in one room, he said, with a bare light bulb hanging down from the ceiling, eating off of two little portable burners. Hubert said it was a bad neighborhood with trash piled up all over the street. But Mary Lou sent him back, and Hubert just about died. Then he married this girl who had always liked him, Marge Ketchum, and they had little baby twin girls right away.

Aunt Helen never mentioned Mary Lou one time in five years, that's how bad it was. One time Mary Lou actually brought that so-called New York artist of hers to see me. I couldn't believe it! The doorbell rang and I thought it was the Jewel Tea man or the boy coming to work in the yard so I opened the door and there stood Mary Lou looking just awful, not even clean, with that hippie boyfriend of hers.

"Well, aren't you going to ask us in?" she said, just like she hadn't done any of it. She had a little bit of Aunt Helen in her, too.

I said, "Come on in." I guess she could tell how I felt.

"This is Jerold Kukafka," Mary Lou said, but I never could bring myself to look right at him. He had wild bushy black hair like a Negro and was wearing some old faded work pants. I would have said something to him only I couldn't think of what to say. He didn't look like any kind of brainy writer to me, but that's what Mary Lou had told Aunt Helen he was, only, of course, he hadn't published anything. Mary Lou sat on the sofa and wrinkled up my antimacassars. She kept pulling at them with her fingers, and her fingernails were all bitten off.

This Jerold Kukafka went walking around and around the room like some kind of skinny jungle cat in a cage at the zoo. I have one whole wall full of shelves where I keep my teacup collection and he kept picking up a teacup and looking at it, then he'd walk away and then he'd come back and look at another one. It made me so nervous.

"You're still collecting your teacups, I see," said Mary Lou.

"Yes, I am," I said.

"You haven't changed a bit," she said. "You still look just the same."

Mary Lou looked around. "This room is the same, too," she said. "You haven't changed anything. Do you remember sitting over there at the table and making paper dolls out of magazines? Do you remember how we used to play gin rummy for hours and hours?"

"Mama and Uncle Louis will be back anytime," I said. "They went over to Junior's to get some salad peas for supper."

"Oh," Mary Lou said.

Jerold Kukafka was looking at my cup from Limoges, France.

"How is my mama?" Mary Lou asked.

"She's all right," I said. "I'd go over there if I was you."

"We went over there," Mary Lou said, "but she wouldn't answer the door."

"She might not be home," I said.

"There's a car in the driveway."

"What kind is it?"

"A blue car," Mary Lou said.

"That's hers all right," I told her. "Buick Skylark." Imagine not knowing what kind of car your own mother drives!

"Well, how is she?" Mary Lou asked again. Mary Lou still had her hair long but pulled straight back in a pony tail, and she was real thin. Her cheekbones stuck out and her eyes looked way too big and they shifted, shifted everywhere.

"Your mother is about as well as you can expect," I said, "considering. Maybe she was taking a nap."

Jerold Kukafka was looking at my cup from the Brussels World Fair. "Let's get out of here," he said. It was the first thing he had said and I jumped. Mary Lou stood right up and went over to him like she was pulled by a magnet and she held his hand.

"Tell Mama I asked about her," Mary Lou said, "and tell her I said I'm real happy." She was happy, too: I believe it. Some people thrive on sin.

Mary Lou left with Jerold Kukafka in the pouring rain not ten minutes before Uncle Louis and Mama came back with the salad peas, and I never said a word. I guess Mary Lou wasn't so happy a year after that because Jerold Kukafka hanged himself dead from an exposed pipe in the bathroom in that place where they lived in New York, and Mary Lou found him herself with his tongue hanging out and all black in the face. Then Mary Lou was in a hospital. Aunt Helen just casually let that drop one day when we were all out on the porch drinking iced tea. Aunt Helen clammed up right away and she wouldn't say *why*, but I'm sure it was mental, myself, or she would have said.

We buried Granddaddy in September and a couple of days after that, here came Mary Lou back home. She was thirty. It was exactly like those years with Jerold Kukafka never had happened at all: here came Mary Lou, looking like she ought to have looked all along. She was wearing dresses and playing tennis at the new country club all of a sudden; she had cut her hair real short, and butter wouldn't melt in her mouth.

One day she walked in the office to see old Earl Graves, the superintendent of schools, and the next week she was teaching senior English at Grundy High. She made a blueberry cheesecake and brought it over to Mama and me. She sold little felt birds at the Women's Club Christmas Bazaar. But I watched her close and noticed things, nothing I could ever put my finger on—she smoked a lot, and her eyes looked funny sometimes. She was back here for almost three years before any rumors started, and I never heard them then. People wouldn't have said a word to me, seeing as how I'm a relative. People are that polite.

The first I heard of it was in the Rexall, where I was having my lunch, when Brenda Looney came bursting in the door. Brenda Looney is a teller at the Levisa Bank and Trust, so she sees everybody and knows what's going on all over town. She wears these harlequin glasses. I never have cared for her myself and I never stand in her line when I go to make my deposits at the bank. But here she came, just slamming into the Rexall on her break, couldn't wait to tell it.

"Did you hear about Hubert? Hubert Blair?" she asked real loud, talking to Mrs. Ritten who works at the cosmetics counter and is a big friend of hers, but of course you could hear her all over the store. "Well!" she went on, and although two counters were in between me and Brenda Looney I could imagine how she looked, how she would draw up her mouth. "Hubert Blair and Mary Lou Stoles have *run off!* Eloped. They say he left a note for his wife."

"Oh, and those poor little twin girls!" cried Mrs. Ritten. "That's just awful. I can't imagine Hubert doing a thing like that."

"Well, that's what they did all right," Brenda Looney said. "I didn't know if you heard it or not."

"That beats everything," Mrs. Ritten said.

"What does?" asked old Mrs. Tyler Rockbridge, coming up, and they told her, and they told everybody that came their way. They said that Marge Ketchum Blair was under heavy sedation and her mother was coming in on the train.

But you can be sure that everybody shut up pretty quick when I got out of my booth and went over to the cash register. They didn't know I was in there. I took my time, too. "I want two packs of Dentyne," I said, "and put it on my bill, please, Sue." I didn't have to tell Sue what I had for lunch. I always have the same thing, a bean salad and a Coke and a small bag of barbecue potato chips. I took my time going out and you could have heard a pin drop. Somebody in this family has got to have some dignity. On my way out of the Rexall I remember that I saw that Coppertone ad up over the lotions, that little girl with her hair in pigtails and a real good tan. I could have cried about Hubert's poor little twins.

Of course, it wouldn't have done any good. Hubert has a lot of money since he's in the coal business now, and he gave Marge the most alimony you ever heard of. Marge built herself a new ranch-style house and then married John Wheeler a year after the divorce went through. John Wheeler is a gynecologist. Hubert and Mary Lou moved fifty miles over to Bluefield, where Hubert has some mines, and they just laid low for a while. Nobody ever said a word about them, at least not to me. It was like they had both fallen into one of Hubert's mines.

They were married, of course—Hubert wouldn't have lived with somebody without marrying them—and about a year after that they had a little boy, and then all of a sudden here came Mary Lou out of retirement. The first thing we knew, she was all over the *Southwest Virginia Mountaineer,* smiling out of the society page every Sunday like she deserved to. Mr. and Mrs. Hubert Blair return from Jamaica! Mrs. Hubert Blair has an intimate luncheon!

Mrs. Hubert Blair is the head of the Heart Fund! That one really cracked me up. I showed it to Mama, who said, "Well, I guess she's turned over a new leaf." Another day Mama said, "Well, they always were in *love*," right in the middle of nothing, but I knew who she was talking about. Mama thought it was romantic.

Mary Lou came back for a visit and brought her little boy, Justin, and that's all I heard from Aunt Helen and Mama for the next two weeks. How cute Justin was, how smart Justin was, how Justin could count to ten on one breath. I was down taking inventory at the hardware store and missed the big visit myself. Then Hubert announced that he was running for Congress and Mrs. Hubert Blair had her picture on the *front* page, just like she was Jackie Kennedy.

In the middle of the campaign Mary Lou came home. This time she came home to stay. Hubert called and called, but Mary Lou wouldn't go back to him. Hubert told Aunt Helen that Mary Lou had left all her diamond rings on the kitchen sink. Hubert came over here in his Lincoln Continental three or four times but Mary Lou wouldn't talk to him. There was a lot of publicity about it in the papers. Finally it go so bad that Aunt Helen was having nervous palpitations of the heart, so I walked over there myself to see what I could do.

Mary Lou was lying on the couch in the front room wearing some old robe that must have been Aunt Helen's. She was smoking a cigarette and looking at the ceiling, that's all. She had all the venetian blinds shut tight.

"Hello," I said. I sat down in the rocker.

"Hello, Agnes," she said. She didn't seem surprised to see me. I rocked for a while.

"Don't you think you'd better go home now and help Hubert run for Congress?" I asked. "Who's taking care of your little boy?"

"He's better off," she said. "Hubert's better off, too." Her voice was flat as a pancake.

"What made you come home?" I asked. Sure I was curious, but I thought I might get at the trouble that way.

"I was heading a campaign to raise money to improve the facilities at Barton," she said in her strange flat voice. Barton is the mental institution for the southwest part of the state. "I had to go over there and take a tour." Her voice stopped, like it was too much effort to go on. I waited.

"They unlocked the door and I was walking through the wards

with the director. Each one we went in was worse than the one before it. Finally we came to the D ward, which was worse than all the others put together. It was the one where they keep the people who are just like vegetables. They keep them in *cribs,* Agnes. These big cribs."

I rocked.

"And I was going along looking at everything with the director, and we stopped by one of the cribs to talk, and this horrible, this, *thing* that was in the crib suddenly sat up and grabbed my hand and looked at me."

"Well," I said. "Poor thing. I guess it was glad to see somebody different."

Mary Lou rolled her head back and forth on the pillow. "No, no," she said. "No. You don't understand. It knew me. It looked right at me and it knew me."

"That's ridiculous," I said.

"No," said Mary Lou. "It knew me."

She wouldn't talk anymore after that so I went home. I still can't figure out why that upset her so much. I bet she made it all up in her head because they bring those people to Barton from all over this part of the state, and the way I look at it, it's about 1,000 to one that any of them would have ever seen her before.

The next day Mary Lou paralyzed herself. They took her in an ambulance to Charlottesville, and then they brought her back. The doctors couldn't find any medical reason for it, they said. They said it was all in her mind. We put her in her old room and Aunt Helen hired two practical nurses, Mrs. Dee and Mrs. Dixon, and they're still there. It's been a year and a half now. Mrs. Dee does the day shift and Mrs. Dixon does the night shift, so she can have some time in the day to work in her garden. I opened a laundromat next to my hardware store.

And Hubert? Everybody felt so sorry for Hubert that he won the election in a landslide victory and now he's sponsoring a strip-mine bill. When ecology came in, Hubert was right on top of it. It's no telling how far he'll go in politics now. He is divorcing Mary Lou quietly—you can't blame him—and he is taking complete care of Justin. He won't even let Aunt Helen look at Justin, much less have a hand in raising him. He told Aunt Helen that he didn't want Justin ever to come in that house and see his mother like she is.

Aunt Helen was real upset because, after all, Justin was the only one she had left. Now Aunt Helen won't have a thing to do with Hubert except sign the checks he sends her, which she says she can barely bring herself to do.

Mary Lou just lies up there in that room everyday like she is lying up there now, with her bed caddy corner so she could look out of the window and see Aunt Helen's climbing rambler rose in full bloom on the trellis if she would turn her head. But she won't. She won't lift a finger. She just lies there. Everybody in town has taken a fancy to it. The preacher, Mr. Sprayberry, comes and sits with her some. He reads her the Bible even though you can't tell if she can hear it or not.

Mama goes and sits with her, and Aunt Helen, and all the ladies in town. People are always bringing congealed salads to Aunt Helen because once Aunt Helen told somebody in the beauty shop that Mary Lou liked them. Mary Lou can eat fine, but you have to feed her. The only one she won't eat for is Mrs. Dee. Some people have said why don't we put her in a nursing home but of course we won't hear of it. Not a one of us has ever died in a nursing home. We can take care of our own.

I go over there and sit and sometimes I think about how we used to play gin rummy and how we used to sneak off and go swimming in the creek, and it's so sad. It's so pitiful the way she lies there. It's a funny thing but she looks almost prettier now than she ever did. Her hair is growing out now and I fix it real pretty. I think about how she looked the night she won Miss Grundy High. I helped Aunt Helen put all her trophies and ribbons up where she can see them. I often think that if she had married Hubert the first time he asked her, if she hadn't gotten all that education, she could be having intimate luncheons for people in Washington right now. But I'm glad she came home.

I talk to her a lot and think she understands everything I say even if she won't make a sign. Everyday when I come home from the store I go over there and sit with her for a long time. It rests me, sitting in that room, it's so peaceful there. It's always real clean and cool, and we've got it fixed up so nice. I try to keep her interested: I told her all about the Burger-O franchise I just bought, and I read the newspaper to her and the *Reader's Digest.* I never do read her anything about Hubert, though. One day I read her "I Am Joe's Nervous System" out of the *Reader's Digest* but her eyes didn't even flicker. A lot of times I just sit and hold her hand, and sometimes I give her a back rub.

And who knows what will happen? It is not given to us, as Mr. Sprayberry says. And who knows if she might not just jump up from that bed one day and go off and get her Ph.D. or do something else crazy? She's not thirty-six now. Or she might stay right there and atrophy to death. What I think, though, is that she's happy. I think she likes to have me hold her hand. Outside her window the seasons come and go, and now Aunt Helen has put a picture of The Last Supper up for her to look at, too. It's so pitiful how she lies there; it would just make you cry.

This story was expanded by the author into the novel Black Mountain Breakdown *(G.P. Putnam's Sons, 1981).*

MY GRANDMOTHER'S GIFT

❧ GLENDA NEEL PENDER

My grandmother wrote a chapter
of her autobiography
with every square
of every quilt she ever made.

They told the story of her life
just as surely as if her needle
had been threaded with ink and
her beautiful evenly spaced stitches
had become words.

What is her story?
Did she have a fragmented life
of
bits
and
pieces?
Scraps of fabric,
some velvet and some cotton?
She is a woman, isn't she?

But she never was a woman
who let the bits and pieces
stay scattered around
or stuffed into an old bag.

She pieced them together
with love and time
and made a spirit quilt
that keeps her warm.

She gave me her quilting frame—
I hope I can find the bolts
that hold it together.

QUILTING WOMEN

∼ JENNIFER MILLER

Bedcovers were the first true art form in America.

Books corroborate this claim for quilts, but they also tend to dwell on patterns used in various regions instead of the particular tastes and talents of the individual artists. Any quilting woman knows that she takes pride in being *different* from her neighbor. In country stores where quilts are being sold women are often heard to exclaim how they would have done that Wild Goose Chase pattern, for example, with a simpler border or fancier stitches or less green. Neighbors may share patterns; they may exchange scraps of materials. But each quilt is an individual creation. It says something about the maker's life.

A quilt is two layers of cloth filled with cotton, polyester, or wool, all stitched together in a pattern that keeps the filling in place. In the past, sewing the layers together (quilting) was often a collective process, requiring that the participating women be friendly, of course, and most of all that their stitches be consistently tight and neat. The back of the quilt is usually one fabric. The "top" is the part that requires the most individual planning and artistic choice. Even at quilting bees, each top was the work of one woman alone.

Women began making quilts in this country as soon as they had enough sewing scraps. Pioneer women kept the family beds piled high with colorful quilts as they struggled to survive the winters in the wilderness of North America. "A woman made utility quilts as fast as she could and as well as she could so her family wouldn't freeze, and she made them as beautiful as she could so her heart wouldn't break. Of all the things she did day in and day out, the quilt was perhaps the only thing that would last longer and be remembered more gratefully than last summer's pickled beets."*

It hasn't been that long since nearly all women did some kind of sewing; depending upon their economic status, they made everything from long underwear to doilies. Black women on Southern plantations did exceptionally fine appliqué work (decorating or trimming one material by sewing on shapes from other cloths), a skill that originated in Dahomey, West Africa. Plantations had superb quilts made by slaves, while Southern farm women made their bedcovers out of whatever sewing scraps or feed bags they had. Whether they were appliquéd velvet and satin or dyed sack patchwork, the quilts were both colorful and necessary.

Women often associated each quilt they made with an event: a wedding, birth, death, going-away. Names of old quilt patterns suggest their origins. Some are from the natural surroundings that have been a joy as well as a hardship to women isolated in the country: North Carolina Lily, Spider's Web, Wild Goose Chase, Bear Paw, Maple Leaf. There are names about daily life (Log Cabin, Barn Raising), about dreams (Around the World), about events (Rocky Road to Kansas, Whig's Defeat). Some are political statements, the kind women weren't supposed to make not so long ago: Jackson's Star, Underground Railroad. One pattern made by some women during the Civil War was called Radical Rose; it featured a black center in each rose, an expression of sympathy for the slaves.

There were patterns with religious names: Tree Everlasting, Forbidden Fruit, Job's Tears. Another favorite was the "crazy" quilt that could be made without any pattern, using all sizes and colors of scrap materials.

Album quilts are for remembrance (sometimes each block is a different story, a family history), and friendship quilts are often "signed" with flowing stitches. There are also death quilts, such as the one made by a woman in Lewis County, Kentucky, in 1839. Elizabeth Roseberry Mitchell pieced a brown cotton quilt that had an intricate picket fence as a border around a cemetery in the center. Inside the cemetery she stitched the shapes of coffins to mark gravesites. There was a path leading from the cemetery to a bottom row of little brown-cloth coffins, each with the name of a member of the family. Whenever one of them died, Elizabeth snipped the coffin and re-sewed it into its place in the cemetery.

---

*Beth Gucheon, *New York Times Magazine,* July 20, 1975.

The advent of an age of cheap blankets and insulated houses eliminated the necessity of quiltmaking for many women. But in rural areas, especially in the South, everyone's mother or grandmother remembers how quilts could brighten a sparsely furnished bedroom. The connotations of hard work, self-sufficiency, patience, love, and durability remain. Plus, quiltmaking is quiet work, peaceful; it requires more imagination than other household work.

In wooden houses in the country some women still make quilts to keep their families warm. But women with "tight" houses make them, too, to use, to give to family and friends, to sell. Some save them, wrapped in plastic, neatly stacked in closets. Maudie Gilbert and her sisters, Mary and Martha, live with their families up on Sandy Ridge, near Campton, Kentucky—mountainous country with icy winter winds. Maudie, Mary, and Martha get together sometimes to do their quilting. Mostly they quilt on their own, though, because Maudie says they do so much talking when they get together that they don't get much done. "You know how sisters are when they've always been close."

Maudie was recounting the winters when she was young and could see the stars through the cracks in the roof, but was still warm under three or four quilts. Her mother made enough quilts for all the family beds, plus some for a woman up the ridge who was well enough off to have others make her quilts. She paid Maudie's mother $2.50 for a double-size quilt, then cut it in half and used it on two beds! Of course, as Maudie says, "Two dollars and fifty cents would buy quite a bunch of groceries at that time. Now you could almost put $2.50 worth of groceries in your pocketbook."

Maudie began quilting when she was seven. Her aunt gave her little pieces of thread and pieces of material too small to be of much use, and Maudie sewed them together. They all quilted, her mother and aunts and two older sisters. When she got married, at eighteen, she started farming with her husband and keeping house; she had six children. "I'd quilt in the fall of the year," she said. "After we got our other work done, then I would make our quilts that we used. Had to make two or three new ones every year because usually there was a new kid to come along every year or two."

Maudie says she'd almost rather quilt than eat.

"After the kids get gone to school I sit right down and start to quilt, and usually it's eleven or twelve o'clock before I even look up. Because, you know, I get so interested in it, just like you really get interested in working a puzzle or something you love and want to see how it's going to turn out; that's how I am about my quilting. It doesn't seem possible, but it's true."

It doesn't seem so impossible, considering the tree quilts and eagle quilts she makes that are famous for their beauty. She and her sisters were picked as the best quilters in the area several years ago. The local co-op asked them to make a quilt for Pat Nixon when her husband was still president; the sisters took it to Washington, D.C., and presented it to her. That one was an eagle quilt.

Now her young son, Joey, helps around the house, washing dishes, sweeping floors, while Maudie quilts ten to twelve hours a day.

"You quilt, quilt, quilt, and you sit right there in that same place all day, and it just takes you *so* long to make one. Of course, the money's good and it's good honest money, but you don't make much. I do it because I love to quilt—and I need what money I do make." She usually gets about $100 for her big quilts and $25 for crib size.

She studied her hands, bending her fingers in and out as if they were stiff. "But I'd make them if I didn't get anything for them. If I sat right down with a piece of paper and a pencil and figured up all the price of everything that's in a quilt, I guess I'd have to quit. But I want to keep doing it till my eyes give out."

She wants to make one special one for each of her children. Plus she needs more for her house because it isn't insulated. It still takes about four quilts on each bed to keep out the cold. But the fancy quilts are not made for daily use; she can't afford to keep the eagle or tree quilts.

A woman whose weakened eyes have ended her quilting days lives about 100 miles east of Maudie, near Whitesburg, Kentucky. The mountains are even more rugged there, and houses balance on cliffs or nestle back in hollows. Mrs. Georgia Fairchild Taylor has always stayed close to her family. She quilted with her sisters, too. Her big old house has closets full of quilts she's made, all light greens and bright yellows and blues and pinks—flower colors. She has always gardened and planted flowers in the spring and summer and made her quilts in the winter. She won't sell them. She only has one daughter. So she saves her quilts, with a special one for her only grandchild, "if he ever gets married."

As a young girl Georgia had to do most of the housework and cooking because her mother was ill for a long time. "There've been things I'd like to do, but I've always been a housekeeper and tended the garden, canned, put up stuff, and I got attached to that kind of work. I'm glad that I did because it's pastime to do some kind of work, whether it's in the garden, doing sewing or quilting, things like that."

Though her house was cold before electricity, quilts aren't as necessary now. But she's proud of the ones she made and thinks "it was the best thing in the world for me to have been home so much," taking care of her ailing parents and, later, a sick husband.

"Family's the most important thing," she said. "Wouldn't you have done the same?"

Passed from mother to daughter, and now to country stores and craft co-ops, quilts are more widely appreciated these days. But most women have been aware of the beauty of what they've done all along. In Madison County, North Carolina, a woman who has quilted to cover her beds and now sells her quilts at a crafts store talked about her early work.

"People back then didn't have the money to buy materials to make fancy tops out of, or even to set it together with," said Leona Rice. "My daddy worked for the Chesterfield Milling Company and over there, they'd bust these flour bags. Every bit of flour was in cloth sacks. So we'd get those flour bags and wash em and we'd strip our quilts together with em." She says they'd even use some of the big sacks for quilt lining.

She remembers carding cotton out of an old mattress that belonged to her grandmother. "We took and tore that mattress up, and Grandmother showed me how to card, and we carded all that cotton, redone it over and put it in little rolls, and that's what we used for my quilts when I was going to get married."

Now she laughs about some of those old quilts, about how she looks at them and thinks, "Oh, Lordy, what stitches I made!" But she avers she's as proud of the old ones as any she'd quilt today.*

Today people are buying quilts like Leona's to hang on their walls. Connor Causey, a young woman in Hillsborough, North Carolina, who quilts and teaches quilting classes, thinks it's great that people are hanging them. "I think they should be treated that way. I'm do-

---

*The interview with Leona Rice was conducted by Laurel Horton, librarian for the Appalachian Room at Mars Hill College and folklore graduate student at the University of North Carolina at Chapel Hill.

ing art and my medium just happens to be material. Though I'm doing a lot of traditional designs now, because there are so many I want to try, someday I'd like to get into some more original designs and even free-form quilting."

Connor's favorite quilts are the patchwork ones; she says the geometry of them is timeless. "You can go back to these patterns that are very old and see that the original designs really took a lot of figuring." One old pattern that is especially complex interested Connor, and she asked her friend with a Ph.D. in physics to separate the pattern into its parts. It took four or five hours. Connor asked, "Now, how could the originator, probably a woman with little or no formal education, figure it out?"

Connor learned to quilt from an older woman in Hillsborough. She usually quilts by herself now, and says that most of the other quilters she knows work alone, too. In the past it was much more of a social function than it is today. At quilting bees the work would go faster, and the women who didn't have telephones and didn't live very close to each other would have a chance to visit. "People get together in many other ways now," says Connor. She works on a frame in her home, and sometimes, when friends drop in to see her, they'll sit and stitch a while with her.

She'll never get tired of quilting, but Connor thinks she probably will get tired of selling them. It makes it "work" to do one to fill an order.

"Nobody quilts for the money. If you break down the hours, you could make more as a waitress." But she has a two-year-old daughter, and quilting has turned out to be a good way to make money at home.

Another young woman, Susan Paterson in Barnardsville, North Carolina, took up quilting when she was pregnant with her first child. Now she has two daughters and quilts so much that her sales help support the family.

"I wanted to make a quilt for my first baby," she said. "I asked a lady who runs a gas station down in Barnardsville how to make a quilt, got her directions, went home, and made a quilt all wrong. It looked pretty good to me for all the mistakes, and the days I spent arranging and rearranging the pieces were so pleasant that I decided to make a full-size quilt."

She was just as happy with her second quilt even though it was lumpy and didn't last long because the thread wasn't heavy enough. Her husband made a quilting frame and she's had a quilt top on it ever since.

At first she made quilts for friends, then began going to some mountain fairs; now she sells through a store in Asheville and Chicago and does a pretty good mail order business. Three years ago she purchased a rubber stamp. Now, she has a price list.

Her mother didn't quilt, but had a big effect on Susan because "she had an eye for handwork." Besides doing all the practical sewing, which she taught to her daughter, she also embroidered, crocheted, and knitted beautifully. "Mother was very confident about being able to do any needlework, and I think that's why when I decided to quilt, I had no doubts about being able to do it."

One turn deserves another, and Susan says she plans to instill that same confidence in her daughters, Emily and Becky. "I'll make sure they can do a little hand sewing and use a sewing machine and help them in any projects they undertake, but I won't sit them down and teach them to quilt unless they ask me."

The way quilting women tell it, a person has to want to quilt to do it well. There has to be an urge to create, and there must be the time and situation that will allow it.

If a woman intends to do all that handwork, it's likely she'll want her quilt to be beautiful, like someone's oil painting. She'll want it to be different from all others, even more so than her own barbecue sauce or apple pie recipe. Most quilts are unique, as are their makers, women like Maudie and Georgia and Leona and Connor and Susan. Quilts were bedcoverings first, born of necessity, but the individual work and creativity has always gone beyond the "necessary."

TWO POEMS FOR MINNIE'S BOY

～ JOYCELYN K. MOODY

I.

Because the white cabbie could see beyond
your anxious eyes and
your weaving wires of fingers
and dared Davis Avenue
on a hot July Saturday afternoon
thinking the whole while
that his mother had raised a fool,
you saw her anyway.
Saw her crawl pass somewhere inside the huge hearse.
Your heart broke out of your throat
in papery sobs
that rustled around the world
while you stood
in all your adult splendor
so noble looking in military uniform—
even if the cap was a little too big,
your chest not as broad as when
you played quarterback for Central High,
and your legs too thin
within the warm trousers—
handsome and grown-up anyway.

Your pouting lips parted
to blurt a boy's fear:
"Mommie, don't leave me!"

II.

Georgie Porgie puddin' pie,
Kissed his momma when she cried;
When poor Minnie passed away,
Most of Georgie also died.

So you managed,
oblivious to her writhings,
to keep steadfast
your grip on her apron strings.
In your grim fist—
clinched like a frightened child's—
they became taut and soiled
from twenty-five more years
of your tugging/twisting/dragging;
ragged and limp with snot,
knotted like an old oak
and as sturdy.

They serve you yet:
as you turn at this mid-life,
the ties you've thinned these long years
bind and bury you.
With mummy tapes
inch by sticky inch
your mother reaps revenge.
For the love of George,
old man,
let go.

SPILLED SALT

◞ BARBARA NEELY

"I'm home, Ma," Junior said.

A weakness spread up Anna Jones's legs and settled in the back of her knees. She pressed down hard on the doorknob, wishing she could slam and lock the door against him. Junior smiled brightly down at her. His large brown eyes and dark freckled skin were so much like her own he was nearly her twin. But he was taller than she remembered—denser.

She'd known he was coming. He'd written to say that he was getting out. She hadn't answered his letter, daring to hope that her lack of response would steer him away from her door. But he was not one to consider what other people wanted. He had already proved that.

"You're here." She stepped back from the door and pretended not to see him reach out and attempt to touch her. But a part of her had leapt to life at the sight of him, no matter what. He at least looked whole and healthy of body. She was grateful for that. She hoped it was a sign that he was all right inside, too.

She tried to think of something to say as they stood staring at each other in the middle of the living room. A fly buzzed against the window screen in a desperate attempt to leave the room.

Will he tell me about it now? Anna wondered. Will he explain how he went from being a boy not long out of high school to whatever it was he became the night he raped that girl?

"Well, Ma, how've . . ."

"I'll fix you something to eat," Anna interrupted. "I know you must be starved for decent cooking." She rushed from the room as though a meal was already in the process of burning.

For a moment she was lost in her own kitchen. The table with its dented metal leg, the green and white curtains and badly battered coffeepot were all slightly familiar-looking strangers. She took a deep breath and leaned against the back of a chair.

In the beginning she'd flinched from the very word. She couldn't even think it, let alone say it. Assault, attack, molest, anything but rape. Anyone but her son, her bright and charming boy, her high school graduate. Her only child.

She'd been sure it was prejudice on the part of the police. Junior would always talk back and he was poor and unemployed. That was enough for them. The girl, of course, was after him—trying to get revenge because he had no interest in her. When these excuses faded in the face of his eventual confession, she'd pacified herself with circumstances: Junior had seen his father beat her. They'd been dirt poor and she'd ultimately had to leave Buddy and raise Junior alone. What had she really known about raising a child? What harm had she done in her ignorance, her impatience and concentration on warding off the pains of her own life? But in the end she kept stumbling over the knowledge of other boys, from far worse circumstances, with mothers too tired and worried to do more than strike out at them, who somehow managed to grow up to do far less harm than Junior had done.

But that was five years ago. Now he was back. Out on the streets. Free.

"I can't sleep. I'm afraid to sleep." The girl had spoken in barely a whisper so that the whole courtroom seemed to tilt as everyone leaned toward her. "Every night he's there in my mind making me go through it all over again."

Would she be free now that Junior had done his time? Or would she still flinch from hands with short square fingers and cry when the first of September came near? Anna moved around the kitchen like an old woman with bad feet.

When the food was ready she watched Junior dump ketchup on his sunnyside-up eggs, like blood staining the yellow. Nausea pushed her away from the table and moved her to the kitchen window. The crisp everydayness of clothes flapping on the line surprised her. A leaf floated into her small cemented yard and landed on a potted pansy. The world was still in spring. Nothing outside had changed.

"I can't go through this again," she mouthed soundlessly to the breeze.

"Come talk to me, Ma," Junior called softly around a mouthful of food.

Anna turned. Nervous hands tugged at her hair and her dress as she walked slowly toward the chair across from him. He smiled an egg-flecked smile that she could not return. She wanted to ask him what he would do now, whether he had a job, whether he planned to stay long, why he'd never made parole. But she was afraid of his answers, afraid of how she might respond if he said he had no job, no plans, no place to stay—except with her, and had not changed in any way.

"I'm always gonna live with you, Mommie. Always," she remembered him saying when he was small. At the time she'd wished it were true, that they could be together always—she and her sweet chubby boy, so full of kisses and love for his mommie. She blinked and shifted her chair at the sudden vision of the young woman he'd attacked as she sat in the courtroom, her shoulders hunched and head hung down like she was the one who ought to be ashamed instead of him. Anna rose abruptly.

"Be right back," she mumbled and scurried down the hall to the bathroom. She eased the lock over so that it made barely a sound.

"He's my son!" she hissed at the drawn-looking woman in the mirror. Perspiration dotted her upper lip and glistened around her hair line.

"My son!" she repeated pleadingly. But the word had less meaning than the memory of that young woman and what he'd done to her. Anna bowed her head and wished him never born before flushing the toilet and unlocking the door.

Nothing had changed in the kitchen except that he had moved to take up her place by the window. There were crumbs on the floor. The salt was spilled. His dishes littered the table.

"It sure is good to look out the window and see something besides guard towers and cons." He stretched, rubbed his belly, and turned to face her.

"It's good to see you, Ma." A smile dented the corners of his mouth. His eyes were soft and shiny.

Oh, Lord, Anna uttered to herself, please let me remember he's my child. Please help me forget all those nights of dreaming, dreaming, dreaming about that girl's face all mixed up with mine!

She began carrying his dirty dishes to the sink, first the plate, then the cup, one by one, drawing out the chore.

"This place ain't got as much room as the old place." She continued to carry dishes.

"It's fine, Ma, just fine."

Oh, Lord! Anna prayed in her mind as she turned to do the dishes.

"Seen Dad?" Junior moved to lean against the stove to her right, causing her to drop the knife and make the dishwater too cold.

"Where would I see *him*?" She tried to put ice in her voice. It trembled.

"Just thought you might know where he is." Junior moved back to the window.

Yes, she thought, where is he? And does he know that his son has outdone even him in pure meanness? She remembered the crippling shock of Buddy's fist against her groin and scoured Junior's plate and cup with a piece of steel wool before rinsing them in scalding water.

"Maybe I'll hop a bus over to the old neighborhood. See some of the guys, how things have changed." He paced the floor behind her. Anna sensed his uneasiness and was pleased.

After he'd gone she fixed herself a large gin and carried it into the living room. Outside, children screamed each other to the finish line of a foot race. She remembered that Junior had always liked to run. So had she, come to that. But he'd had more time for playing than she'd had. She'd been hired out as a mother's helper by the time she was ten. She didn't begrudge him his fun. It just seemed so wasted now.

She wished she could talk to him about it. She'd tried when he first went to jail. But he would only say that he knew he'd been wrong.

"But why?" she'd kept asking him. Silence was his only response. Perhaps that was best, especially now, after so long. Anything could happen if they'd let five years' accumulation of words on the subject come rolling out of their mouths. She might not be able to stop or even control which of her thoughts got turned into words. Worse yet, he might begin to question her, might ask her what there was about her mothering that made him want to treat a woman like a piece of toilet paper. And what would she say to that?

Tears slid down her cheeks, tears for the as-good-as-dead child her son had been, tears for the child's mother—the girl who had not understood that he needed most special handling to keep him from becoming a man she did not care to know. The kind of handling, it occurred to her now, that no woman may know how to provide.

Anna drained her gin, left Junior a note reminding him to leave her door key on the kitchen table, and went to bed.

Of course, she was still awake when he came in. He bumped into the coffee table, ran water in the bathroom for a long time, then quiet. Anna lay awake in the dark blue-gray night searching for sounds. She found the refrigerator, the hot water heater, and the rumble of a large truck on a distant street. *He* made no sound from where he lay on the opened out sofa, among her sewing machine and dress dummy, marking tape and pins. Was he asleep or waiting to make sure she was asleep so he could sneak out of the house as he had that other time?

She twisted and turned and rolled across her bed. But she could not evade the knowledge that despite what he'd done, she had not stopped loving him, just as she could not stop hating the girl he'd raped. If it had not been for her. . . . No. She knew better. Then why hadn't she seen the signs? And how come no one told her about this possibility and how to ward against it? Chicken pox, diphtheria, cowardice, and peeping through bathroom keyholes were all covered by the baby books or the seasoned mothers who passed along the do's and don'ts. But no one had warned her against this cruel vicious sickness. She pressed clenched fists against her lips to keep from crying out. And still she could not help but love at least the memory of him, or the memory of the person she'd thought he was. Now she no longer knew, no longer trusted herself to judge. She had already been so wrong about him and, therefore, about herself.

Anna woke to a cacophony of church bells. She could hear Junior moving around in the kitchen. It was late. She would have to hurry or miss church service. In the same moment she knew she wasn't going. She could not leave him alone in her house.

His tap on the door startled her. She cleared her throat and resisted the urge to clutch the covers around her flannel nightgowned chest before calling for him to come in.

The coffee he carried smelled weak. The toast was limp. But it was the first time she'd had breakfast in bed since he'd been arrested. She couldn't hold back the tears or the flood of memories of many mornings, just so—him bending over her with a breakfast tray:

"You wait on people in the restaurant all day and sit up all night making other people's clothes. You need some waiting on, too."

Had he actually said that, this man as a boy? Could this man have been such a boy? She nearly tilted the tray in her confusion.

"I need to brush my teeth." She averted her face and reached for her bathrobe.

She stayed in the bathroom till she heard him leave her bedroom and turn on the TV in the living room.

When Junior once again came to her door she called out to him that she had a sick headache and had decided to stay in bed with a cool compress on her forehead. He was immediately sympathetic, offering a neck massage or tea. She wanted only to be alone.

All afternoon she lay on her unmade bed, her eyes on the ceiling or idly roaming the room, while her mind moved across the surface of these new-old pains, so amazingly fresh after all these years. First there was Buddy. He had laughed at her, punched her, and finally driven her and their child into the streets. Then there was his son. Her baby. His son. He had dragged a young girl off the street and ruined a great lot of her life. And now he'd come back to spill salt in her kitchen.

For five years she'd been free of this too-familiar heaviness in her life. She'd put "widowed" on her job application and never mentioned a son to new people she met. Once she'd left the silent accusations of the old neighborhood she'd permitted herself to believe that her monthly letters, and the three times a year she hired a jitney to drive her the long distance to the maximum security prison where he'd been kept, was all that would be demanded of her in the way of payment for her part in the crime.

I'm home, Ma, homema, homema. His words echoed in her inner ear.

Her neighbors would want to know where he'd been and why. Fear and disgust would creep into their faces and voices. Her nights would be full of listening. Waiting.

Anna knelt beside the bed, dragged out her old green Samsonite, and plopped it on the bed. She dusted it with the tail of her bathrobe before lifting the lid. The smell of leaving and good-bye flooded the room. She hurried from dresser drawer to closet, choosing her favorites: the black knit skirt that once had a jacket, the silky red blouse not worn for ages, her comfortable gray shoes. She packed in a rush, as though her bus or train was even now pulling into the station.

When she'd packed her clothes, she walked to the wall on the left side of her bed where the shiny metal and wooden crucifix hung. Its Aryan plaster of paris Christ seemed to writhe in bittersweet agony. In the past the Lord had always been her port of last resort. After fussing and drinking and trying to work her troubles away she'd invariably turned to God. She'd always found a resting place with Him—a place where He knew and did what was best and she, therefore, could not be blamed. In the past she'd always been able to fall before His son where he hung on her wall and soothe the jagged edges of her heart. But it occurred to her, now, that if God could create Junior and Buddy and allow them to act as they did, perhaps this particular worry was not one that He could understand. She ran her finger down the slim muscular body, then lifted the cross from the wall. She put it, not as she'd originally intended—in her suitcase—but on the shelf in her closet among two old hats and a musty sweater she could never afford to have cleaned. Her son had died, too.

When she'd finished dressing Anna sat down in the hard straight-backed chair near the window in her room to wait for dark. Junior tapped at her door a number of times until she was able to convince him that she was best left alone and would be fine in the morning. When dark came she waited for the silence that reigns with sleep, then quietly left her room. She set her suitcase by the front door, tiptoed by Junior where he slept on the sofa, and went into the kitchen. By the glow from the back alley street light she wrote him a note and propped it against the sugar bowl:

"Dear Junior, I'm sorry, but I just can't be your mother right now. Maybe someday. Much love, Anna Jones."

Junior flinched and frowned in his sleep as the front door clicked shut.

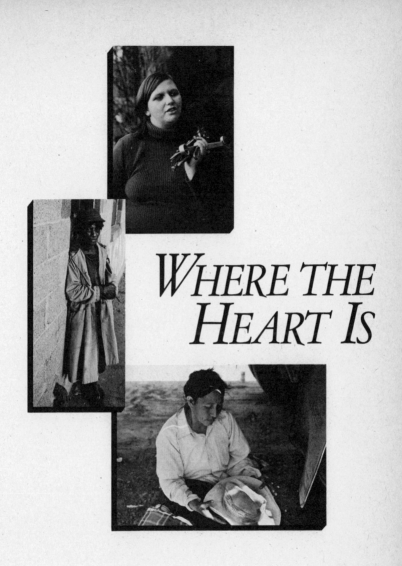

WHERE THE HEART IS

PART SIX

Sometimes I feel like a motherless child
A long ways from home.
　　　　　—Traditional Negro Spiritual

Migration has been one of the universal responses to internal community pressures, and the Southern experience is no exception. Women of all races and classes have chosen or been forced to leave the region, trying to escape from economic dead ends, fleeing racial persecution, haunted by ghosts from their own past, even threatened with violence or death. For many of these exiles, the South has a bitter taste. Yet, surprisingly, many also stay attached to the region in a relationship that transcends mere nostalgia. There are families that remain, and there are memories and obligations—both real and assumed—that continue to influence their lives and work. Gloria Anzaldúa, speaking as much from her Tejana-Chicana roots as from any of her other experiences, encourages women to write, particularly those who have been told for so long that they have nothing to say.

The ascendancy of conservatism in the eighties and the increasing respectability of overt racism, promoted in part by elected Southern officials and Southern-based organizations, suggest that migration from the South may increase as we move into the upcoming decades. We may expect that the issues raised by those who leave will remain with us, and that they will take on new dimensions as the notion of who is a Southerner is challenged by changing demographics. While political, racial, and economic conditions encourage a continuing *outward* migration, immigrants *to* the South bring new faces, histories, and hopes. Chief in this new wave are people from South and Central America, the Caribbean, Asia, the Middle East, and Africa. They arrive in flight from war, hunger, and poverty, all too often related to the militarism of this government. Our notions about race will continue to be challenged by the added presence of these newcomers, who don't fit into the old bi-racial mold. We can benefit from these new migrants, who bring ideas, skills, and new perspectives that have the potential to enrich our own culture.

The challenge of new ideas, the determination to make tangible visions of a social order that challenges the old stereotype, is generally a painful but profitable process. Sara Evans's account of the alienation experienced by white women, particularly Southerners, who participated in the Southern civil rights movement clearly demonstrates that their distress was as acute as any suffering that may have precipitated the outward migration of Southern women. Her analysis of the role that movement played in the elevation of women's consciousness of our own peculiar oppression makes it clear that alienation, exile, and other forms of displacement are often the forerunner to profound social change.

THE PRODIGAL CHILD'S HOMECOMING: CALIFORNIA TO GEORGIA, 1980

↝ BEVERLY BURCH

daughter of suitcases, she comes
glittering with new clothes, eager to see
them dazed by her strangeness

& stunned by her sharpness
of words, watch them cringe at their own
soft, southern sounds, shapeless, ashamed

flies home as a queen, sleek
in her pride & dream-blind, she is
swallowed defenseless

back in the belly
the loving beast leaves her crawling
recalling herself in this house
sees only her shadow
hiding bold in their eyes

chooses one faded dress
and goes to the table, her chattering
family, the feast in her honor
slips into the seat no one noticed
was empty

beaming, believing, they pass her
cornbread and chicken

SWING THRU THE SOUTH JOURNAL, FALL 1981: WE DIDNT MISS NO AIRPLANES OR NO GIGS. WE DIDNT PAY NO OVERWEIGHT. WE GOT PAID ALL OUR MONEY.

✒ HATTIE GOSSETT

*Since the days of vaudeville, when entertainers were booked on the T.O.B.A. circuit (*Theater Owners Booking Agency*), being on the road has been considered* Tough On Black Asses. *Hurried schedules, inadequate accommodations, hastily consumed meals, inadequate sleep, and the frightening possibility of not getting paid are some of the minor hazards. And on tours through the South, the constant threat of racial conflict underscores other tensions. While the Jim Crow laws that made traveling such a hell for blacks have been eliminated, the racial attitudes that spawned them are very much alive.*

One of the essential persons on a tour is the road manager. It is that person's job to see to it that everything happens on time, everybody gets paid, instruments get "loaded in," and reasonably cordial relationships are maintained with the local producers. In the fall of 1981, hattie gossett toured the South while working as road manager for a New York–based jazz band. The fast-paced road life and interaction with the all-male band and local folks are described in these excerpts from her journal.

richmond va

a quiet country coltrane lookin dude also from nc is driving us from the airport and tells us he is a music student at the gig/school doing a masters on gene ammons and sonny stitt. what?! yes indeed! welcome to the south! immediately go to work and tell him about the schomburg and the jazz institute and other places for research and urge him to come to nyc and chi. the white dude in the back also a grad student is doing bird and cannon. very heady and wonderful conversation on the way into town. not only that but they were on time.

richmond is hip and very friendly. bank vast and empty during height of lunch hour on thursday. 5 grand in cash please miss. some 100s a few more 50s and lots of 20s. please. smile. no we dont want a cashiers check. we have a payroll to meet. (the check is drawn on this bank.) murray calmly drawing on his aromatic pipe is the last bad smooth muthafucka from chi southside. a richard wright type post office alumnus cum night school ergo dr. nigga dean of the arts with 2400 students and smoked blue gray glasses and tweeds. stop! he got the white folks game down without losing anything. i am counting it out at the window. the star is complimenting me on t c b. so he dont have to sweat. work girl work!

the water has got algae which has been happening for 2 weeks tho nobody told us that before we left home. nassssstyyyy! one of 2 blemishes on a very smooth tho slow starting 2 days. the other being: yr rooms wont be ready for at least an hour cuz you got here too early. so we go up to the 3rd floor rest-rant for eggs. the water even fucks up my herbal tea! horrible! otherwise everything is very cool.

the richmond jazz society is black and white. the women mostly sit at the tables in the lobby selling buttons cooking w/jazz cookbooks books of matches records etc. the dudes all walk around a lot. only one or two women walk around. everyone is very nice. on wednesday nite they take us out for a nice dinner. after the gig on thursday they take us to a charming fixed up waterfront area to a hip bar that has cuevo gold tequila. enjoy meeting 2 local brothers—40ish—at the bar. one recently returned home to richmond after 15 years in california and the other is a local musician who has written a novel which some new york literary agency charged him $100 to read and reject.

miami

torn between hanging out in the cuban and black areas vs tea and 9pm bed-ie bye on the first nite here i reluctantly pick the latter. a sign of latent maturity? i am tired. the airplane takes it all away from me and wears me out.

there are still those little wooden houses in the poor black area like there were when i was a teenager and i am 39 now. didn't see poor white area. lots of construction downtown. coconut grove used to be black town according to our guide who grew up here. the waterfront part of it got snatched for urban renewal/nigger removal and now consists of $1/4million co ops.

at university of miami clinic the next day while the band is clinicing i walk the tropical campus grounds and see lots of asians and latins and blacks. also see representatives from those whose neighborhood this is sitting around the big campus pond fishing. mostly middleaged black women doing serious fishing probably for dinner. reggae music coming from somewhere. earlier was a live rock band. relish this lolling on the grass tho am afraid to really stretch out for fear of losing it altogether.

during the guided tour yesterday when the guy said and now we are approaching pause breath the inner city pause where the riots were pause and i said oh good we are going home he didn't get it. he thought i misunderstood him to mean going back to the hotel so i said no *home.* he still didnt get it so i had to explain to him that the inner city is *my home* wherever i may be.

slick concert hall at university.

jackson miss

sunday. feels so familiar. i know this place. never been here. am conscious of it as a warzone like saigon or joburg. and we are here with folks-es! staying in the notell motel called sun&sand motel and lounge (as opposed to bar) right behind the big house/capitol bldg. immediately upon deplaning and checking in we head for the piccadilly a black southern food cafeteria in the mall. a big negro baroque space filled with working class after church folks and the food is really good and cheap. the musicians are beaming conversation about older women and younger men. confessions of being turned out by older women. my period starts in the piccadilly.

the gig is in the community arts exchange a real community center type of place—plain and spacious. good people vibes. lots of black folks and even some white folks which i didnt expect in this town. mostly 20s and 30s. people have driven here from places 300 miles away and such. the vibe is very good like at the left bank in baltimore or the church basement on 141 street in harlem.

home. tables and chairs. red and white checked tablecloths. wine bottles with candles.

meet some really great sisters here who photograph and print and public relations etc. on the second day ellen takes me to spend an afternoon with margaret walker who even remembers what she ate—french style beefstew—at our redbook magazine expense account luncheon 15 years ago. and i was worried that she wouldnt remember me from all that time. she is doing HER richard wright book which sounds like a great (to me anyway) analysis of the post ww2 black male intellectual and all his little runnings away as personified by wright and countless others. she breaks him down into 5 parts: existentialism and marxism and pan africanism and freudianism and science-ism (einstein et al.). go on girl.

before going to her house we dropped the band off at jackson state university for a workshop and stayed long enough to make sure everything was going cool. a real black southern beginning with at least 5 important people speaking *before the workshop begins!* almost like they are praying which is still a common thing to do before any kind of event here. someone says its the southern sense of ritual and ceremony. i have forgotten much of this cuz i have been able to keep away from it as an adult but its all coming back to me now. there are music students here from other black schools all over the state.

on tuesday the 3rd day we go downtown for special biscuits for breakfast at a place owned by a brother. then we drive up to starkville to ole miss. beautiful beautiful road called the natchez trace. miles and miles of big pine trees interspersed with fields of dried cotton stalks tho we do see a few patches of still unpicked cotton. nearly every house has a big big woodpile next to it and we see many trucks hauling cut logs. the sunlight as filtered thru the pines is very delicate and subtle which contrasts with the brightness of the open fields. the trace was once an old native american trail i am told. now it is a 2 lane blacktop historical site with picnic tables parks and lakes and no stores or billboards.

this trip is starting to remind me of schooldays bus trips. someone is always telling a joke or making a wise crack. i am being treated very well. i am not allowed to lift or carry anything too heavy. no cursing is allowed in front of me. someone will remember my presence and say oh hattie is here be cool. i wish it was possible for things to be another way. the dichotomy of virgin/ mammy vs whore is a trap. either way you lose cuz you cant be who you really are. but at this moment in time i guess this might be the most one can hope for. sigh. as long as nobody asks me to sew any buttons or saute any bean sprouts or fry any pork chops i guess i am ok. sometimes because i feel like it i do carry some of the drums and the drummer teasingly threatens to have me carry the trapcase (the heaviest one) and the piano player tells me to strap the next good steinway we run into onto my back.

starkville ole miss is a big campus which john who is the husband of ellen and who is driving us today says is loaded and powerful. this is footballville where the white boy athletes eat whole cows and pigs for breakfast man—according to the drummer a southerner who attended black southern schools—while the black students/schools get dry white bread and baloney. well this theater is dry white bread and baloney. it has an old musty smell. the paint is peeling. the ragged curtain is safety pinned together in places even though this is a mostly white school. the stadium probably has massage shower heads in all the wall to wall carpeted climate controlled locker rooms which also probably have piped in good ole boy foot stompin music on the 32 track quad super sound system. oh well.

the stewardess from miami to atlanta (changing there for jackson) is striking for her ordinary everydayness and her obvious mature older womanness. little make up. very pleasant in a genuine manner rather than a plastic one. very unusual in my experience.

nashville

nothing is together here overall tho there are some individual bright moments. cuevo gold. steak & eggs. george tidewell. the red bearded guy. the black guy who asked the band to play something out during the workshop. the bands little sillies. finding tapes by sonny rollins and by philly joe at the music store. getting tape heads cleaned. the untogetherness started with the pickup an hour late at the airport. one driver running out of gas and the doctor having to give him $$$$$$$. tapes being chewed up by filthy tape heads. cant get a wardrobe together for the evening and wearing day clothes. no lite in the dressing room or closet at the hotel. 2 musicians having to wait all afternoon for their rooms. the sloppy looseness of these white college kids and their arrogance. and their arrogance again. oh well i guess theres bad days too. jackson was nice cuz of ellen and john and the other community people there. also i havent rested today. probably wont get to bed before 1 or 2 then on the bus at 7 am tomorrow for kentucky which means up at 5 or 5:30.

nashville sunday

off/travel day means i can stay in bed today till 10 or so and get room service and take a long steamy hot shower and wash my hair tho the room is not quite as warm as i would like in this fancy radison plaza of the radison collection pause breath not chain which is so tacky and gross and commercial according to the very classy in house promo pamphlet in the room. but they really aint got no class at all cuz when the bus driver went to pay his phone and food bills just now at 11 am the asst mgr came to my room and tried to bogart me into letting her in or me coming down to the lobby at once to pay his room bill. the nerve of this bitch on a sunday morning. even after i tell her everything is cool and that i would take care of the bill when i take care of mine she is still standing there outside my door and trying to tell me i got to come now or in a half hour. so then i tell her i have just showered and shampooed and that i will be down in an appropriate amount of time to settle. check out time isnt till 1 and of course when we got here at 1 or so yesterday our rooms were 2 hours late (phone rings and asst mgr says shes coming with cops) and now heres this bitch at my door with a cop are you ready for this shit! fortunately my boss gets here while they are here and takes over. they are demanding a list of everyones name and demanding that everyone pay now right now or else. no i am not ready. so much for a quiet morning in the nice hotel on the day off. i want to get out of here. now!

on the other hand who do i think i am telling these white people i will be down when i get ready and refusing to give everybodys name? am i crazy? have i forgotten who i am and what my role is? or course miss anne honey come rite in my lil room while i am dripping wet and my hair is standing all over my head. i dont need no privacy. yeah i must be getting carried away with myself or something. better watch it. not just becuz its the south either. this could have happened in the north just as easily. yeah i better watch myself and remember who i am. it could have been worse. they could have dragged me out before my boss got here or searched the room or anything. as a matter of fact they were surprisingly polite and calm.

   my boss who is a bad white girl from new york who is not easily intimidated takes the wallet from me which contains a couple grand in cash and marches the white girl asst mgr and white boy cop down to the front desk where she starts screaming and yelling racism and then throws a grand in cash all over the desk and the floor and tells them to take out for everybody right now cuz we are leaving this sad-ass place. of course the hotel people back right up and beg her to please take the money back and put it away please. they havent even totaled up none of the bills and dont know how much anybody owes and have to scramble around while my boss and all the cats (who she has assembled) stand there glaring at them. yeah. i really forgot myself there for a minute.

williamsburg/corbin ky

now its sunday nite after nashville up in the hills hi enuff to make my ears pop. dry country and thick hill country cracker accents. the star is threatening to go off again. the driver says its serious up here. so serious hes not even gonna look at no black womens let alone no white womens. now thats serious cuz he loves white ladies better than a pig loves slops.

   the wksp is attended by what look like hi & jr hi band kids most of whom dont appear to be paying any attention to the music but are twitching around in their seats. theres a steinway here but its not good enuff so i dont have to pack it up and put it on my back. in the crowd of about 50–75 i see one black boy and one very very brown looking girl. will this crowd of kids grow up to be the polyester folks at the concert in bowling green the other nite who applauded politely but werent really there?

the bus and the driver

the bus was built in 1968. its a fullsized thing painted in silver blue waves on both sides of the outside with a big old sailing ship rocking in deep waters. going down the hiway you cant miss it. on the c b people say things like whats that big ole stagecoach lookin thang and who be in it? inside is divided into 3 areas. in front is a lounge—couches on either side of the aisle a built in table and benches windows with thick curtains for privacy a microwave oven a betamax deck an audio tape deck a color tv a cold box and a bathroom. next comes the sleeping compartment which has no windows and which has 12 bunks with curtains for privacy. surprising how good you can sleep too. finally is the back lounge—more couches another audio tape deck. the last and only word in custom private group surface travel. down this way mostly all entertainers use a vehicle like this to get around. ours isnt that elaborate when you think of what presley had or what dolly parton has. theirs feature king sized beds with canopies closet space for extensive stores of costumes etc. full kitchens etc. many people live completely on their buses on the road not like us who eat in restaurants and stay in hotels every nite. a country boy the driver says of himself. born in richmond or somewhere in va and living in baton rouge. with his millionaire boss. been drivin these buses for near bout 15 years. says he has been up to the top as high as elizabeth taylor.

barborsville ky

monday morning. did i panic this morning or what? i wasnt ready at all when i woke up feeling low. then on the bus at 8 and getting lost looking for diesel fuel for the bus on the way to a 10 am school lecture demo. finally get to the school to be told gig is moved to church cuz of better piano and acoustics. these school people didnt even know band was coming till yesterday mr blue said. out! out! out! but this is improvisational music so the cats improvise off center on the right side of the pulpit of the white baptist church cuz the piano is in a little built in compartment in the rite corner. they set up in no time at all and hit with bye bye black bird real mellow and pretty on this gloomy monday. the pianist looks kinda funny and nice boxed in this little compartment with only his head and shoulders showing and with these white gladiolas in front framing his very black face. another all white group of hi school kids who seem more attentive. arent there any black kids in these schools? where are they?

i miss walking. i never walk further than from the hotel door to the bus and from the bus to the door of the gig. and i never have any time for exercises. also being around these men all the time is wearing even tho i am a heterosexual and like men in general. but not this much. and not to the exclusion of women so totally. theres a lot of stuff i cant talk about with them. a lot i cant say. theres little real conversation about anything other than music or the world series or sugar ray leonards fight. after the gig when all the kids are gone the pianist favors us with a long gospel selection at the piano.

pineville ky

here we are in a big ole gym of bell county hi school with the entire student body at 2 in the afternoon packed into the bleachers. they applaud like mad but the bus driver says they dont know what theyre listening to. the piano bench has 4 legs and the left front one looks like its going to snap any moment now. and the pianist sits to the left on the bench. and leans to the left. real hard. oh but excuse me. mr m is slyly slipping his left hand down to slide the leg back in place in the middle of his bow. excuse me. must not be too many of us in the area. but no. the principal who says the gym was built in 45 or so and who has been here since 46 and who looks like a modern version of the 19th century russian provincial school inspector in a boyish grin and a faded purple suit with mud spattered cuffs runs down how unfortunately all the blacks live in town in pineville and go to *town* school but that the bobcat den is a *county* school and that for some strange reason all the whites live out in the county. sound familiar? only 2 blacks—1 girl and 1 boy in the whole school. and he takes pains to say how pleased they are with the 2 black kids and to name others in previous generations of their families who he has seen in his time. oh yes. we would sure like to have more blacks. indeed we would. but theres nothing we can do about it. i think i came in on this line.

on the bus some of the cats allow as how maybe reggie jackson wasnt completely wrong for punching out the black woman who asked him for an autograph while he was with a white woman after all womens have these mouths that say these things that can really get to a man so tuff he gotta hit her. they dont see anything to get excited about really cuz after all womens do have these mouths and we do insist on saying these things and whats a po boy to do?

tuesday morning. these people aint ready either. no one has told them what/who they are getting. am in a small old fashioned methodist college that looks and feels like palmer institute with the most blacks we have seen anywhere in the area all dudes maybe 5 including a couple africans. one of these dudes with overdeveloped muscles and underdeveloped bodily covering struts down the center aisle just as the concert starts to a front row seat and proceeds to pull out his copy of some newspaper and start to read. ugh! ugh! then to lunch at the only the original colonel sanders kentucky fried chicken shop in corbin. smells just like the one that moved out the drugstore food section on 157 and bway run by 2 black women who fried real chicken in real black cast iron frying pans with clean grease and cooked real collard greens etc. etc. of course the colonel put an end to all that. oh do i wanna go home. i am tired. the star went off and tried to beat the bus again today. the same door again and then another door. driver calls his boss and i have to speak and guarantee $$$$$.

[then afterwards] my nerves are plucked between the star and the gigs and i make the mistake of answering the sponsor lady when she asks me how everything is going and asking her how cum everybody was so unprepared and how cum there were no blacks at any of the 4 schools? very stupid mistake. shes a dignified very reserved little lady and she didnt like it at all. said that when her board plans who (bands theater companies etc.) to send to which school they never think about making sure blacks get exposed. no they dont think about that. and no it isnt her fault no blacks are in any of the 4 schools we go to. who am i to say these things to her anyway? and its not her responsibility to make sure the teachers get info on what's happening so they can prepare their students. after all as she righteously lets me know theyve had integration in this area before anybody else in the country ever thought about it. and they never had any racial incidents or problems. (read riots rebellions welfare cheats etc.) its not her fault and she shouldn't be asked to be responsible for seeing to it that black kids get exposed to culture. government funded culture. especially government funded black culture.

on the other hand or maybe on the same one the nice old old white lady i met with the sponsor lady last nite just after the concert and her slightly younger buddy thought they were delivering ultimate compliments when they asked me if there is an anatomical (geneological?) difference between blacks and whites which makes you nigras have such a wonderful sense of rhythm (i am not lyin!) and why it is that every one of you i have ever met could sing or dance or something? yeah they thought they were asking me a deeply serious question and they expected an answer. and when i said that white folks have some stuff that is different and also okay like ballet and blue grass music they got right adamant and said oh no oh no. they werent having none of my liberal bullshit. oh no they said. we have been watching and we know. white people just dont have that what you all have. the last thing the elder one said before telling the doctor that a couple weeks before she had seen her first uprite bass in life in a concert by this big white classical bassist and that the doctor was her 2nd uprite in life and that she thought he was just as good as the white boy.

anyway the sponsor lady put me in my place by saying the music is too out and that ⅓ left at intermission at the cumberland evening concert cuz of that so what do i mean about preparation and about black participation?

south eastern kentucky is a starkly pretty place. hills of multicolored trees out of the windows. along the sides of the hiways high huge jagged abstract sculpture looking rocks in grays and blackbrowns and blacks. too bad the weather is so shitty. raining and foggy and damp the whole time. lunch (again) in a place that features pinto beans cornbread and coffee for $1. the most expensive thing on the menu is the $6 ribeye steak. in the land of country and western i am thrilled to find stevie wonders reggae tune on the box along with some old doo wops and manhattan transfer doing confirmation. in this place i don't have to think about schedules and pianos and such so i have time to check out the people who have a rugged look that i like. there are pinball machines which the cats leap right onto. the little daughter of the owners plays the machines with the cats and beats them all. very nonchalantly too. she doesn't seem scared of the cats at all. great. some of the white people catch on to how i am monopolizing the box and beat me to the draw by a few seconds and theres a tense moment as we are flooded by twang twang. but after a few beats we hear the heavy backbeat on the tune coming through loud and clear like 50s rhythm and blues and the white boys singing like they just came out of rev chickenlegs jump for joy church. amazing. i feel comfortable enough to lean over to 2 white women next to us who have been trading smart remarks with some white guy over on the other side and keeping him in his place and ask them the name of the record and the artist. they look at me for a second and at first dont say anything. then they tell me and its cool and we start to talk a little. they give us directions for how to get to the school we have to go to that afternoon. i like them. they have a dry understated way of talking that is very funny and very deep at the same time. and i can tell from the lines in their faces and from their eyes that they havent had an easy time in this life either. i remember that this is the coal mining region and that we havent seen any mines or signs of that life cuz we have been pretty close to the interstate the whole time here and not too far up into the back hills. there are so many layers and layers and no time to investigate.

DELTA

✦ RAYMINA Y. MAYS

The last time Delta went home she went on a Greyhound bus.
When she had arrived and bathed and settled in a rocking chair on
her mother's porch with a glass of lemonade, surrounded by her
aunts who had all gathered to give her mother and each other some
back up for the long list of stories that they would tell, she was told
a story about her arrival. The aunts and her mother sat and encouraged each other, added missing details, and supplied the right
voices, walks, and facial expressions. When her little sister, Beth
Ann, was told she was coming home, she sang a little song called
"My sister is coming home on a Greyhound bus."

"Now I know them songs them babies sing when they jumpin
rope," one aunt said. "And that wasn't hardly one of em. I say,
Bell, come out here. I b'lieve this baby out here makin up new
rhymes. Don't you know this girl had them kids jumpin rope to
you comin home?"

This time when Delta called to tell her sister she was coming
home on the bus, she was asked if she couldn't get there sooner.
Couldn't she take a plane?

Delta was so caught up in her memories that she didn't realize
that she was in town until the bus driver announced "Haytown."
The bus stop was still a bench in front of the pharmacy, and the
faded Greyhound Bus sign was still pasted to the window. The bus
driver put Delta's bags on the sidewalk next to the bench.

Delta saw her mother's Continental parked not far from where
she stood. She waved to the figure behind the wheel and waited
impatiently for the door to open and her sister, Beth Ann, to get
out of the car. She walked toward Beth Ann. Almost ran toward

her. When she couldn't seem to get to her fast enough Delta let out a joyful holler from where she stood. People turned their heads, some smiled.

When Delta reached Beth Ann she hugged her hard and then pushed her back so she could eye the changes. Beth Ann was a woman who looked much like Delta. Busy eyes. Cheekbones and nose. All a lot like her own. When she had her eyes filled she reached for Beth Ann again. They cried in each other's arms and Beth Ann whispered, "Momma's dead." And they hugged so tightly that Delta forgot where her tears ended and Beth's began.

Once the bags were loaded into the trunk of the car, Beth Ann drove through the town so that Delta could see what had changed and what had remained the same. Between questions Beth Ann would point out different people old and new. It seemed that before Delta could answer one question, Beth Ann had another one.

Did she still live with that woman up in New York? Why didn't she call or write more often? Miss Perry and them still live in that green house. Mrs. Sara still gets drunk and can't find her way home. What happened when word got to her that her momma died of a heart stroke? Did she cry? They only had three aunts left and not four as before. Aunt Lovie died last year of the same thing momma died of. Delta's friend Sonja Jean didn't ever leave town. She had taken to going to the Illusion bar, only bar in town. And Sonja be sittin up in the bar in the middle of the day drinkin beer out of a Styrofoam cup with folk who didn't have no job. Sonja slept with women and her husband nearly beat her to death when he found out and took her kids away from her. Had she slept with Sonja? Did she want to go by Sonja's house when she got rested and the funeral was over? Delta tried to answer all of Beth's questions and to save her questions for later.

Delta had wished first that her mother hadn't died. But she wished second that death would have slipped up on her in the flower garden and not while scrubbing some woman's floors. When Beth Ann parked the car Delta walked in search of her mother's garden. She was amazed at her mother's ability to grow flowers that would grow past a tall person's knees. She picked flowers for the table inside but dropped them because she didn't want to look at the table.

Delta entered the house from the back porch. She walked through quickly, not looking at the furniture or pictures or at the room that she and Beth Ann had shared as children. She made her way to the front porch. She heard the laughter of her Aunt Beth and Aunt Delta and Aunt Martha. She pushed the screen door open and the laughter stopped.

"Looooorrd," Aunt Delta said pulling at Delta's army coat, "if this ain't Bell's child then I don't know who is." Delta leaned over so that the woman whose name she had been given could kiss her. She went to her other aunts one at a time and waited until they positioned their snuff so that they could say hello. Then she sat in a chair next to her Aunt Delta and waited for the questions.

What happened to that woman you brought down the last time you was here? Did you feel bad bout being away for this many years? You married? What's New York like? You still teach? You still smart?

Delta looked at her Aunt Delta. She remembered her for being good with making her comfortable when she really wasn't. Taking away a fair amount of girlhood pain. Understanding when no one else seemed to.

"Loooorrd, Jesus. The girl just got in town and yall tryin to get her whole life story. Leave her lone," Aunt Delta persuaded. "Rean they questionin you so close is cause they think you gonna go to the funeral then leave right away. Leave her be I said."

"You gonna stay a while?"

Delta said yes, though she told her lover before leaving New York that she would leave when the funeral was over. She could not stay in her mother's house. Her mother had said never come home again and she took her word for it and the fact that she was dead didn't make it any easier to come home.

When Delta looked away from her aunts, Beth was standing behind the screen door beckoning her from the porch. She excused herself then followed Beth to their mother's room. She looked at the dresser to briefly see herself in the mirror. She was nauseated by seeing herself in her mother's mirror. She was in the one room where she and Beth had not been allowed. If they went in that room when her mother was away visiting or shopping she always knew and punished them.

Beth Ann hugged Delta. "Stay. It's summer and since you and the woman who you're with teach and schools out, she can come here too." Delta wanted to be with Beth, too, and she knew that Beth Ann would like her lover.

For a long time she had wanted to talk with Beth about growing up, telling secrets, swimming naked in the pond, getting mad at their momma for being nice to that other woman's children and having the patience as long as a short stick when it came to her and

Beth. She wanted to talk about how when their father died the walls seemed to pick up their mother's grief and places in the floor creaked where they never had before and how they seemed so close to their mother then. Delta told Beth that she would stay for the summer and maybe she could meet her womanfriend.

"Momma kept a direy," Beth Ann said. "I read it. She talked about you mostly. You're probably mentioned on every other page. I'll keep our aunties company while you look at the books. She wrote about ten."

Delta couldn't imagine her mother with a journal. The first page was dedicated "For Mrs. Johnson, who told me to keep this." Mrs. Johnson was the woman she worked for.

There was a slip of paper in one of the pages and Delta turned to that one and began to read:

"Today is the day Delta came home from school up north. She change. her hair is bushy. her clothes not cleaned or ironed. I am ashame of her to come in here with her aunties here dressed like that. Her friend look no better. She live bout 50 mile south of here but stayin here with Delta before she go home. I don't know who her people are."

Delta skipped pages and read more.

"They was in Delta bed like they was married. This the only way I can explain it. Kissing and holding. I don't allow that in my house. If I hadda been able to sleep last night I wouldn't know. Who woulda tole me?"

Delta skipped more pages.

"Delta called. She cried. I told her I would kill myself for making her like that if I did it. I think I did. I hate myself. Queer. Folk in town know. Go to the hairdresser and things get hushed. Beth Ann got picked on in school. I got to watch Beth Ann so she won't be one too."

On another page was a passage that read: "I hate myself. I called Delta today. I tell her to come on home and don't bring that woman. Told her Mrs. Johnson know a doctor for her sickness. I love her. I hate myself. She hung up in my face."

Delta lay across her mother's bed consumed by the journal. She was holding a year of her mother's thoughts in her hand. She would ask Beth Ann if she could keep the journals.

As Delta continued to read she came to a page about Sonja Jean. She couldn't imagine that her mother would write anything about Sonja Jean except that she hated her.

"Melvira's girl Sonja is like Delta, but when she found out she

married Ruth's boy. They got babies. Sonja stay in and out of the
hospital. Her mind is nearly bout gone. Folk say she leave town to
sleep with womens. Melvira and them say the girl crazy. If I say
Sonja Jean crazy then I have to say Delta crazy and I know Delta
ain't crazy. That is the one reason I didn't like Sonja cause she was
too smart like Delta and the two of them together was enough to
make my pressure rise. I want to call Delta and tell her they put
Sonja away tonight. She said don't call and it be about two in the
morning so I might call tomorrow anyway. Don't care what she
say."

Delta's mother never called.

"They say Sonja called Delta's name one or two times while she
was under the needle. Delta didn't go to Sonja's wedding folks say
because there was a big fight last time Delta came home. I didn't
know nothing about this. Show how folk talk behind your back.
Sonja must have been the first one for Delta. Why didn't I know?"

Delta wiped away bitter tears. Where was Sonja's house? Beth
Ann would take her there. Delta searched for the last journal. She
turned pages, though she did not know exactly what she was looking for. Finally she began to read.

"She may not be a mental case. It sure ain't natural though.
Someone I brought into the world sleeping with women and doing
only god knows what."

Delta frantically turned more pages. She read: "I couldn't accept
it. I'll go to my grave not accepting that someone who came out of
me sleeps with women."

SPEAKING IN TONGUES:
A LETTER TO THIRD WORLD WOMEN WRITERS

✒ GLORIA ANZALDÚA

21 mayo 80

Dear *mujeres de color,* companions in writing,

I sit here naked in the sun, typewriter against my knee trying to visualize you. Black woman huddles over a desk in the fifth floor of some New York tenement. Sitting on a porch in south Texas, a Chicana fanning away mosquitos and the hot air, trying to arouse the smoldering embers of writing. Indian woman walking to school or work lamenting the lack of time to weave writing into your life. Asian American, lesbian, single mother, tugged in all directions by children, lover, or ex-husband, and the writing.

It is not easy writing this letter. It began as a poem, a long poem. I tried to turn it into an essay but the result was wooden, cold. I have not yet unlearned the esoteric bullshit and pseudo-intellectualizing that school brainwashed into my writing.

How to begin again. How to approximate the intimacy and immediacy I want. What form? A letter, of course.

My dear *hermanas,* the dangers we face as women writers of color are not the same as those of white women though we have many in common. We don't have as much to lose—we never had any privileges. I wanted to call the dangers "obstacles" but that would be a kind of lying. We can't *transcend* the dangers, can't rise above them. We must go through them and hope we won't have to repeat the performance.

Unlikely to be friends of people in high literary places, the beginning woman of color is invisible both in the white male mainstream world and in the white women's feminist world, though in the latter this is gradually changing. The *lesbian* of color is not only invisible, she doesn't even exist. Our speech, too, is inaudible. We speak in tongues like the outcast and the insane.

Because white eyes do not want to know us they do not bother to learn our language, the language that reflects us, our culture, our spirit. The schools we attended or didn't attend did not give us the skills for writing or the confidence that we were correct in using our class and ethnic languages. I, for one, became adept at and majored in English to spite, to show up, the arrogant racist teachers who thought all Chicano children were dumb and dirty. And Spanish was not taught in grade school. And Spanish was not required in high school. And though now I write my poems in Spanish as well as English I feel the rip-off of my native tongue.

Who gave us permission to perform the act of writing? Why does writing seem so unnatural for me? I'll do anything to postpone it—empty the trash, answer the telephone. The voice recurs in me: *Who am I, a poor Chicanita from the sticks, to think I could write?* How dare I even consider becoming a writer as I stooped over the tomato fields bending, bending under the hot sun, hands broadened and calloused, not fit to hold the quill, numbed into an animal stupor by the heat.

How hard it is for us to *think* we can choose to become writers, much less *feel* and *believe* that we can. What have we to contribute, to give? Our own expectations condition us. Does not our class, our culture as well as the white man tell us writing is not for women such as us?

The white man speaks: *Perhaps if you scrape the dark off of your face. Maybe if you bleach your bones. Stop speaking in tongues, stop writing left-handed. Don't cultivate your colored skins or tongues of fire if you want to make it in a right-handed world.*

I think, yes, perhaps if we go to the university. Perhaps if we become male women or as middle class as we can. Perhaps if we give up loving women we will be worthy of having something to say worth saying. They convince us that we must cultivate art for art's sake. Bow down to the sacred bull-form. Put frames and meta-frames around the writing. Achieve distance in order to win the coveted title "literary writer" or "professional writer." Above all do not be simple, direct, or immediate.

Why do they fight us? Because they think we are dangerous beasts? Why *are* we dangerous beasts? Because we shake and often break the white's comfortable stereotypic images they have of us: the Black domestic; the lumbering nanny with twelve babies sucking her tits; the slant-eyed Chinese with her expert hand, "They know how to treat a man in bed"; the flat-faced Chicana or Indian, passively lying on her back, being fucked by the Man *á la* La Chingada.

The Third World woman revolts: *We revoke, we erase your white male imprint. When you come knocking on our doors with your rubber stamps to brand our faces with DUMB, HYSTERICAL, PASSIVE PUTA, PERVERT, when you come with your branding irons to burn MY PROPERTY on our buttocks, we will vomit the guilt, self-denial, and race-hatred you have force-fed into us right back into your mouth. We are done being cushions for your projected fears. We are tired of being your sacrificial lambs and scapegoats.*

I can write this and yet I realize that many of us women of color who have strung degrees, credentials, and published books around our necks like pearls that we hang onto for dear life are in danger of contributing to the invisibility of our sister-writers. "La Vendida," the sell-out.

The danger of selling out one's own ideologies. For the Third World woman, who has, at best, one foot in the feminist literary world, the temptation is great to adopt the current feeling fads and theory fads, the latest half-truths in political thought, the half-digested new age psychological axioms that are preached by the white feminist establishment. Its followers are notorious for "adopting" women of color as their "cause" while expecting us to adapt to *their* expectations and *their* language.

How dare we get out of our colored faces. How dare we reveal the human flesh underneath and bleed red blood like the white folks. It takes tremendous energy and courage not to acquiesce, not to capitulate to a definition of feminism that still renders most of us invisible. Over and over I have found myself to be the only Third World woman at readings, workshops, and meetings.

We cannot allow ourselves to be tokenized. We must make our own writing and that of Third World women the first priority. We cannot educate white women and take them by the hand. Most of us are willing to help but we can't do the white woman's homework for her. That's an energy drain. More times than she cares to remember Nellie Wong, the Asian-American feminist writer, has been called by white women wanting a list of Asian-American women who can give readings or workshops. We are in danger of being reduced to purveyors of resource lists.

Coming face to face with one's limitations. There are only so many things I can do in one day. Luisah Teish, addressing a group of predominantly white feminist writers, had this to say of Third World women's experience:

> If you are not caught in the maze that [we] are in, it's very difficult to explain to you the hours in the day we do not have. And the hours that we do not have are hours that are translated into survival skills and money. And when one of those hours is taken away it means an hour that we don't have to lie back and stare at the ceiling or an hour that we don't have to talk to a friend. For me it's a loaf of bread.

Why am I compelled to write? Because the writing saves me from this complacency I fear. Because I have no choice. Because I must keep the spirit of my revolt and myself alive. Because the world I create in the writing compensates for what the real world does not give me. By writing I put order in the world, give it a handle so I can grasp it. I write because life does not appease my appetites and hunger. I write to record what others erase when I speak, to rewrite the stories others have miswritten about me, about you. To become more intimate with myself and you. To discover myself, to preserve myself, to make myself, to achieve self-autonomy. To dispel the myths that I am a mad prophet or a poor suffering soul. To convince myself that I am worthy and that what I have to say is not a pile of shit. To show that I *can* and that I *will* write, never mind their admonitions to the contrary. And I will write about the unmentionables, never mind the outraged gasp of the censor and the audience. Finally I write because I'm scared of writing but I'm more scared of not writing.

Why should I try to justify why I write? Do I need to justify being Chicana, being woman? You might as well ask me to try to justify why I'm alive.

The act of writing is the act of making soul, alchemy. It is the quest for the self, for the center of the self, which we women of color have come to think of as "other"—the dark, the feminine. Didn't we start writing to reconcile this other within us? We knew we were different, set apart, exiled from what is considered "normal," white-right. And as we internalized this exile, we came to see the alien within us and too often, as a result, we split apart from ourselves and each other. Forever after we have been in search of that self, that "other" and each other. And we return in widening spirals and never to the same childhood place where it happened, first in our families, with our mothers, with our fathers. The writing is a tool for piercing that mystery but it also shields us, gives us a margin of distance, helps us survive. And those that don't survive? The waste of ourselves: so much meat thrown at the feet of madness or fate or the state.

Returning after I've stuffed myself. Writing paragraphs on pieces of paper, adding to the puzzle on the floor, to the confusion on my desk making completion far away and perfection impossible.

26 mayo 80

Dear *mujeres de color*

I feel heavy and tired and there is a buzz in my head—too many beers last night. But I must finish this letter. My bribe: to take myself out for pizza.

So I cut and paste and line the floor with my bits of paper. My life strewn on the floor in bits and pieces and I try to make some order out of it working against time, psyching myself up with de-caffeinated coffee, trying to fill in the gaps.

Leslie, my housemate, comes in, gets on hands and knees to read my fragments on the floor and says, "It's good, Gloria." And I think: *I don't have to go back to Texas, to my family of land, mesquites, cactus, rattlesnakes, and roadrunners. My family, this community of writers. How could I have lived and survived so long without it. And I remember the isolation, relive the pain again.*

"To assess the damage is a dangerous act," writes Cherríe Moraga.* To stop there is even more dangerous.

It's too easy, blaming it all on the white man or white feminists or society or our parents. What we say and what we do ultimately comes back to us, so let us own our responsibility, place it in our own hands, and let us carry it with dignity and strength. No one's going to do my shitwork, I pick up after myself.

It makes perfect sense to me now how I resisted the act of writing, the commitment to writing. To write is to confront one's demons, look them in the face and live to write about them. Fear acts like a magnet; it draws the demons out of the closet and into the ink in our pens.

The tiger riding our backs (writing) never lets us alone. *Why aren't you riding, writing, writing?* It asks constantly till we begin to

*Cherríe Moraga, "La Güera," in *This Bridge Called My Back: Writings by Radical Women of Color,* eds. Cherríe Moraga and Gloria Anzaldúa (Watertown, Mass.: Persephone Press, 1981).

feel we're vampires sucking the blood out of too fresh an experience; that we are sucking life's blood to feed the pen. Writing is the most daring thing I have ever done and the most dangerous. Nellie Wong calls writing "the three-eyed demon shrieking the truth."*

Writing is dangerous because we are afraid of what the writing reveals: the fears, the angers, the strengths of a woman under a triple or quadruple oppression. Yet in that very act lies our survival because a woman who writes has power. And a woman with power is feared.

> What did it mean for a black woman to be an artist in our grandmother's time? It is a question with an answer cruel enough to stop the blood.†

I have never seen so much power in the ability to move and transform others as from that of the writing women of color.

I say *mujer magica,* empty yourself. Shock yourself into new ways of perceiving the world, shock your readers into the same. Stop the chatter inside their heads.

Your skin must be sensitive enough for the lightest kiss and thick enough to ward off the sneers. If you are going to spit in the eye of the world, make sure your back is to the wind. Write of what most links us with life, the sensation of the body, the images seen by the eye, the expansion of the psyche in tranquillity: moments of high intensity, its movement, sounds, thoughts. *Even though we go hungry we are not impoverished of our experiences.*

> I think many of us have been fooled by the mass media, by society's conditioning that our lives must be lived in great explosions, by "falling in love," by being "swept off our feet," and by the sorcery of magic genies that will fulfill our every wish, our every childhood longing. Wishes, dreams, and fantasies are important parts of our creative lives. They are the steps a writer integrates into her craft. They are the spectrum of resources to reach the truth, the heart of things, the immediacy, and the impact of human conflict.‡

---

*Nellie Wong, "Flows from the Dark of Monsters and Demons: Notes on Writing," *Radical Woman Pamphlet* (San Francisco, 1979).
†Alice Walker, "In Search of Our Mothers' Gardens: The Creativity of Black Women in the South," *Ms.*, May 1974, p. 60.
‡Wong, *ibid.*

Many have a way with words. They label themselves seers but they will not see. Many have the gift of tongue but nothing to say. Do not listen to them. Many who have words and tongue have no ear, they cannot listen and they will not hear.

There is no need for words to fester in our minds. They germinate in the open mouth of the barefoot child in the midst of restive crowds. They wither in ivory towers and in college classrooms.

Throw away abstraction and the academic learning, the rules, the map and compass. Feel your way without blinders. To touch more people, the personal realities and the social must be evoked —not through rhetoric but through blood and pus and sweat.

Write with your eyes like painters, with your ears like musicians, with your feet like dancers. You are the truthsayer with quill and torch. Write with your tongues of fire. Don't let the pen banish you from yourself. Don't let the ink coagulate in your pens. Don't let the censor snuff out the spark, or the gags muffle your voice. Put your shit on the paper.

We are not reconciled to the oppressors who whet their howl on our grief. We are not reconciled.

Find the muse within you. The voice that lies buried under you, dig it up. Do not fake it, try to sell it for a handclap or your name in print.

Love,
Gloria

This letter is excerpted from This Bridge Called My Back: Writings by Radical Women of Color, *eds. Cherríe Moraga and Gloria Anzaldúa (Watertown, Mass: Persephone Press, 1981).*

231·

WOMEN'S CONSCIOUSNESS AND THE SOUTHERN BLACK MOVEMENT

❧ SARA EVANS

Twice in the history of the United States the struggle for racial equality has been midwife to a feminist movement. In the abolition movement of the 1830s and 1840s and again in the civil rights revolt of the 1960s, women experiencing the contradictory expectations and stresses of changing roles began to move from individual discontents to a social movement in their own behalf. Working for racial justice, they developed both political skills and a belief in human rights which could justify their own claim to equality.

Moreover, in each case, the racial and sexual tensions embedded in Southern culture projected a handful of white Southern women into the forefront of those who connected one cause with the other. In the 1830s, Sarah and Angelina Grimké, devout Quakers and daughters of a Charleston slave-owning family, spoke out sharply against the moral evils of slavery and racial prejudice. "The female slaves," they said, "are our countrywomen—*they are our sisters;* and to us as women, they have a right to look for sympathy with their sorrows, and effort and prayer for their rescue. . . . Women ought to feel a peculiar sympathy in the colored men's wrong, for like him, she has been accused of mental inferiority, and denied the privileges of a liberal education."

Through the nineteenth century and into the twentieth, religious commitment led a series of middle-class women to engage in social action, though they continued to accept many conventional attitudes about women and blacks. A new set of circumstances in the late fifties and early sixties, however, forced a few young Southern white women into an opposition to Southern culture more comparable to that of the Grimké sisters than to their immediate predecessors. During this period, student ministries and the YWCA fostered a growing social concern and articulated, in the language of existential theology, a radical critique of American society and Southern segregation. The ethos of the Southern civil rights struggle perfectly matched this spirit of religious insurgency which motivated a generation of white students. When the revolt of Southern blacks began in 1960, it touched a chord of moral idealism and brought a significant group of white Southern women into a movement which would both change their lives and transform a region.

Following the first wave of sit-ins in 1960, the Southern Christian Leadership Conference (SCLC), at the insistence of its assistant director, Ella Baker, called a conference at Shaw University in Raleigh, North Carolina, on Easter weekend. There black youths founded their own organization, the Student Nonviolent Coordinating Committee (SNCC) to provide a support network for direct action. SNCC set the style and tone of grassroots organizing in the rural South and led the movement into the black belt. The spirit of adventure and commitment which animated the organization added new vitality to a deeply rooted struggle for racial equality.

In addition to this crucial role within the black movement, SNCC also created the social space within which women began to develop a new sense of their own potential. A critical vanguard of young women accumulated the tools for movement building: a language to describe oppression and justify revolt, experience in the strategy and tactics of organizing, and a beginning sense of themselves collectively as objects of discrimination.

The clash between the heightened sense of self-worth which the movement offered to its participants and the replication of traditional sex roles within it gave birth to a new feminism. Treated as housewives, sex objects, nurturers, and political auxiliaries, and finally threatened with banishment from the movement, young white Southern women responded with the first articulation of the modern challenge to the sexual status quo.

The Decision

The first critical experience for most white women was simply the choice to become involved. Such a decision often required a break with home and childhood friends that might never heal. It meant painful isolation and a confrontation with the possibility of violence and death. Such risks were not taken lightly. They constituted forceful acts of self-assertion.

Participation in civil rights meant beginning to see the South through the eyes of the poorest blacks, and frequently it shattered supportive ties with family and friends. Such new perceptions awakened white participants to the stark brutality of racism and the depth of their own racial attitudes. One young woman had just arrived in Albany, Georgia, when she was arrested along with the other whites in the local SNCC voter registration project. By the time she left jail after nine days of fasting, the movement was central to her life. Her father suffered a nervous breakdown. But while she was willing to compromise on where she would work, she staunchly refused to consider leaving the movement. That, it seemed to her, "would be like living death."

Anguished parents used every weapon they could muster to stop their children. "We'll cut off your money," "You don't love us," they threatened. The women who refused to acquiesce often responded with loving determination. On June 27, 1964, a young volunteer headed for Mississippi wrote:

Dear Mom and Dad:

This letter is hard to write because I would like so much to communicate how I feel and I don't know if I can. It is very hard to answer to your attitude that if I loved you I wouldn't do this. . . . I can only hope you have the sensitivity to understand that I can both love you very much and desire to go to Mississippi. . . . There comes a time when you have to do things which your parents do not agree with.

Even activist parents, who themselves had taken serious risks for causes they believed in, were troubled. Heather Tobis's uncle wrote that her work in Mississippi compared with the struggle against fascism in the 1930s and 1940s. "We are proud to claim you as our own," he said. But her parents asked angrily over the phone, "Do you know how much it takes to make a child?" Whether they kept their fears to themselves or openly opposed their children's participation, the messages from parents, both overt and subliminal, were mixed: "We believe in what you're doing—but don't do it." Their concern could only heighten their daughters' ambivalences.

The pain of such a choice, however, was eased by the sense of purpose with which the movement was imbued. The founding statement of SNCC rang with Biblical cadences:

"Through nonviolence, courage displaces fear; love transforms hate. Acceptance dissipates prejudice; hope ends despair. Peace dominates war; faith reconciles doubt. Mutual regard cancels enmity. Justice for all overcomes injustice. The redemptive community supersedes systems of gross immorality."

The goals of the movement—described as the "redemptive community," or more often, the "beloved community"—constituted both a vision of the future obtained through nonviolent action and a conception of the nature of the movement itself.

Within SNCC the intensely personal nature of social action and the commitment to equality resulted in a kind of anarchic democracy and a general questioning of all the socially accepted rules. When SNCC moved into voter registration projects in the Deep South, this commitment led to a deep respect for the very poorest blacks. "Let the people decide" was about as close to an ideology as SNCC ever came. Though civil rights workers were frustrated by the depth of fear and passivity beaten into generations of rural black people, the movement was also nourished by the beauty and courage of people who dared to face the loss of their livelihoods and possibly their lives.

One white, female civil rights worker in Mississippi wrote that the Negroes in Holly Springs were incredibly brave, "the most real people" she had ever met. She continued, "I'm sure you can tell that the work so far has been far more gratifying than anything I ever anticipated. The sense of urgency and injustice is such that I no longer feel I have any choice . . . and every day I feel more and more of a gap between us and the rest of the world that is not engaged in trying to change this cruel system."

New Realities

The movement's vision translated into daily realities of hard work and responsibility which admitted few sexual limitations. Young white women's sense of purpose was reinforced by the knowledge that the work they did and the responsibilities they assumed were central to the movement. In the beginning, black and white alike agreed that whites should work primarily in the white community.

They had an appropriate role in urban direct action movements where the goal was integration, but their principal job was generating support for civil rights within the white population. The handful of white women involved in the early sixties either worked in the SNCC office—gathering news, writing pamphlets, facilitating communications—or organized campus support through such agencies as the YWCA.

In direct action demonstrations, many women discovered untapped reservoirs of courage. Cathy Cade attended Spelman College as an exchange student in the spring of 1962. She had been there only two days when she joined Howard Zinn in a sit-in in the black section of the Georgia legislature. Never before had she so much as joined a picket line. Years later she testified: "To this day I am amazed. I just did it." Though she understood the risks involved, she does not remember being afraid. Rather she was exhilarated, for with one stroke she undid much of the fear of blacks that she had developed as a high school student in Tennessee.

Others, like Mimi Feingold, jumped eagerly at the chance to join the freedom rides but then found the experience more harrowing than they had expected. Her group had a bomb scare in Montgomery and knew that the last freedom bus in Alabama had been blown up. They never left the bus from Atlanta to Jackson, Mississippi. The arrest in Jackson was anticlimactic. Then there was a month in jail where she could hear women screaming as they were subjected to humiliating vaginal "searches."

When SNCC moved into voter registration projects in the Deep South, the experiences of white women acquired a new dimension. The years of enduring the brutality of intransigent racism finally convinced SNCC to invite several hundred white students into Mississippi for the 1964 "freedom summer." For the first time, large numbers of white women would be allowed into "the field," to work in the rural South.

They had previously been excluded because white women in rural communities were highly visible; their presence, violating both racial and sexual taboos, often provoked repression. According to Mary King, "the start of violence in a community was often tied to the point at which white women appeared to be in the civil rights movement." However, the presence of whites also brought the attention of the national media, and, in the face of the apparent impotence of the federal law enforcement apparatus, the media became the chief weapon of the movement against violence and brutality. Thus, with considerable ambivalence, SNCC began to include whites—both men and women—in certain voter registration projects.

The freedom summer brought hundreds of Northern white women into the Southern movement. They taught in freedom schools, ran libraries, canvassed for voter registration, and endured constant harassment from the local whites. Many reached well beyond their previously assumed limits: "I was overwhelmed at the idea of setting up a library all by myself," wrote one woman. "Then can you imagine how I felt when at Oxford, while I was learning how to drop on the ground to protect my face, my ears, and my breasts, I was asked to *coordinate* the libraries in the entire project's community centers? I wanted to cry 'Help' in a number of ways."

And while they tested themselves and questioned their own courage, they also experienced poverty, oppression, and discrimination in raw form. As one volunteer wrote:

> For the first time in my life, I am seeing what it is like to be poor, oppressed, and hated. And what I see here does not apply only to Gulfport or to Mississippi or even to the South. . . . This summer is only the briefest beginning of this experience.

Some women virtually ran the projects they were in. And they learned to live with an intensity of fear that they had never known before. By October 1964, there had been fifteen murders, four woundings, thirty-seven churches bombed or burned, and over 1,000 arrests in Mississippi. Every project set up elaborate security precautions—regular communication by two-way radio, rules against going out at night or walking downtown in interracial groups. One woman summed up the experience of hundreds when she explained, "I learned a lot of respect for myself for having gone through all that."

New Role Models

As white women tested themselves in the movement, they were constantly inspired by the examples of black women who shattered cultural images of appropriate "female" behavior. "For the first time," according to one white Southerner, "I had role models I could respect."

Within the movement many of the legendary figures were black women around whom circulated stories of exemplary courage and audacity. Rarely did women expect or receive any special protection in demonstrations or jails. Frequently, direct action teams were equally divided between women and men, on the theory that the presence of women in sit-in demonstrations might lessen the violent reactions. In 1960, slender Diane Nash had been transformed overnight from a Fisk University beauty queen to a principal leader of the direct action movement in Nashville, Tennessee. Within SNCC she argued strenuously for direct action—sit-ins and demonstrations—over voter registration and community organization. By 1962, when she was twenty-two years old and four months pregnant, she confronted a Mississippi judge with her refusal to cooperate with the court system by appealing her two-year sentence or posting bond:

> We in the nonviolent movement have been talking about jail without bail for about two years or more. The time has come for us to mean what we say and stop posting bond. . . . This will be a black baby born in Mississippi, and thus wherever he is born he will be born in prison. I believe that if I go to jail now it may help hasten that day when my child and all children will be free—not only on the day of their birth but for all their lives.

Perhaps even more important than the daring of younger activists was the towering strength of older black women. There is no doubt that women were key to organizing the black community. In 1962 SNCC staff member Charles Sherrod wrote the office that in every southwest Georgia county "there is always a 'mama.' She is usually a militant woman in the community, outspoken, understanding, and willing to catch hell, having already caught her share."

Stories of such women abound. For providing housing, food, and active support to SNCC workers, their homes were fired upon and bombed. Fannie Lou Hamer, the Sunflower County sharecropper who forfeited her livelihood to emerge as one of the most courageous and eloquent leaders of the Mississippi Freedom Democratic Party, was only the most famous. "Mama Dolly" in Lee County, Georgia, was a seventy-year-old, gray-haired lady who could "pick more cotton, slop more pigs, plow more ground, chop more wood, and do a hundred more things better than the best farmer in the area." For many white volunteers, they were also "mamas" in the sense of being mother figures, new models of the meaning of womanhood.

The Undertow of Oppression

Yet new models bumped up against old ones: self-assertion generated anxiety; new expectations existed alongside traditional ones; ideas about freedom and equality bent under assumptions about women as mere houseworkers and sexual objects. These contradictory forces finally generated a feminist response from those who could not deny the reality of their newfound strength.

Black and white women took on important administrative roles in the Atlanta SNCC office, but they also performed virtually all typing and clerical work. Very few women assumed the public roles of national leadership. In 1964 black women held a half-serious, half-joking sit-in to protest these conditions. By 1965 the situation had changed enough that a quarrel over who would take notes at staff meetings was settled by buying a tape recorder.

In the field there was a tendency to assume that housework around the freedom house would be performed by women. As early as 1963 Joni Rabinowitz, a white volunteer in the southwest Georgia Project, submitted a stinging series of reports on the "woman's role."

> Monday, 15 April: . . . The attitude around here toward keeping the house neat (as well as the general attitude toward the inferiority and "proper place" of women) is disgusting and also terribly depressing. I never saw a cooperative enterprize [sic] that was less cooperative.

Those women who had joined the young movement when it included only a handful of whites knew the inner circles of SNCC through years of shared work and risk. They had an easy familiarity with the top leadership which bespoke considerable influence. Yet women like Casey Hayden and Mary King could virtually run a freedom registration program and at the same time remain outside the basic political decision-making process.

Mary King described herself and Hayden as being in "positions of relative powerlessness." They were powerful because they worked very hard. According to King, "If you were a hard worker and you were good, at least before 1965 . . . you could definitely have an influence on policy."

The key phrase is "at least before 1965," for by 1965 the positions of white women in SNCC, especially Southern women whose goals had been shaped by the vision of the "beloved community," was in steep decline. Ultimately, a growing spirit of black nationalism, fed by the tensions of large numbers of whites, especially women, entering the movement, forced these women out of SNCC and precipitated the articulation of a new feminism.

Racial-Sexual Tensions

White women's presence inevitably heightened the sexual tension which runs as a constant current through racist culture. Southern women understood that in the struggle against racial discrimination they were at war with their culture. They reacted to the label "Southern lady" as though it were an obscene epithet, for they had emerged from a society that used the symbol of "Southern white womanhood" to justify an insidious pattern of racial discrimination and brutal repression. They had, of necessity, to forge a new sense of self, a new definition of femininity apart from the one they had inherited. Gradually they came to understand the struggle against racism as "a key to pulling down all the . . . fascist notions and mythologies and institutions in the South," including, as Dorothy Burlage said, "notions about white women and repression."

The entrance of white women in large numbers into the civil rights movement could hardly have been anything but explosive. Interracial sex was the most potent social taboo in the South. And the struggle against racism brought together young, naive, sometimes insensitive, rebellious, and idealistic white women with young, angry black men, some of whom had hardly been allowed to speak to white women before. They sat-in together. If they really believed in equality, why shouldn't they sleep together?

In many such relationships there was much warmth and caring. Several marriages resulted. One young woman described how "a whole lot of things got shared around sexuality—like black men with white women—it wasn't just sex, it was also sharing ideas and fears, and emotional support. . . . My sexuality for myself was confirmed by black men for the first time ever in my life, see . . . and I needed that very badly. . . . It's a positive advantage to be a big woman in the black community."

On the other hand, there remained a dehumanizing quality in many relationships. According to one woman, it "had a lot to do with the fact that people thought they might die." They lived their lives at an incredible pace and could not be very loving toward anybody. "So [people] would go to a staff meeting and . . . sleep with whoever was there."

Sexual relationships did not become a serious problem, however, until interracial sex became a widespread phenomenon in local communities in the summer of 1964. The same summer that opened new horizons to hundreds of women simultaneously induced serious strains within the movement itself. Accounts of what happened vary according to the perspectives of the observer.

Some paint a picture of hordes of "loose" white women coming to the South and spreading corruption wherever they went. One male black leader recounted that "where I was project director we put white women out of the project within the first three weeks because they tried to screw themselves across the city." He agreed that black neighborhood youth tended to be sexually aggressive. "I mean you are trained to be aggressive in this country, but you are also not expected to get a positive response."

Others saw the initiative coming almost entirely from males. According to historian Staughton Lynd, director of the freedom schools, "Every black SNCC worker with perhaps a few exceptions counted it a notch on his gun to have slept with a white woman—as many as possible. And I think that was just very traumatic for the women who encountered that, who hadn't thought that was what going south was about." A white woman who worked in Virginia for several years explained, "It's much harder to say 'no' to the advances of a black guy because of the strong possibility of that being taken as racist."

Clearly the boundary between sexual freedom and sexual exploitation was a thin one. Many women consciously avoided all romantic involvements in intuitive recognition of that fact. Yet the presence of hundreds of young whites from middle- and upper-middle-income families in a movement primarily of poor, rural blacks exacerbated latent racial and sexual tensions beyond the breaking point. The first angry response came not from the surrounding white community (which continually assumed sexual excesses far beyond the reality) but from young black women in the movement.

A black woman pointed out that white women would "do all the shit work and do it in a feminine kind of way while [black women] . . . were out in the streets battling with the cops. So it did something to what [our] femininity was about. We became amazons, less than and more than women at the same time." Another black woman added, "If white women had a problem in SNCC, it was not just a male/woman problem . . . it was also a black woman/ white woman problem. It was a race problem rather than a woman's problem." And a white woman, asked whether she experienced any hostility from black women, responded, "Oh tons and tons! I was very, very afraid of black women, very afraid."

Soon after the 1964 summer project, black women in SNCC sharply confronted male leadership. They charged that they could not develop relationships with the black men because the men did not have to be responsible to them as long as they could turn to involvement with white women.

Black women's anger and demands constituted one part of an intricate maze of tensions and struggles that were in the process of transforming the civil rights movement. SNCC had grown from a small band of sixteen to a swollen staff of 180, of whom half were white. The earlier dream of a beloved community was dead. The vision of freedom lay crushed under the weight of intransigent racism, disillusion with electoral politics and nonviolence, and differences of race, class, and culture within the movement itself. Within the rising spirit of black nationalism, the anger of black women toward white women was only one element. It is in this context that Ruby Doris Smith Robinson, one of the most powerful black women in SNCC, is said to have written a paper on the position of women in SNCC.

Ruby Doris Smith Robinson was a strong woman. As a teenager she had joined the early Atlanta demonstrations during her sophomore year at Spelman College. That year, as a participant in the Rock Hill, South Carolina, sit-in she helped initiate the "jail–no bail" policy in SNCC. A month in the Rock Hill jail bound her to the movement with a zeal born of common suffering, deepened commitment, and shared vision. Soon she was a battle-scarred veteran, respected by everyone and feared by many; she ran the SNCC office with unassailable authority.

As an early leader of the black nationalist faction, Robinson hated white women for years because white women represented a cultural ideal of beauty and "femininity" which by inference defined black women as ugly and unwomanly. She was also aware that women had from time to time to assert their rights as women. In 1964 she participated in and perhaps led the sit-in in the SNCC office protesting the relegation of women to typing and clerical work. Thus, when a anonymous paper entitled "The Position of Women in SNCC" circulated at the tension-filled Waveland conference in the fall of 1964, most of the speculation about its authorship centered on Robinson. She died of cancer in 1968, and we may never know her own assessment of her feelings and intentions in 1964. We do know, however, that tales of the memo generated feminist echoes in the minds of many. And Stokely Carmichael's reputed response that "the only position for women in SNCC is prone" stirred up even more discontent. The persisting myth among white feminists that Robinson wrote and presented this first overt attack on sexism in the movement remains a testimony to the powerful image of black women and of Robinson in particular. It has become a staple in accounts of the revival of feminism. In fact, however, the anonymous author was a Southern white woman who had been active in civil rights since the late 1950s, Casey Hayden.

Rebirth of Feminism

A year later, Casey Hayden and Mary King wrote a signed memo on the same subject, but its tone was more philosophical and conciliatory. As Southern white women who had devoted several years of their lives to the vision of a beloved community, they found the rejection of nonviolence and the trend toward a more ideological, centralized black nationalist movement to be bitterly disillusioning. The second memo was addressed to black women and to some of their friends in the Northern new left in the vain hope of finding a common ground. In it they argued that women, like blacks, "seem to be caught in a common-law caste system that operates, sometimes subtly, forcing them to work around or outside hierarchical structures of power which may exclude them. Women seem to be placed in the same position of assumed subordination in personal situations too. It is a caste system which, at its worst, uses and exploits women."

Hayden and King set the precedent of contrasting the movement's egalitarian ideas with the replication of sex roles within it. They noted the ways in which women's position in society determined women's roles in the movement—like cleaning houses, doing secretarial work, and refraining from active or public leadership. At the same time, they observed, "having learned from the movement to think radically about the personal worth and abilities of people whose role in society had gone unchallenged before, a lot of women in the movement have begun trying to apply those lessons to their own relations with men. Each of us probably has her own story of the various results."

They spoke of the pain of trying to put aside "deeply learned fears, needs, and self-perceptions . . . and . . . to replace them with concepts of people and freedom learned from the movement and organizing." In this process many people in the movement had questioned basic institutions, such as marriage and childrearing. Indeed, such issues had been discussed over and over again, but seriously only among women. The usual male response was laughter, and women were left feeling silly. Hayden and King lamented the "lack of community for discussion: nobody is writing, or organizing, or talking publicly about women, in any way that reflects the problems that various women in the movement came across." Yet despite their feelings of invisibility, their words also demonstrated the ability to take the considerable risks involved in sharp criticisms. Through the movement they had developed too much self-confidence and self-respect to accept passively subordinate roles.

In some ways, the memo was a parting attempt to halt the metamorphosis in the civil rights movement from nonviolence to nationalism, from beloved community to black power. It expressed Hayden and King's pain and isolation as white women in the movement. The black women who received it were on a different historic trajectory. They would fight some of the same battles as women, but in a different context and in their own way.

Their statement represented a flowering of women's consciousness that articulated contradictions felt most acutely by middle-class white women. While black women had been gaining strength and power within the movement, white women's position—at the nexus of sexual and racial conflicts—had become increasingly precarious. Their feminist response, then, was precipitated by loss in the immediate situation, but it was a sense of loss against the even deeper background of new strength and self-worth which the movement had allowed them to develop. Like their foremothers in the nineteenth century, they confronted this dilemma with the tools which the movement had given them: a language to name and describe oppression; a deep belief in freedom, equality, and community soon to be translated into "sisterhood"; a willingness to question and challenge any social institution which failed to meet human needs; and the ability to organize.

It is not surprising that the issues were defined and confronted first by Southern women whose consciousness developed in a context which inextricably and paradoxically linked the fate of women and black people. These spiritual daughters of Sarah and Angelina Grimké kept their expectations low in November 1965. "Objectively," Hayden and King wrote, "the chances seem nil that we could start a movement based on anything as distant to general American thought as a sex-caste system." But change was in the air and youth was on the march.

In the North there were hundreds of women who had shared in the Southern experience for a week, a month, a year, and thousands more who participated vicariously or worked to extend the struggle for freedom and equality into Northern communities. These women were ready to hear what their Southern sisters had to say. The debate within Students for a Democratic Society (SDS) which started in response to Hayden and King's ideas led, two years later, to the founding of the women's liberation movement.

Thus, the fullest expression of conscious feminism within the civil rights movement ricocheted off the fury of black power and landed with explosive force in the Northern, white new left. One month after Hayden and King mailed out their memo, women who had read it staged an angry walkout of a national SDS conference in Champaign-Urbana, Illinois. The only man to defend their action was a black man from SNCC.

This article is based largely on personal interviews conducted during the early seventies with participants in the Southern civil rights movement, and on papers from their personal files.

FOR THE CHILDREN'S SAKE

~ PART SEVEN

Even while we forge new links among women in the changing, diversifying South, we are compelled to keep examining the existing institutions that have influenced and shaped our current conditions. We are and will continue to be called upon to change those institutions in order to ensure that they become or remain responsive to the needs and aspirations of at least half of the population—women. As we look at where we are today, we are increasingly aware of the impact our schoolrooms, our churches, our laws, and our technology exert on our personal experience, and on our future. The struggle to extricate ourselves from the crippling influence of English common law that stubbornly clings to the definition of women as property of men is taking place in legislatures and the courtrooms. Susan Bright takes that struggle into the classroom with a play that examines the roots of our legal status and the ongoing efforts to challenge them, and to bring about a change. But even as we reshape laws, attitudes and assumptions do not always follow swiftly. We still must confront the racial and sexual stereotypes that divide us, depriving us of the individual and collective creativity we need in order to flourish—to survive.

While we are living in an age of wondrous technology, we are fearful and threatened by its destructive potential. Marilou Awiakta reminds us that it is not the nature of a thing itself that breeds destruction but a lack of respect for its nature, as she tries to comprehend the power of the atom within the context of the holistic philosophy of the Cherokee. Again, we are challenged to know, to discover, to share what we find. The vision of a more just world has inspired teachers of every era, and the teachers of today are no different. They see the potential of our young people, and, as we see in the efforts of one teacher, we can't ignore older people either. We are sure to need the energies of both, if we want to mold unifying institutions that take advantage of our natural differences to replace the old, divisive ones.

Among the many voices of the women of the South, a common note is rising. It calls out sometimes loudly, sometimes softly, always firmly, and tells of the growing desire to harmonize with the voices of women around the world. Our goal, our legacy, is a better tomorrow.

THE CHALLENGE

❧ CHRISTINA DAVIS

In the morning when I rise each day
I raise my eyes to the skies
And say, there's some struggle in this life
just to live it. . . .
Yes, in the morning when I rise each day
And I raise my eyes to the skies
I say, it's the struggle in this life
That keeps us going . . . going . . . going

There are sisters, women, mothers who are under attack
By a system that is trying to bring slavery back
There are workers who are trying to stop the lies
In a fight for compensation that's no compromise
In our struggles to unite and fight for the cause
We are threatened with division thru tactics and laws
There's a challenge that's been issued that we now must take
If the world will be maintained for the children's sake
So listen sisters, women, mothers there can be no doubt
That for united struggle is what we all must be about

MOCK TRIAL

⚬ SUSAN BRIGHT

Cast of Characters

> ELDER: one who voices the ethics or values of a culture (six readers)
> LEGISLATOR: one who makes laws (twelve readers)
> JUDGE: one who interprets the law, a branch or agency of the state (eight readers)
> PLAINTIFF: one who places a complaint before a court of law (three readers)

Setting

> Western Civilization

Story

> One in which women have been stereotyped as
> 1) wife and mother
> 2) infantile and incompetent
> 3) seductive and immoral
> 4) nonpersons and nonentities

Stage Directions

> Seat three Plaintiff women along one side of the square. On the other three sides, respectively, seat the Elders, the Judges, and the Legislators (comprising the rest of the readers)

· · ·

PLAINTIFF 1: . . . before our government can be a true democracy
. . . the civil and political rights of every citizen must be practically
established. (Susan B. Anthony, 1863)

ELDER 1: A daughter is less desirable than a son. (Lev. 12)

ELDER 2: A daughter can be sold for debt by her father. (Exod. 21)

ELDER 3: A daughter can be made a prostitute by her father.
(Judg. 19)

PLAINTIFF 2: Woman was and is condemned to a system under
which the lawful rapes exceed the unlawful ones a million to one.
(Margaret Sanger, *Woman and the New Race,* 1920)

ELDER 4: Let the woman learn in silence with all subjection. But
suffer not a woman to teach, nor usurp authority over the man; but
be in silence. (1 Tim.)

ELDER 5: Wives, submit yourselves unto your own husbands, as
unto the Lord. For the husband is the head of the wife. (1 Cor.)

JUDGE 1: By marriage, the husband and wife as one person in law:
that is, the very being or legal existence of the woman is suspended
during marriage, or at least is incorporated and consolidated into
that of the husband, under whose protection, and cover, she per-
forms everything, and is therefore called in our law *femme covert,*
covert-baron, or under the protection and influence of her husband, her baron, or lord. (*Blackstone's Commentaries on the Laws of
England,* 1800)

PLAINTIFF 3: Witness the records of the courts with the wife-beat-
ers and slayers, the rapists, the seducers, the husbands who have
deserted their families, the schemers who have defrauded widows
and orphans—witness all these and then say if men are the natural
protectors of women. (Susan B. Anthony, *History of Woman Suffrage,* IV, 1902)

ELDER 6: The woman is to keep silent and is the transgressor. (1
Tim.)

PLAINTIFF 1: This perception of woman as inferior, subservient, silent, and obedient became part of English law, and Blackstone, in his eighteenth-century *Commentaries on the Laws of England,* a document that had great influence on the American legal system, describes women as:

> ... chattels, in effect slaves, their legal existence suspended during marriage, with limited freedom of movement, little right to property or earnings, no control over the children, and no political or civil rights of any kind. Blackstone's quip (slightly paraphrased) that "Husband and wife are one and that one is the husband" was no idle jest. At the very moment when a man met his bride at the altar and said to her, "With all my worldly goods I thee endow," he was actually taking every cent she possessed. ... He could beat her with a stick "no bigger than the wedding ring." All this on account of her "Defectum sexus."

(American Civil Liberties Union from a brief prepared in 1961 for Gwendolyn Holt, who had been tried and found guilty of murder in Florida by an all-male jury.)

LEGISLATOR 1: All men are created equal. (Thomas Jefferson, Declaration of Independence, 1776)

PLAINTIFF 2: Men wrote the Constitution; women were expressly excluded in intent and content. (Wilma Scott Heide to U.S. Senate Subcommittee on Constitutional Amendments, 1970. *Equal Rights,* U.S. Government Printing Office)

LEGISLATOR 2: Words in the masculine gender shall embrace a female as well as a male, unless a contrary intention may be manifest. (Mississippi Code: General Provisions)

PLAINTIFF 3: I should like to practice law in Virginia. (Belva Lockwood, 1893)

LEGISLATOR 3: ... any person duly authorized and practicing as counsel or attorney at law in any State or Territory of the United States, or in the District of Columbia, may practice as such in the courts of this State. (Virginia Statute, 1893)

JUDGE 2: In the above statute the word *person* refers to males and therefore Belva Lockwood shall not be admitted to practice law before the Virginia Supreme Court of Appeals. (*Lockwood* v. *The Virginia Court of Appeals,* U.S. Supreme Court Decision, 1893)

LEGISLATOR 4: A person qualified to vote for representatives to the general court shall be liable to serve as a juror. (Massachusetts Statute, 1931)

JUDGE 3: The court agrees in the general sense "person" includes women and that the word by itself is an equivocal word; however, by the true construction of the statutes of this commonwealth, in the light of relevant constitutional provisions, women are not eligible to jury service. (*Commonwealth of Massachusetts* v. *Welosky,* 1951)

LEGISLATOR 5: To give her [women] the ballot is to unsex her and replace the tender, loving, sweet-featured mother of the past with the cold, calculating, harsh-faced, street corner scold of politics. (Suffrage Debate, United States House of Representatives, Congressman Frank Clark of Florida, 1915)

LEGISLATOR 6: But, Mr. Speaker, she is not to go out in the world to meet its trials, engage in its struggles, and fight its battles, and I venture to remark, without the slightest fear of successful contradiction, that no instance in American life can be found where any woman ever did this voluntarily who had a husband who was worth the powder and lead that would be required to kill him. (Suffrage Debate, United States House of Representatives, Congressman Frank Clark of Florida, 1915)

PLAINTIFF 1: A sister has well remarked that we do not believe that man is the cause of all our wrongs. We do not fight men; we fight bad principles. (Ernestine L. Rose, Fourth National Woman's Rights Convention, 1853, *History of Woman Suffrage,* I, 1881)

LEGISLATOR 7: I am absolutely safe in asserting that practically all the women in America who are happily married are opposed to suffrage. In opposing this measure, I am speaking for that vast multitude of American wives and mothers who love their husbands and their children and who prefer to reign as queen of the home rather than to grovel in the slums of politics.... (Suffrage Debate, United States House of Representatives, Congressman Frank Clark of Florida, 1915.)

PLAINTIFF 2: We hold that whatever is essentially wrong for women to do, cannot be right for man. (J. Elizabeth Jones, "Address to the Women of Ohio," 1850, *History of Woman Suffrage,* 1, 1881)

PLAINTIFF 3: The real goddesses of Liberty in this country do not spend a large amount of time standing on pedestals; they use their torches to startle bats in political cellars. (Ella S. Stewart, speaking of Bartholdi's Statue of Liberty at the National American Woman Suffrage Association Convention, 1909, *History of Woman Suffrage,* V, 1922)

LEGISLATOR 8: Nature destined woman to be the homemaker, the child rearer, while man is the moneymaker. The most sacred and potential spot on earth is the fireside shrine. Here the child receives its morals, its religion, its character; and over this shrine the devoted mother presides as the reigning sovereign, the uncrowned queen ... (Suffrage Debate, United States House of Representatives, Congressman Edwin Webb, 1915)

PLAINTIFF 3: The law, it seems, has done little but perpetuate the myth of the helpless female best kept on her pedestal. In truth, however, that pedestal is a cage bound by a constricting social system and hemmed in by layers of archaic and antifeminist laws. (Faith Seidenberg, "The Submissive Majority: Modern Trends in the Law Concerning Women's Rights," *Cornell Law Review* IV, January 1970)

LEGISLATOR 9: I am opposed to it [women's suffrage] because it would thrust the ballot into the hands of millions of ignorant Negro women. (Texas Suffrage Debate, Texas State Legislature, Congressman Martin Dies, January 12, 1915)

PLAINTIFF 1: It is not the intelligent woman versus the ignorant woman; not the white woman versus the black, the brown, and the red—it is not even the cause of woman versus man. Nay, woman's strongest vindication for speaking is that the world needs to hear her voice. (Anna Julia Cooper, a black woman of the South, *A Voice From the South,* 1892)

LEGISLATOR 10: I wish to speak against this amendment on behalf of the millions of American mothers who are detained at home on more important business. No doubt some of these absent mothers are busy extracting splinters from the toes of future congressmen, hearing the lessons of future Supreme Court judges, boxing the ears of future generals, buttering the bread of future senators, or soothing with a lullaby the injured feelings of a future president. (Texas Suffrage Debate, Texas State Legislature, Congressman Martin Dies, January 12, 1915)

LEGISLATOR 11: I have no doubt that if women handled the cleaver at the beef stalls we would get cleaner steaks, but what man wants to court a butcher? [Laughter] No doubt women would make excellent peace officers, but what man wants to marry a policeman? [Laughter] It may be that the entrance of pure women into dirty politics would have a cleansing effect upon the politics, but I cannot believe that it would have that effect upon the women. And in a case of that kind we had better have soiled linen than soiled laundresses. (Texas Suffrage Debate, Texas State Legislature, Congressman Martin Dies, January 12, 1915)

PLAINTIFF 3: It has always been thought perfectly womanly to be a scrubwoman in the legislature and to take care of the spittoons; that is entirely within the charmed circle of woman's sphere, but for women to occupy any of these official seats would be degrading. (Susan B. Anthony, National American Woman Suffrage Association Convention, 1895, *History of Woman Suffrage,* IV, 1902)

PLAINTIFF 1: The fear of sacrificing femininity at the altar of success has kept thousands of girls in their place. (Letty Cottin Pogrebin, *How to Make It in a Man's World,* 1970)

PLAINTIFF 3: You may tell us that our place is in the home. There are 8 million of us in these United States who must go out of it to earn our daily bread, and we come to tell you that while we are working in the mills, the mines, the factories, and the mercantile houses we have not the protection that we should have. You have been making laws for us and the laws you have made have not been good for us. (Leonora O'Reilly, address to joint session of the Senate Judiciary Committee and Senate Committee on Woman Suffrage, 1912, *History of Woman Suffrage,* V, 1922)

PLAINTIFF 1: The war-horses of the fight for suffrage sometimes complain, indeed, that the young take the vote, and so on, for granted. So they should. Its denial is an outrage. Its possession is elementary justice and common sense. The younger women have a hard enough task before them. They have got to win the next stage—real equality of opportunity and freedom of choice. (Mary Agnes Hamilton, *Women at Work,* 1941)

PLAINTIFF 2: . . . to be tried by a jury of my peers, for example.

LEGISLATOR 12: Women do not wish their rights to be passed upon by women. . . . They know the leniency of men. (Congressman

Stanley Bowdie of Ohio, United States House of Representatives, January 12, 1915)

PLAINTIFF 3: We are speaking of very basic human rights.

JUDGE 4: The name of no female person shall be taken for jury service unless said person has registered with the clerk of the circuit court her desire to be placed on the jury list. (Florida Supreme Court, 1959)

PLAINTIFF 1: Of my two handicaps, being female put many more obstacles in my path than being black. (Shirley Chisholm, *Unbought and Unbossed*, 1970)

JUDGE 5: The legislature has the right to exclude women from jury duty to protect them from the filth, obscenity, and noxious atmosphere that so often pervades a courtroom during a jury trial. (Mississippi Supreme Court, 1966)

PLAINTIFF 2: Masculine ethics, colored by masculine instincts, always dominated by sex, has at once recognized the value of chastity in the woman, which is right; punished its absence unfairly, which is wrong; and then reversed the whole matter when applied to men, which is ridiculous. (Charlotte Perkins Gilman, "Charlotte Perkins Gilman's Dynamic School Philosophy," *Current Literature*, July 1911)

LEGISLATOR 1: Men shall be chosen over women to administer the estate of a person dying in the state [without having made a will]. (Provision I. C. 15.314 Idaho Statute)

PLAINTIFF 1: It is my family. I am the correct person to administer the estate. (Sally Reed, *Reed* v. *Reed*, Idaho Supreme Court, 1950)

JUDGE 6: Philosophically it can be argued with some degree of logic that the provisions of I. C. 15.314 do discriminate against women on the basis of sex. However, nature itself has established the distinction, that in general men are better qualified to act as administrators of estates than are women. (*Reed* v. *Reed*, Idaho Supreme Court, 1970.)

PLAINTIFF 3: Discrimination because of one's sex is just as degrading, dehumanizing, immoral, unjust, indefensible, infuriating, and capable of producing social turmoil as discrimination because of one's race. (Pauli Murray, *Discrimination*, U.S. Government Printing Office, 1971)

PLAINTIFF 1: I'm going to Tuscaloosa and get me a damn job and you can take the baby! (Words spoken in a public place by Gertrude Price, Alabama, 1948—for which offense she was sentenced to jail, Haig Bosmajian, *Sexism and Language,* National Council of Teachers of English, 1977)

JUDGE 7: The evidence shows that women were present at the time the defendant [arresting police officer] claims she used the word in the café. Whether a girl or woman actually heard the word *damn* was not important, according to the court, for "to constitute a violation of such provision it is not necessary to show that a female heard the language used. It is the fact of presence, subject to insult if the language is heard, which is the essence of the offense. (*Price* v. *McConnell,* Alabama Supreme Court, 1948)

PLAINTIFF 2: Allowing men stronger means of expression than are open to women further reinforces men's positions of strength in the real world; for surely we listen with more attention the more strongly and forcefully someone expresses opinions, and a speaker unable—for whatever reason—to be forceful in stating views is much less likely to be taken seriously. (Robin Lakoff, *Language and Woman's Place,* 1975)

PLAINTIFF 3: I recognize for myself no narrow sphere. Where you may work, my brother, I may work. (Lucy N. Coleman, Women's National Loyal League, 1863)

JUDGE 8: . . . trying to hold a married woman liable on a contract that under the law of Texas she is incapable of making is no more reasonable than to hold that a minor, or one of unsound mind, could be held liable to a contract. (*United States* v. *Yazell,* 1964)

PLAINTIFF 1: Once the status of women was identified in legislation and court opinions with that of children (and slaves and the insane), denying the female the rights and duties expected by and from a male became not only easier but apparently logical and legal. It was a simple matter of definition, and the person who had the power to define controlled the destiny of those being defined. (Haig Bosmajian, *Sexism and Language,* National Council of Teachers of English, 1977)

PLAINTIFF 2: Only one thing can make me see the justness of women being classed with the idiot, the insane, and the criminal and that is, if she is willing, if she is satisfied to be so classed. It is idiotic not to want one's liberty; it is insane not to value one's inalienable rights, and it is criminal to neglect one's God-given responsibilities. (Judith Hyams Douglas, 1908, *History of Woman Suffrage, V,* 1922)

PLAINTIFF 1: We have all been thrown down so low that nobody thought we'd ever get up again; but we have been long enough trodden now; we will come up again.... (Sojourner Truth, Woman's Rights Convention, 1853, *History of Woman Suffrage,* I, 1881)

PLAINTIFF 2: We have declared in favor of a government of the people, for the people, by the people, the whole people. Why not begin the experiment? (Elizabeth Cady Stanton, to Senate Judiciary Committee, 1872, *History of Woman Suffrage,* II, 1882)

The text for this reading draws heavily on two sources: "Sexism in the Language of Legislatures and Courts," by Haig Bosmajian, in Sexism and Language *(National Council of Teachers of English, 1977) and* Feminist Quotations: Voices of Rebels, Reformers, and Visionaries, *compiled by Carol McPhee and Ann Fitzgerald (Thomas Crowell, 1979).*

THE LONESOMES AIN'T NO
SPRING PICNIC

✎ BIRTHALENE MILLER

Me and Candy sitting in the swing pumping it slow and easy, float-
ing out in air so full of spring that if we close our eyes we can smell
the grass growing. We're counting together, aiming on going up to
a thousand for no reason at all, except to show Jeffrie and Jimmie
and Rhodie that there is one more thing that we can do that they
can't. Just letting the devil git ahold of our souls, Grandpop would
say. We stop when he come out into the yard.

He's got on his best dark blue marking-for-death suit, and he
carry his pearl-handled walking stick in one hand and the Bible in
the other. Candy and me cross our fingers and watch him walk
down the street. When he's out of sight I open my mouth and my
breath comes popping out like soap bubbles. I'm that relieved.

I look at Candy and she's shaking. "Why you still scared?" I say.
"He done gone past your house."

Candy say, "I hear a screech owl last night right outside my window."

"You hold your wrist and choke it till you make it quit hollering
and tell it to go away and mark somebody else for bad luck or dying?"

"Yeah, but what if the devil git me alive for doing it the way
your grandpop always preaching?"

"I druther the devil git me alive than he git me dead," I say, but
I whisper it so that Rhodie can't tattletale it the way she do everything, even the time she catch me and Candy with our hands on
each other doing a thing that Grandpop say is an admonition to the
Lord and eternal damnation to our souls. We still do it sometimes.

We try not to, though, cause we're scared of what God'll do to us if He catch us.

Candy is thinking of that now, I know, cause she look worried and I start worrying, too. We start up the swing again but there's no joy in it now. The world that smell so clean and green and sweet just smell sad like funerals now, and we git down and go into the kitchen.

Grandma is baking custard pies. She's got a streak of flour, white as death's pale horse, smeared across her face. She's looking toward us but her eyes are going on through us, and she's mumbling to herself.

"Grandma?" I ask. "Grandma, who is it going to die?"

Grandma don't answer but start in rolling out the dough and I see she's mad or upset from the heavy way she is leaning on the dough roller.

"Grandma, who is it going to die?" I say again, and Grandma look at me finally and say, "Ain't nobody going to die, if the Lord be merciful." But her eyes got that look of her body being here and her mind over yonder someplace, like she's two people at once. Make a chill run up and down my spine. What Miz Rose call a possum walking over my grave. But I don't want to think about no graves now, especially my own, and I grab Candy's hand.

We just the other side of the door when Grandma start in mumbling again. "Lord, pore little Sue Ellen ... Lord, all alone and scared."

"Sue Ellen?" Candy ask, but I can't answer because of the catball that's suddenly caught in my throat. We go out and set on the front steps. Just quiet and holding hands. It is the first time we ever know Grandpop to mark someone so young for dying. Sixteen.

After a long while Candy ask, "Why'd he want to go and do that to her?"

I say, "He don't do the choosing. The Lord do that. Grandpop just points out them that the Lord say to."

Candy say, "I wonder what she dying from?"

"I know," Rhodie say, crawling out from under the steps beneath us. "She dying from forcation."

"What?" me and Candy say together, and then I say, "Look here, Rhodie, Grandpop is going to git you for saying ugly words like that."

Rhodie say, "He say it hisself."

"That's different. Preachers have got to say what the Lord tell them to and if He tell them to say a bad word, they gotta say it."

Rhodie plops the bottle against her doll's painted lips and asks, "Why is forcation a bad word?"

"Cause ... just cause it is," I say, trying to sound knowing. "And another thing, if you keep telling them lies, Grandpop is gonna strap you."

"What lies?" Rhodie cry, looking like she don't even know what I'm talking about. Sometimes I wonder how she can be my sister, she's so dumb.

I say, "Them lies you tell about Sue Ellen dying from—"

"Ain't lies," Rhodie say. "Sue Ellen dying from forcation. Deacon Riddell say it hisself and she his own daughter."

"Niece," I say. "Just cause she live with them don't make them her parents. And the word is fornication, dummy. Don't nobody die from it."

"Do too. Grandpop and Deacon both say Sue Ellen dying from it."

"When they say that?" I ask.

"A few minutes ago. When they come up the street. They in the church now."

I can see the church door open. "What else they say?"

"Deacon tell Grandpop he raise her up in the straight and narrow, and he never allowed her to smoke or drink or paint her face or wear short skirts or mess around with boys."

I wonder again how Sue Ellen stayed so gay and friendly living with two people what always go round like their mouth full of straight pins and they afraid to smile for fear they swallow one.

I see Grandpop and Deacon come out of the church and go into the cemetery.

"Picking out a spot for the grave," Candy say.

"Don't have to pick one. They'll put her beside her mama and daddy," I say, but the two men walk past Sue Ellen's parents' graves and on to the far corner of the cemetery. Deacon bend down and start driving down the burial stake.

There ain't no graves at all in that section and I think of Sue Ellen with her pretty face and smile being put off all by herself and my eyes run over with tears and Candy keeps asking over and over, "Why they putting her there, Mary Anne? Why they putting her there?"

She look at me and see I'm crying and she start crying, too. We don't want to watch no more, and we go round the house and set on the bench beneath the bare wisteria vines that crook over into themselves like they got a hurt, too, like me and Candy has. I got a worry, also, that keep gnawing at me. I say, "Don't see how Sue Ellen . . . I mean, how she can . . . what with her not going with no boys."

"And no men, neither."

"Lizzie Beth Collins . . . she all the time with her. She the one. Got to be."

Me and Candy look at each other. Then we both move down the bench as far away as we can from each other and Jeffrie and Jimmie sneak up behind us and start shouting, "Bang! Bang! You dead!"

They stop hollering suddenly and I look up and see Grandma standing on the steps. She say, "For shame . . . Lord, as if there ain't enough killing and dying in this world without you two play-acting it. You, Jeffrie, you Jimmie, throw them sticks down right now!"

Grandma ain't quite five feet tall, not much more'n me and Candy and we eight—or almost—years old. But Grandma's voice got ten feet of do-what-I-say in it, and the boys throw the gunsticks down quicker'n they be red hot coals.

Grandma say, "Candice, your mama want you and the boys to go home now, and Mary Anne, you and Rhodie's dinner is on the table. Pearl and me are taking some pies over to Miz Rose's and the Deacon's."

After Rhodie finally git through dawdling over dinner I go outside and Candy come over. We set on the steps but far apart. After a while Grandma and Miz Pearl come back. As they coming up the walk Grandma saying, "But Lord, a coat hanger!"

Miz Pearl look at me and Candy, and she poke Grandma in the ribs. They go up the steps past me and Candy. They set down in the rockers and Miz Pearl say, "That Deacon Riddell . . . expecting any minute for the corpse to be brought back from the undertaker, and all he can talk about is the disgrace." Her and grandma whisper to each other.

When they hush whispering Grandma say, "You see what I see? Two cats so full of curiosity that they going to bust open in a minute. Friday and the last spring holiday from school and you two waste it just setting around eavesdropping."

"We ain't eavesdropping. We watching them dig Sue Ellen's grave."

"And they digging it in the far corner," I add.

"Mary Anne, what are you talking about? Her parents buried in the middle."

"Yes'm, I know, but. . . ."

"They burying her in the new ground they take in. Way over at the far end of it," Candy burst in ahead of me.

Miz Pearl and Grandma both get up and look.

Grandma say, "Lord, they right, Pearl. That pore motherless. . . ." She moan and press her hands against her belly like she got a pain in it somewhere.

Grandpop come into the yard and up the steps like he don't even see Grandma or Miz Pearl or me or Candy, though we got to quick jerk back to keep his death-marking clothes from touching us.

"Mr. Robinson, may I have a word with you, please?" Grandma say, low and respectful, like Grandpop preach in the pulpit that it's the duty of a woman to be that way cause she neath her husband, being only his rib and he got to all the time stand with his shadow between her and God.

"Speak ahead, woman," Grandpop say.

"Private. Please," she say.

"All right, but it will have to be fast," Grandpop say. His eyes have that look they always git when he's working on one of his pulpit-thumping, window-rattling, hellfire breathing sermons.

Grandma shut the door behind her and Grandpop. We can't hear what she saying but we hear him plenty good through the open window.

"Fitting? Fitting? A fornicator and a murderer. What would be a more fitting place for us to bury her? Less'n we bury her outside the cemetery altogether?"

"But just a child." Grandma talking louder now. "What if it was Mary Anne or Rhodie? In a few years they will be young ladies . . ."

"And it will be the church's duty to make them and all other young folks know that the wages of sin is death everlasting."

"Mr. Robinson!" Grandma cry. "You're not fixing to preach a hell damnation sermon over that poor girl's body, are you?"

"The Lord puts the words in my mouth. I only say them."

"But . . ."

"Enough, woman. I got to be about the Lord's work."

Grandpop come back out and go across to his church. After a while we hear Grandma talking on the phone. She's on the phone a long time, forever it seem, and the warm spring afternoon run quickly toward cold sunset. The air so still and heavy with flower smell and sunshine and wet, I feel like I'm looking through glass. Lying on my side in a goldfish bowl and looking across the yard and the cemetery at the grave diggers and the water so quiet and heavy over me that I can hear the thud-thump of the hard shovels against clay and the far-off distant sound of Grandma talking.

When she finally come out, her eyes shining with mad. She say, "Lord! Men! The tribulation of them." She walk up and down the porch. And down and up it. She moan as she walk. "Lord . . . that pore . . . Lord, that lily-livered woman wanting to do better but always obeying that rockhearted man of hers."

She stop pacing finally and stand staring at the church. "Lord, why you lay such a burden on womenfolks by putting that obeying thing in?"

After a while, she turn and go into the house and start rattling the pots, and Miz Pearl tell Candy to come along and help her get supper, cause afterward they all going over to the Riddells'. Candy look at me and I see how bad she hate the thought of going. I reach out my hand to her. Our hands are all but touching when we remember and jerk them back.

I watch her go and the loneliness is a boil inside me aching to pop itself. I go inside. Grandma hears mine and Rhodie's prayers and tucks us into bed. I ain't sleepy and I git up and go to the bathroom. When I pass the opened door of Grandpop's and Grandma's room I peep inside and see Grandma sitting all alone and quiet and reading the Bible.

Seeing her like that gives me a bad case of the lonesomes. But everywhere is going to be lonesome from now on without Candy, I think, and I crawl under the quilt beside Rhodie. I think of Sue Ellen and the lonesomeness of her grave off by itself. I think of all the lonesomeness in the world. Then I think of dying and hellfire and I throw the covers back and pull my gown up and look at my body. I expect to see the red flickering of flames on it, but the streetlights coming in through the shades make it look green. And I think that maybe it's poisonous for me or anybody else to touch ever again.

In the morning Grandma and Grandpop don't say nothing to each other. After we all dress up in our funeral-going clothes we set in the living room and wait for the hearse to bring the corpse. Grandma set with her black purse in one hand and her Bible in the other and with the quiet all around her. Grandpop keep looking at her. Finally he say, as if he can't stand it no more, "Idie, what is it? What's ailing you?"

Grandma set on as though she don't even hear him, even though I know she do and even though she always before pay heed to every word he say, like the Bible says to. That's the reason I decided I ain't never going to git married but just always have lots of boyfriends.

Grandpop ask, "Is it the grave?"

Grandma don't say nothing and Grandpop say, "Idie, you know that I got to say and do the things the Lord tell me to."

"And I got to do and say the things He tell me to," Grandma speaks at last.

Grandpop open his mouth wide to say something but just then he see the hearse coming and he grab his hat up and run out.

Grandma follow him and me and Rhodie follow Grandma. Candy join me in the church yard and we follow the people inside. When we all seated I look up and see Grandpop standing at one end of the casket and Grandma standing at the other end. I don't understand that cause everybody but the preacher is supposed to be setting. And I don't understand it even more when Grandpop go up into the pulpit and Grandma go up behind him and stop in front of the pulpit stand so she between Grandpop and the congregation. Everybody look at her, not understanding. Everything so quiet you could drop a straight pin point down and hear it hit.

Grandma open her mouth and speak and her voice is as quiet and peaceful as winter rain dripping past a bedtime window. She say, "I know that most, maybe even all of you, think it sinful for a woman to speak in church. Preacher"—she nod over her shoulder at Grandpop—"Reverend Robinson say it and I respect him as my husband and my preacher. But there is somebody else I respect, too. Some people. Though many say they don't need or deserve respect. I say they do. I say until they git their respect this world going to go on being messed up."

People look at Grandma and some begin to shift around and clear their throats, small noises grating against the quiet, cracking the thick hull of it.

Grandma look at the crack in the quiet and she draw the quiet closer around herself. She say. "Women—that's who I'm talking about. Women all the time git blamed for every sin done under the sun. Some we do. Some we don't. But nearly always the sin we do we don't do alone. There's a man do it with us and he just as guilty. Only he, being a man, don't git the blame heaped on him like us women do."

She look down into the slowly widening crack and she say, "There's someone, a man, or a boy what think he's a man, who ain't one bit less guilty than Sue Ellen. But I don't see nobody pointing him out, accusing him of his sins. And he, more'n likely, setting right here among us."

The people turn slowly from looking at Grandma and begin alooking at each other and I see them wondering as I am. A boy or a man, I think—and not Lizzie Beth Collins. The worry that has been corked up inside me comes spewing out like half-frozen Coke.

Grandma say, "Sue Ellen in years scarcely more than a child. But she die the death of a woman. If there be any woman here today what can love or pity her because of, or despite of, what she did, I invite that woman to step forward and help me in burying this, our dead sister."

Grandma stand waiting in the quietness that is so thick that I feel I can reach out and touch it, so soft and deep that I can put my whole hand in it. Grandpop still standing behind her, and he look like he don't know what to do or say, and the people all look at Grandma and nobody move. Then suddenly Miz Pearl git up quick and go stand beside Grandma. Lizzie Beth and several other girls and some women go up. Me and Candy go up, hand in hand.

Deacon Riddell jump up. The frowns in his face so deep you could plant a turnip patch in them. He cry, "Preacher, I object to such unorthodox proceedings."

Grandpop don't say nothing, and Grandma go down and stand at the head of the casket. We follow her and I look down at Sue Ellen's face. It look as calm and peaceful and quiet as Grandma's. And so beautiful. The beautifulest face I ever see. Except Grandma's now with the softness on it like light. She say, "Let us pray."

After the service Miz Pearl and five other women act as pallbearers. They start to carry the casket toward the red mound of dirt in the far corner of the graveyard, but Grandma stop them. She pick Miz Riddell out of the crowd following along behind us. She say, "You, Lucille. You Sue Ellen's only blood kin. You decide where you want her buried—alongside her parents or way off in the corner by herself." She point to the two mounds of dirt—one that we see yesterday and a new one in the middle of the cemetery. I stare at the nearest mound and Miz Riddell and everybody else stare at it. All except Grandma, who look as if there ain't nothing unusual about a grave gitting dug all by itself in the middle of the night.

Miz Riddell look at the grave, "Please," she say. "She has been a daughter to me for twelve years." Tears come running down her face.

"An admonition unto the Lord," Deacon interrupt. "I say she is to be buried in the grave I pick for her."

"No!" Miz Riddell say. She say it low at first. Then she say it louder. "No!" And her sobbing overtakes her.

Deacon say, "The Bible says wives obey their husbands."

"The Bible says it all right," Grandma say. "But it say a lot of other things, too, like love and mercy and he without sin casting the first. . ."

"Right in God's own Book. It say wives obey their husbands and. . . ."

"Maybe it say that just cause it's written there by men," Grandma say.

Deacon's face quiver like there is water under it boiling. "Heresy!" he screech. "Preacher! A heretic!"

Grandpop been standing back in the crowd. He step forward now and lay a big hand upon Deacon's shoulder. He say, "No member of my church going to call no other member a heretic. Especially no one going to call my wife one." He look around at the crowd and then back down at Deacon. "The women have taken it upon themselves to conduct this funeral. Let us let them carry on with it," he say and turn and walk slowly out of the cemetery and into his church.

Deacon stare after Grandpop. Then he spit upon the ground and march out of the cemetery, too.

When we pass the church after finishing burying Sue Ellen, I see Grandpop setting in his study. Even after it is dark out and the spring air is thick with a misting of rain, I still see him setting alone and lonesome looking.

I lay awake a long time thinking of the day and Grandma and the strange ways of women and men. Rhodie flops over toward me and abandons her pillow and burrows into mine. I start to push her away but don't. I lay breathing her breath and it smell warm and rich and sweet like the hot chocolate Grandma give us before putting us to bed. I think of Candy and, with the secret fear and guilty worry that Sue Ellen's death brought gone, the thought of her is warm and gentle and sweet again in my mind.

QUEEN OF THE ROAD

⤳ LIZ WHEATON

Unlike most young girls thirty years ago, Edna Kilgo dreamed of becoming a truck driver. She collected model trucks; she studied the mammoth eighteen-wheelers and felt butterflies rise in her breast when she saw them, heard them, and smelled them on the road. She married a trucker and longed to ride with him across the hills of Georgia to places she'd read about in books—everywhere a gutsy woman and a magnificent machine could travel.

Edna rode with her husband, and even drove a few times, before the babies started coming.

Her marriage eventually disintegrated, but Edna's white line fever didn't abate. The model truck collection grew as did her four children, and eventually she met a man—not a trucker—who loved and accepted Edna, the children, and the dream. They married in 1967.

For eight long years Edna lived her dream vicariously; she worked as a secretary for a Florida trucking firm. Meanwhile, she kept trying for a driver's slot. "I offered to work for nothing to learn how to drive. I even offered to buy my own insurance on the truck and the load I would carry." But the response was always the same: Come back when you've got driving experience.

Edna's big break came in 1975—or so she thought. An eight-week, state-certified truck driving course was offered at a county vocational school near her home in Florida. Edna registered immediately.

Then came the first setback: the Kilgo family had to move to Atlanta. During the six months before the course began Edna raised the extra money she would need to attend school away from home.

She worked odd jobs. "Anything that was legal," she said. "I asked no one for help, not even my husband." This was *her* dream. On the day Edna towed her fifteen-foot camper from Atlanta to school in Eagle Lake, Florida, she had 700 hard-earned dollars in her pocket.

Edna relished school. "I wouldn't trade anything for the experience," she said. She studied and listened and learned; she took the school's eighteen-wheeler on test drives and practiced maneuvering through back roads, city traffic, and parking lots; she learned standard maintenance procedures and emergency driving techniques.

When she returned to Atlanta, with diploma in hand and the sweet taste of victory in her mouth, every other member of her class had a driving job lined up, including the four other women who were "going doubles" with their husbands. Her instructors had warned that it would be virtually impossible for a woman to break into the trucking industry on her own, but Edna was confident that the situation in Atlanta would be different from that in rural Polk County, Florida.

Fourteen months and over a hundred trucking companies later, Edna had not been allowed to take the first driving test and only one firm had so much as given her an application to fill out. "I worked and scrimped and saved, and I graduated near the top of my class. But what did I graduate to? To be told that I needed anywhere from six months to four years all-weather, over-the-road experience."

Edna knew that most men can find trucking jobs without over-the-road experience, and she knew that laws prohibit discrimination against women. At forty-five years of age and a grandmother, Edna approached the Southern Regional Office of the American Civil Liberties Union in Atlanta in early 1979.

ACLU attorney Christopher Coates recognized that this unique case could help break the trucking industry open for women. With financial and legal support from the ACLU Women's Rights Project, Coates filed *Kilgo* v. *Bowman Transportation* on April 23, 1979.

Self-assured and beaming with pride, Edna spoke at the news conference called to announce the class-action lawsuit: "I want the feel of the wheel in my hand, smell the diesel smoke, eat greasy food and complain about it, get upset over weekend layovers, and all the other things that make up the world of trucking. I've got white line fever, and when I'm under the wheel of the eighteen-wheeler I feel like I'm queen of the road. I may never be able to drive an eighteen-wheeler again, but maybe in some way it will help other women to break into the trucking industry."

Edna Kilgo's statement was prophetic. On May 20, 1983, in the Federal District Court in Atlanta, Georgia, the judge ruled in favor of Kilgo. The ruling against Bowman struck down as discriminatory the experience requirement which had been used to keep blacks and women out. A number of other practices used by Bowman to discourage women were also declared illegal. Although Edna Kilgo died in October 1979, she left a legacy to the other women who will be the beneficiaries of her courageous action.

LISTEN!!

✣ MAXINE ALEXANDER

LISTEN!!
LISTEN TO ME!

they've poisoned the water
we can no longer drink the water
they've stripped the trees of foliage
they've stripped the beaches of dunes
and wage daily war against the rainforests
they are killing the seeds of the future
already the fruits of the earth grow twisted
and deceptively plentiful to the eye
our bodies reek
we are afraid to bathe
in the poisoned waters

and the fingers of our grandchildren no longer number five

PLEASE LISTEN!

they are terrorizing our people
with their barbarous medicine
with their shiny implements of death
and noxious drugs
the mother's breasts are dry
the babies are starving
they've poisoned the very womb

and hear me now
they've poisoned the *minds* of our people
some among us even bow down
and worship the monster
who devours the flesh of our mothers
drinks the blood of our fathers
and defecates destruction for our children's children
and o my earth my mother
poisons your sweet waters

so that the grandchildren's fingers no longer number five

CAN YOU HEAR ME!!

i say we live in fear
there are those among us wearing our faces
who have been trained by the enemy
to blind the eyes of our sisters
steal the hearts of our brothers
rape our daughters and teach our sons to kill for money
have we no shame
and haven't you seen
that the hands of the children
are not like the hands of the old ones
that the old ones live alone
at the mercy of our enemies
and it is not to our comfort
that they cannot see

that the grandchildren's fingers no longer number five

I LEAD TWO LIVES: CONFESSIONS OF A CLOSET BAPTIST

~ MAB SEGREST

I lead a double life. By day I'm a relatively mild-mannered English teacher at a Southern Baptist college. By night—and on Tuesdays and Thursdays and weekends—I am a lesbian writer and editor, a collective member of *Feminary,* a lesbian-feminist journal for the South. My employers do not know about my other life. When they find out I assume I will be fired, maybe prayed to death. For the past four years my life has moved rapidly in opposite directions.

When I started teaching English at my present school, five years ago, I knew I was a lesbian. I was living with Sue, my first woman lover. But I wasn't "out" politically. I had not yet discovered the lesbian culture and lesbian community that is now such an important part of my life. The first time I had let myself realize that I was in love with Sue I sat under a willow tree by the lake at the Girl Scout camp where we both worked and said aloud to myself in the New York darkness: "I am a lesbian." I had to see how it sounded, and after I'd said that, gradually, I felt I could say anything. When, three years ago, Sue left to live with a man, I knew my life had changed. I read lesbian books and journals with great excitement. I joined the collective of *Feminary,* then a local feminist journal, and helped turn it into a journal for Southern lesbians. I started writing. I did all this while working for the Baptists, feeling myself making decisions that were somehow as frightening as they were inevitable. Early issues of *Feminary* record the process. First there is a poem by "Mabel." Then an article by "Mab." Then the whole leap: "Mab Segrest." I knew if I could not write my name, I couldn't write anything. I also knew: if I can't be myself and teach, I won't teach.

It is fall as I write this, and September brings back memories of new plaid cotton dresses, clean notebooks, pencils sharpened to fine points, and especially a stack of new books full of things I didn't know yet. Since my junior year in college, over a decade ago, I have wanted to be a teacher. For a long time—before Sue and I both made the brave, reckless leap that a woman makes when she loves another woman for the first time—teaching was the most important thing in my life. I have always liked school. And I always—always!—loved to read. During my childhood—which if it was full of small-town life and summers with my brother in the woods near the lake was also full of the deep loneliness of being queer—I spent many hours with books on the front porch swing or in my father's chair by the gas heater. I have always pondered things in long conversations with myself walking home from school, my hands slightly waving as I held forth to some invisible audience. Now in my classes I love the challenge of looking out over a sea of consciousness, watching eyes focus and unfocus, as words register or float out the back window, every period the necessity to generate interest, every hour a hundred tiny failures and successes. Teaching is the work I love best. I can bring much of myself to it, and much of it into myself. But as a lesbian teacher in a society that hates homosexuals—especially homosexual teachers—I have learned a caution toward my students and my school that saddens me. The things my life has taught me best I cannot teach directly. I do not believe that I am the only one who suffers.

The first time homosexuality came up in my classroom it was a shock to my system. It was in freshman composition, and I was letting a class choose debate topics. They picked gay rights, but nobody wanted to argue the gay side. Finally three of my more vociferous students volunteered. I went home that day shaken. I dreamed that night I was in class, my back to my students, writing on the board (I always feel most vulnerable then), and students were taunting me from the desks—"lesbian! queer!" The day of the debate I took a seat in the back row, afraid that if I stood up front *IT* would show, I would give myself away: develop a tic, tremble, stutter, throw up, then faint dead away. I kept quiet as my three progay students held off the Bible with the Bill of Rights, to everyone's amazement, including my own. (I certainly knew it could be done; I just hadn't expected them to do it. No one else in the class had figured any legitimate arguments were possible.) Then the antigay side rallied and hit on a winning tactic. They implied that if the opponents *really* believed their own arguments, they were pretty "funny." I called an end to the debate, and the progay side quickly explained how they didn't mean anything they had said. Then one of my female students wanted to discuss how Christians should love people even when they were sick and sinful. I said the discussion was *over* and dismissed the class. The only time I had spoken during the entire debate was in response to a male student behind me who had reacted defensively to a mention of homosexuality in the army with, "Yes, and where *my father* works, they castrate people like that." I turned with quiet fury—"Are you advocating it?" All in all I survived the day, but without much self-respect.

The next year, on a theme, a freshwoman explained to me how you could tell gay people "by the bandannas they wear in their pockets and around their necks." She concluded, "I think homosexuals are a menace to society. *What do you think?*" A pregnant question, indeed. I pondered for a while, then wrote back in the margin, "I think society is a menace to homosexuals." I resisted wearing a red bandanna the day I handed back the papers.

Sometimes friends ask me why I stay. I often ask myself. I'm still not sure. A Southern Baptist school is not the most comfortable place for a gay teacher to be—sitting on the buckle of the Bible Belt. A few years ago Anita Bryant was appointed a vice-president of the Southern Baptist Convention. I stay partly because teaching jobs are hard to come by, especially in this vicinity where I'm working on *Feminary.* I have begun to apply for other jobs, but so far without success. I wonder how different it would be in other places, where bigotry might be more subtle, dangers more carefully concealed. Mostly I stay because I like my students. They remind me, many of them, of myself at their age: making new and scary breaks from home and its values, at first not straying very far and needing to be told, "There's a bigger world. Go for it." Teaching them is like being a missionary, an analogy many of them would understand.

Two years ago I came out for the first time to a student. I had resolved that if any gay student ever asked me to identify myself, I would. So when Fred came up to my desk before Christmas vacation, sporting one new earring and wanting to talk about bars in Washington, I knew it was coming.

"Where do *you* go to dance?" he asked. (At the time, there was one gay disco in the vicinity.)

"Oh," I evaded, "you probably wouldn't know it. What about you?"

"Oh, you wouldn't know it either." Then, quickly, "It's between Chapel Hill and Durham."

Me: "I think I do. It starts with a C?"

Him: "Yes. *You* go there?" His eyes lit up.

Me: "Yep."

Him, politely, giving me an out: "You probably just went one time and got disgusted??"

Me: "Nope."

By this time the class was filling with students, milling around my desk and the blackboard behind us. I suggested to Fred that we finish the conversation after class. We did—in the middle of campus on a bench from which we could see anyone coming for at least half a mile. I felt a sudden sympathy for the CIA. He asked me if he could tell his friends. I took a deep breath and said yes. But they never came to see me. I still don't know how far word had spread; every now and then I have the feeling I exchange meaningful glances with certain students. I would like for gay students to know I am there if they need me—or maybe just to know I am there—but I do not take the initiative to spread the word around. I have made the decision to be "out" in what I write and "in" where I teach, not wanting to risk a job I enjoy or financial security; but it is not a decision I always feel good about. I see the unease of most college students over sexuality—whether they express it in swaggering and hollow laughter over "queer" jokes or in timidity or in the worried looks of married students from back rows—and I know that it is part of a larger dis-ease with sexuality and the definitions of "men" and "women" in this society. I see how they, and most of us, have been taught to fear *all* of our feelings. And I understand all too well, when I realize I am afraid to write—to even know—what I think and feel for fear of losing my job, how money buys conformity, how subtly we are terrorized into staying in line.

The closest I ever came to saying what I wanted to was in an American literature class last year. Gay rights came up again—I think I may have even steered the discussion in that direction. And a student finally said it to me, "But what about teachers? We can't have homosexuals teaching students!" I resisted leaping up on the podium and flashing the big L emblazoned on a leotard beneath my blouse. Instead, I took a deep breath and began slowly. "Well, in my opinion, you don't learn sexual preference in the classroom. I mean, that's not what we are doing here. *If* you had a gay or lesbian teacher, he or she would not teach you about sexual preference." I paused to catch my breath. They were all listening. "What he or she would say, *if you had* a gay teacher, is this . . ." (by now I was lightly beating on the podium) ". . . don't let them make you afraid to be who you are. To know who you are. She would tell you, don't let them get you. Don't let them make you afraid." I stopped abruptly, and in the silence turned to think of something to write on the board.

And if they ever *do* have a lesbian teacher, that is exactly what she will say.

THERE'S NOT A CHILD THAT CAN'T LEARN

~ REBECCA McCARTHY

Minnie Palmore House sits on a knoll overlooking the Aiken-Augusta Highway in Aiken County, South Carolina. The House is a one-of-a-kind school offering a variety of educational experiences to children from preschool through junior high. A steady stream of students flows into the red-brick building for the morning and afternoon tutoring sessions, where the children spend several hours reading, counting, writing, and reciting—"getting the basics," says teacher Abelle Palmore Nivens. She's the school's founder, a woman in her mid-sixties with a vibrant energy belying her age.

"So many children are missing out on education in public schools for one reason or another," she comments. "There's not a child who can't learn; there are only children who haven't been taught." That philosophy guided Mrs. Nivens through forty-three years of first-grade teaching in Aiken County and then prompted her to found her own school a few years ago. "I was spending more time with forms and paperwork than with actual teaching. I couldn't give the children what I wanted to give them. When I retired I said I was leaving that classroom but not education."

In 1978, with financial help from her sister, Mrs. Nivens bought an old army barracks and transported it from nearby Fort Gordon to its current location. Friends and family have helped with its ongoing renovation; teachers, civic groups, and neighbors have donated books, toys, materials—and time. Some people volunteered as teachers' assistants when the school opened.

During the school year about twenty-five two- to five-year-olds attend Minnie Palmore House. Some attend only a morning or afternoon session; others stay all day while their parents work. Kindergarten is not mandatory in South Carolina, and children often have trouble finding a kindergarten class with space available. Minnie Palmore House helps fill that need.

In the summers the number of students swells to around forty, as many school-aged children come to polish their academic skills during the vacation months. Many of these older children need "the basics" as urgently as the preschoolers; Mrs. Nivens mentions a fifteen-year-old girl who came because she hadn't yet learned to read.

The inside of the school is functional, not fancy—charts of numbers and letters and posters with words and days of the week cover the walls, and well-thumbed textbooks line the shelves of the front room. A back room has tables for math and art classes, and the hall is crowded with desks and blackboards. Kids are everywhere: three-year-olds spelling and writing their names, four-year-olds working with numbers, five-year-olds sounding out words in fourth-grade science books. Mrs. Nivens works with each child on his or her own level and has a seemingly magical ability to inspire them to new vistas of achievement. "Give me a child for a year and he'll be ready for anything," she says.

Many of the students come from New Hope, the predominantly black neighborhood surrounding the school. But others travel from as far as fifteen miles away, attracted by the school's high reputation. Students who can afford it pay the $5 an hour fee; those who can't pay less or nothing. The money buys supplies and pays Mrs. Nivens's assistants. "I can afford to teach for free," explains Mrs. Nivens. "I've got my pension. I'm still teaching because I love it."

The school is named after Mrs. Nivens's mother, who taught kindergarten in her home in New Hope until she was nearly ninety years old. Teaching runs in the family—Mrs. Nivens's grandmother, mother, and eight of her sisters all taught. Mrs. Nivens completed a B.A. degree at South Carolina State College, then earned a master's degree in early childhood education at Columbia University in New York City, and returned to teach in Aiken County. She married, had two children, and continued her career, working first with black students and later with students of both races. She preferred first grade because, she says, "That's where everything happens. Children know when someone believes in them and in their abilities."

Mrs. Nivens smiles. "I give them a sense of who they are, self-esteem. With that, they can do anything."

MAXINE ALEXANDER, a beginning genealogist in Durham, North Carolina, has traced six generatons of her family in North Carolina. She is currently compiling a special issue of *Southern Exposure* on Indians of the South and searching for a publisher for her book of poems, *New Time Blues and Other Colors*.

GLORIA ANZALDÚA is a "Tejana Chicana poet." Together with Cherríe Moraga she edited the anthology *This Bridge Called My Back: Writings By Radical Women of Color*. She is now living in New York and at work on her novel *Andrea*. In her spare time she teaches, read the Tarot, and doodles in her journal.

MAUDY BENZ is a visual artist, sculptor, and writer in Chapel Hill, North Carolina. She has participated in a number of art shows and readings. She recently had a poem published in *Southern Poetry Review*, won honorable mention in a fiction contest, and had a painting in the Spring 1984 Raleigh Museum Show.

ALMA BLOUNT is the photography editor for the *North Carolina Independent*, an alternative weekly newspaper in Durham that began publication in 1983. She is also a freelance writer and a regular contributor to *Southern Exposure*.

MARGARET JONES BOLSTERLI is a cultural historian and a professor of English at the University of Arkansas. She has written extensively on various aspects of Southern life and culture.

ANNE BRADEN is a Louisville-based journalist who has been active for more than three decades in Southern social justice movements. She is a frequent contributor to *Southern Exposure* and currently cochairs the Southern Organizing Committee for Economic and Social Justice.

SUSAN BRIGHT is a poet, art-based learning consultant, and English instructor in Austin, Texas.

BEVERLY BURCH works as a psychotherapist in Berkeley, California. She spent most of her life in the South and was editor and founder of *Women's Free Express,* published in Nashville, Tennessee, during the 1970s.

VICTORIA MORRIS BYERLY has worked on the staff of a number of publications. In undertaking the oral-history project on women in mill villages she moved from editor to independent journalist and began to explore her own culture and heritage. She lives in Jamaica Plains, Massachusetts.

CHRISTINA DAVIS is an activist and community educator. She uses songs as a way of teaching and organizing, much like the earlier singers of the civil rights, peace, and women's movements. She is on the promotions team at the Institute for Southern Studies in Durham.

AMELIA DIAZ ETTINGER grew up in Puerto Rico, where she was educated "through endless years at a Catholic school." She joined a group of environmentalists and became the first woman wildlife manager for the island. She began to write in earnest after moving to Durham, North Carolina, where her daughter was born, and now lives in La Grande, Oregon.

SARA EVANS teaches in the history department at the University of Minnesota. She has been active in both the civil rights and women's movements, and is the author of *Personal Politics.*

CLARA D. FORD is a poet and freelance writer who draws on her experiences growing up in small Southern towns and her family's storytelling tradition for her work. She taught in public schools briefly but resigned to devote more time to her writing, her husband, and her twin children in McConnells, South Carolina.

CONSTANCE GARCIA-BARRIO is a freelance writer with fond memories of her Southern heritage. She lives in Old Bridge, New Jersey.

DEE GILBERT is a freelance writer and magazine editor from the New Orleans area. The abbreviated oral histories here are part of a larger, book-length work in progress. She is director of *Patchwork,* a New Orleans oral history project. She credits Elizabeth Cousins Rogers, an activist for six decades, with inspiring her to collect women's oral histories.

hattie gosset. work experience herstory: babysitter paid companion office girl waitress cleaningperson. for information about forthcoming collection of writings: presenting sister noblues contact editorial department wild wimmins archives post office box 661 lincolnton station harlem new york 10037.

RAYNA GREEN is a writer, scholar, and political activist who works on issues of interest to American Indians, women, and scientists. She is currently developing an American Indian program for the Museum of American History, Smithsonian Institution. Her most recent books are *That's What She Said: A Collection of Contemporary Fiction and Poetry by Native American Woman* and a bibliographical work on Native American women.

JACQUELYN DOWD HALL is the author of *Revolt Against Chivalry: Jesse Daniel Ames and the Women's Campaign Against Lynching* and is the director of the Southern oral history program and associate professor of history at the University of North Carolina at Chapel Hill. She was also one of the three editors of "Generations," the special issue of *Southern Exposure* from which this book developed.

MELISSA HIELD is currently director of People's History in Texas, Inc., a nonprofit educational organization, and an executive assistant at the Texas State Treasury. She is also a Ph.D. candidate in American Civilization at the University of Texas at Austin. Research for her article was sponsored by a grant from the N.E.H. Youth Grant Program and one from the Texas Committee for the Humanities for the Oral History of Texas Women Labor Organizers Project, 1976–79. A previous version of her article appeared in *Frontiers* (Vol. IV, No. 2, Summer 1979).

ELLESA CLAY HIGH's book *Past Titan Rock,* from which her article is excerpted, received the 1983 Appalachian Award from the University Press of Kentucky for the best manuscript concerning the region. Her poetry, fiction, and nonfiction have appeared in a number of magazines, and she teaches English at the University of West Virginia, in Morgantown.

LEE HOWARD was born in eastern Kentucky; her book *The Last Unmined Vein,* an oral history, captures the voice and spirit of many of her people there. Her work has appeared in *Southern Exposure* and the anthology *Women Surviving Massacres and Men.* She now lives in Oak Ridge, Tennessee.

MARIE STOKES JEMISON lives in Birmingham, Alabama, where she helped create the Southern Women's Archive at the Birmingham Public Library. She was raised to be a Southern belle, but in 1955 the Montgomery bus boycott drew her into the civil rights movement.

VIVIAN M. LOKEN has published two books of poetry, *World Spun* and *String My Harp, David.* Her work has appeared in a variety of publications and been anthologized in *Full Circle, Full Circle II and III* and *On Being Black.* She has been a natural mother, foster mother, and grandmother. She is now sharing her writing and experience through lectures and workshops in Minneapolis, Minnesota.

REGINA M. K. MANDRELL is a genealogist and a member of a number of historical societies and writing clubs in Fair Hope, Alabama. She has worked for various professional organizations producing pamphlets, brochures, and educational materials.

SUE MASSEK arrived in the Appalachias in the early 1970s from Topeka, Kansas, in search of music. She has found it an ideal place to learn to use music for political purposes, and is now living in Lexington, Kentucky. She is recording her fourth album as a member of the musical group The Real World, which will appear on the Flying Fish Label.

RAYMINA Y. MAYS is a fiction writer and co-founder of a third-world women's newsletter, *Between Ourselves.* The first issue is expected to be published this year. She lives in Washington, D.C.

REBECCA MC CARTHY is a freelance writer in Athens, Georgia.

MARY MEBANE recently received grants from the National Endowment for the Arts and the Milwaukee Artists Foundation to pursue her creative-writing career. Her autobiographical books *Mary* and *Mary, Wayfarer* were published by Viking. She has taught English at a number of universities and lives in Milwaukee.

BIRTHALENE MILLER has had her work published in a number of magazines and was nominated for a Pushcart Award for a short story which appeared in the *Black Warrior Review.* She lives in Mississippi with her family.

JENNIFER MILLER recently edited a special edition of *Southern Exposure* on the folklife, traditional communities, and environment of the Southern Coast. She began the syndicated newspaper column *Facing South,* published by the Institute for Southern Studies, and is now living in Durham again after a sojourn in New Orleans.

JOYCELYN K. MOODY is the current editor of *Facing South.* She is a Cancer, a mother, a fantastic cook, a poet, and a beginning visual artist, not necessarily in that order.

MARAT MOORE was born in east Tennessee and has worked in the coal mines of West Virginia, where she lived for a number of years. She is now a photographer and writer for the United Mine Workers, in Washington, D.C. Her article is excerpted from her forthcoming book on women coal miners in Appalachia.

BARBARA NEELY is an African of American slave descent and lives in

Durham, North Carolina. She is currently at work on a novel about working-class black women and a nonfiction work on the sociopolitical roots of black male sexism.

MATTIE MAE NELSON's niece, Darnell Arnoult Stone, discovered this letter by her aunt and thought it worth sharing. Stone lives in Chapel Hill, North Carolina.

GLENDA NEEL PENDER grew up in Florida and is now living in Dahlonega, Georgia, where she is a natural health care practitioner and owns a health-food store. Her grandmother, about whom her poem is written, was one of several special Southern women in her life, and died in February, 1984.

PHAYE POLIAKOFF is a freelance writer and independent radio producer. Originally from Spartanburg, South Carolina, she now lives in Durham and is continuing her research on women in the sex industry.

CARMINE PRIOLI is an associate professor of American literature and folklore at North Carolina State University in Raleigh. His work has appeared in a number of journals. He and his wife, Elizabeth Hood-Prioli, are building their own house in Chapel Hill.

RUTHANN ROBSON is an attorney with Florida Rural Legal Services in Jupiter, Florida, where she concentrates on feminist issues. Her work has appeared in many feminist and alternative periodicals, including *Kalliope, New Pages, Maenad, Feminary, Social Anarchism* and the *Minnesota Review.*

MAB SEGREST is a writer, activist, and teacher who recently quit her job at a Southern Baptist university. She is currently working with an organization to oppose racial and religious violence. She is a member of *Feminary,* a Southern lesbian-feminist journal in the Chapel Hill area.

MARILYN SEWELL is forty-two years old and the mother of two sons. She has worked as a teacher, psychotherapist, magazine editor, and women's-center program director. She is presently studying to become a Unitarian Universalist minister in Berkeley, California.

LEE SMITH is the author of two novels, *Oral History* and *Black Mountain Breakdown.* She lives in Chapel Hill and is teaching in the English department of North Carolina State University.

LUISAH TEISH is a writer, lecturer, actor, and feminist activist from Louisiana. She is the author of the forthcoming book *Working the Mother: Personal Charms and Practical Rituals for the Natural Woman.* Her work has appeared in a number of journals. She now works with cultural and political groups in Berkeley, California.

WENDY WATRISS is a freelance photojournalist and writer whose work has appeared in *Life, Geo, Smithsonian, Mother Jones,* Time-Life books, and many other national publications. She has also been a newspaper reporter and has produced documentaries for NET on such topics as refugees in the Sahel, black cowboys, and Agent Orange. She now lives in Houston, Texas.

LIZ WHEATON is on leave from the Institute for Southern Studies to write a book on the 1979 Klan-Nazi killings of five anti-Klan demonstrators in Greensboro, North Carolina, where she is now living.

SARAH WILKERSON is a graduate student in history at the University of North Carolina in Chapel Hill. She is also a freelance writer and contributor to *Southern Exposure.*

PHOTO CREDITS

We are grateful to the following for supplying or allowing us to use their photographs:

Maxine Alexander: page 1(t)
Baldwin/Watriss: pages ii(t), 1(m), 163(t), 203(b)
Alma Blount: page 115(b)
Victoria Morris Byerly and the Southern Textile Workers Oral History Project: pages ii(b), 163(b)
Becky Chavaria-Gomez: page 73(b)
Wendy Ewald: page 31(b)
Elana Freedom: pages 31(t), 247(m)
Georgia Department of Archives and History/Vanishing Georgia Project: page 73(t)
Dee Gilbert: page 1(b)
Laurel Horton: page 163(m)
Marie Stokes Jemison: page 31(m)
Steven March: page 203(m)
Marat Moore: pages 73(m), 115(m), 247(b)
National Women's Education and Employment Project, Inc.: page 247(t)
Marilyn Peterson: page 203(t)
Vina Wadlington Webb and Suite Five Productions: page ii(m)

(t) top
(m) middle
(b) bottom

WOMEN'S STUDIES IN PAPERBACK FROM PANTHEON

THE CHARLOTTE PERKINS GILMAN READER:
The Yellow Wallpaper and Other Fiction
edited by Anne Lane (1980)
A collection of the work of the nineteenth-century feminist.
0-394-73933-7 $4.95

EVE AND THE NEW JERUSALEM:
Socialism and Feminism in the Nineteenth Century
by Barbara Taylor (1983)
"A breaktakingly detailed recovery of a lost chapter in the history
of socialism and feminism."
—Elaine Showalter
0-394-71321-4 $9.95

FEMINIST THEORISTS: *Three Centuries of Key Women Thinkers*
edited by Dale Spender (1984)
Celebrates the rich but neglected tradition of feminist thought.
0-394-72197-7 $10.95

HERLAND: *A Lost Feminist Utopian Novel*
by Charlotte Perkins Gilman (1979)
Herland describes a society of women discovered by three male ex-
plorers who then must re-examine their assumptions about women
and their roles in society. "A pure delight . . . a serendipitous discovery."
—Susan Brownmiller
0-394-73665-6 $2.95

MOSCOW WOMEN: *Thirteen Interviews*
by Carola Hansson and Karin Lidén (1983)
Lively, candid and often moving interview with women from the
Soviet Union.
0-394-71491-1 $7.95

NEVER DONE: *A History of American Housework*
by Susan Strasser (1982)
The first complete history of the American housewife, American
household technology, and the ideas about housework.
0-394-70841-5 $11.95

OLD MISTRESSES: *Women, Art and Ideology*
by Rozsika Parker and Griselda Pollock (1982)
"An important, intelligent, and provocative study of women's position in the history of art . . . a major achievement."
—Linda Nochlin
0-394-70814-8 $10.95

THE SOCIOLOGY OF HOUSEWORK
by Ann Oakley (1975)
Oakley challenges the conventional trivialization of housework.
0-394-73088-7 $3.95

STORMY WEATHER:
The Music and Lives of a Century of Jazzwomen
by Linda Dahl (1984)
"The definitive work on women in music—an incredible job of research."
—John Hammond
0-394-72271-X $11.95

STRONG-MINDED WOMEN AND OTHER LOST VOICES
OF NINETEENTH-CENTURY ENGLAND
by Janet Horowitz Murray (1982)
A stunning collective portrait of women's lives in nineteenth-century England.
0-394-71044-4 $11.95

SUBJECT WOMEN
by Ann Oakley (1981)
A richly documented assessment of where women stand today—economically, politically, socially, emotionally.
0-394-74904-9 $7.95

WE WERE THERE:
The Story of Working Women in America
by Barbara Wertheimer (1977)
A narrative history of women's work from pre-colonial times to the present. "The best single volume of the history of American working-class women."
—Herbert Gutman
0-394-73257-X $7.95

WOMEN: *The Longest Revolution*
by Juliet Mitchell (1984)
A collection of Mitchell's best essays and lectures on women, psychoanalysis, and literature.
0-394-72574-3 $9.95

WOMEN'S WORK, WOMEN'S HEALTH:
Myths and Realities
by Jeanne M. Stellman (1978)
Lays to rest several historical myths about women's working and childbearing years.
0-394-73452-1 $5.95

WORKING IT OUT:
23 Women Writers, Artists, Scientists and Scholars
Talk About Their Lives and Work
edited by Sara Ruddick and Pamela Daniels (1977)
Candid assessments of the rewards and dilemmas of creative work.
0-394-73452-1 $6.95